WHAT PSYCHOTHERAPISTS
LEARN FROM THEIR CLIENTS

WHAT PSYCHOTHERAPISTS LEARN FROM THEIR CLIENTS

SHERRY L. HATCHER, PHD, ABPP, EDITOR

To order additional copies of this book, contact:
Xlibris
1-888-795-4274
www.Xlibris.com
Orders@Xlibris.com
698315

Table of Contents

With love and appreciation to my dear husband Robert, and to our daughters, their husbands, and our grandchildren: Jessamyn, Michael, and Willa; Juliet, Kevin, Quinn, and Zev

Acknowledgments

Thanks to the Provost's Office at Fielding Graduate University for initial support of Dr. Hatcher's research project and to Marlene Zimels and Louise Keeler for their assistance with implementing that support. Appreciation goes to Rebecca Ditmore who guided our cover design for this book, Jessica Ditmore for the cover artwork, and for copy editing by Margaret Bonanno.

We recognize Kelly Usselman and Patricia Gingras, who participated in earlier stages of this project, including some of the data collection, and for a presentation of initial findings at a Fielding Graduate University National Session.

The Editor also wishes to express thanks for the hard work and perseverance of the contributors represented in this volume, including Dr. Margaret Cramer whose introduction to the book so graciously honors our research efforts.

Finally and quite importantly, we want to express our immense gratitude to the psychologist participants who gave so generously of their time and thoughtful reflections. Each was invited to review the transcript of his/her interview and given the option to choose a pseudonym by which he or she is represented throughout this volume.

The Contributors

Jason H. Boothe, M.A. is a doctoral student at Fielding Graduate University; he holds master's degrees in both Health Psychology and Clinical Psychology. Jason has previous publications to his credit and currently works in the Career and Counseling Services at the University of Houston-Clear Lake in Texas.

Margaret Cramer, PhD, ABPP is a member of the faculty in Psychology at Fielding Graduate University. She has authored peer-reviewed articles in _The American Journal of Psychotherapy_ and _Psychotherapy: Theory, Research, Practice,_ and has won numerous awards for teaching, clinical supervision, and clinical writing. She received the Innovator Award for Contributions to the Treatment of Women and Children from the Center for Substance Abuse Treatment in Washington, DC.

Joan M. Frye, PhD earned her doctorate from Fielding Graduate University and works at the Vanderbilt University Psychological and Counseling Center in a post-doctoral position. She has previously published with our research group and presented several times at the Annual Convention of the American Psychological Association.

Claudia Hinojosa, M.A. holds master's degrees in both Psychology and Mental Health Counseling and is completing her doctorate in Clinical Psychology at Fielding Graduate University. She has worked in various clinical settings, including as a Research Technician in the Department of Psychiatry at Columbia University College of Physicians & Surgeons in New York. Ms. Hinojosa has published previously in peer-reviewed journals.

Sherry L. Hatcher, PhD, ABPP (Editor) is currently Faculty Chair in the Clinical Psychology Program at Fielding Graduate University. She previously edited another book while on faculty at the University of Michigan where she earned Excellence in Education awards in three separate years. Dr. Hatcher has authored numerous articles in peer-reviewed psychology journals such as _Psychotherapy; Teaching of Psychology;_ and _PsycCRITIQUES,_ for which journal she serves on the Editorial Board. For seven years Dr. Hatcher served on the Michigan Psychological Association Ethics Committee, and she teaches on that topic, among others such as Psychotherapy Research, Clinical Interviewing, and Supervision.

Adriana Kipper-Smith, PhD has a doctorate in Clinical Psychology from Fielding Graduate University. She works as a clinical psychologist at the Vanderbilt University Psychological and Counseling Center and has previous publications in both American and international peer-reviewed psychology journals.

Katherine Tighe, M.A., MSW is a therapist with a primary interest in working with adolescents with co-occurring disorders. She is an advocate for animal-assisted therapy (AAT) and integrates dogs and other animals into her practice, as well as contributing to research on the effectiveness of AAT.

Mechtild Uhe, M.A. is a doctoral candidate in the Clinical Psychology Program at Fielding Graduate University. She holds a master's degree in Clinical Psychology from the Westphalian Wilhelm's University, Germany and another from Fielding Graduate University. Over the last 15 years, she has provided interventions and assessments in various settings including hospitals, school boards, private practice, and law enforcement agencies.

Manuela L. Waddell, M.A. Manuela Waddell is a doctoral candidate at Fielding Graduate University, having completed her pre-doctoral internship at the St. Louis Psychoanalytic Institute. She has previously published in a number of peer-reviewed journals, including on the subject of addictions, and she has given a number of presentations at professional conferences.

Joanne S. West, PhD Joanne West holds a doctorate in Clinical Psychology. She has served as a visiting professor in a doctoral psychology program at Medaille University and has also been the director of the Psychology Master's program there. Dr. West has provided psychological services in private practice, community mental health, and college settings. Her professional interests include therapist factors in the therapeutic relationship and the impacts on development of Intimate Partner Violence.

Introduction

"Be kind; everyone you meet is fighting a great battle."

(Ian MacLaren, 1897)

How I wish I'd had the benefit of *What Psychotherapists Learn from Their Clients* several decades ago. This book illuminates a seldom-discussed but crucial area of the treatment relationship. The popular notion, held by patients and clinicians alike, is that the therapist is there to "treat" the patient. S/he is the expert, the seer holding all the answers, the keys to the basement, and the combination to the vault where all the secrets are kept. Embedded in this way of thinking is also something of a pretense that, because the psychotherapist is present in the role of clinician, s/he is not involved in the process and certainly not affected by the client other than in a countertransferential manner. Perhaps the traditional focus in our training—that therapy is not a social relationship, that boundaries are an essential and ethical part of practice, and that we must learn and adhere to role-appropriate behavior—results in our learning to avoid an awareness of our patients' influence on us, and of what we learn from them, not just about them. Largely hidden from this perspective is the fact that one of the operative terms in the idea of the treatment relationship is *relationship*. The therapist is 50% of the dyad, fully one half of the enterprise. And among psychotherapists, it is a widely known secret that being in the privileged position of learning about the private struggles, secret torments and desires, and fundamental heartbreaks of other human beings affects us deeply and throughout our lives.

Anthony Storr writes in *The Art of Psychotherapy* that you can't get to know someone without really learning to like him/her. Storr suggests that it may well be that one of the conditions of change involves "the conviction that there is at any rate one person who is entirely on the patient's side; who is . . . wholly dedicated to one's interests" (Storr, 1979, p. 69). Indeed, it is now recognized that "analyst and patient simply cannot avoid having an impact on each other, even if they are totally silent" (Ehrenberg, 1992, viii). It's clear that the work of treatment requires intimacy and, as that intimacy develops, we learn to care deeply for our patients.

While it is now well understood that the experience within the treatment dyad is mutually co-constructed, it was D.W. Winnicott (1971) who first emphasized that it was neither patient nor therapist, but something in between the two, a transitional space, that became the vehicle for change as well as the arena into which the core conflict was delivered. Psychotherapist and patient were equal composers of this experiential narrative, albeit from different vantage points and through different roles in the treatment enterprise. In his exploration of creativity and creative apperception, Winnicott suggested that, "it is creative apperception more than anything else that makes the individual feel that life is worth living" (p. 65). The alternative to living authentically and creatively is a life of compliance to the demands of external reality. What is essential to note here is that Winnicott was not referring to the end point of the process, that is, the final decision, but to the process itself which must feel creative. Such creativity requires the spontaneity and sense of jeopardy of play, a set of interactions during which neither partner knows precisely what will happen next.

As Sherry Hatcher and her research team reveal in this important and deeply engaging book, the recognition that therapists care about, and engage in cooperative endeavor, with the individuals with whom they work is only the beginning. In 2008 and 2009, Dr. Hatcher and her group entered the world of the psychotherapist's internal experience with the goal of more deeply understanding the depth and types of learning acquired from work with clients during the course of psychotherapy. Through semi-structured interviews with 61 psychologists from all four major theoretical orientations, the team explored the ways that the reciprocal experience of mutual influence becomes a central part of successful treatment. In fact, the ability to learn from clients appeared to be part of most psychologists' professional development and continued engagement in the work of treatment. Those committed to continued growth and development seemed to utilize lessons learned from the people with whom they work as an ongoing avenue for increased self-knowledge. Study participants represented the four major theoretical orientations; psychodynamic, cognitive-behavioral, humanistic, and integrative orientations were represented by those interviewed and, notably, the findings of the project reiterate those of the common-factors research in that there were no large differences found regarding theoretical approach or clinical model.

Although a few previous studies have explored the effect of clients on therapists, this volume provides evidence of the particular ways these 61 participants have been affected by the people they've known in treatment, and the relationship of lessons learned to stage of professional development and personal growth. We are allowed to listen in on a type of personal reflection to which we are seldom privy and which is seldom encouraged. Dr. Hatcher's skilled and clinically astute interviewers invite and encourage their participants to discuss their heartfelt thoughts and feelings about the more reciprocal influence that lies within every psychotherapy relationship. Questions are open-ended; there is an inductive method of investigation here that creates a parallel sense of intimacy for the reader. Our participants are opening up and we are opening up along with them.

While the editor and principal investigator of this study, Sherry Hatcher, is a well-known scholar, an accomplished researcher, and a master clinician, the precise manner in which she inhabits these various roles creates a special type of mentor for graduate students in psychology. I have known Sherry for 14 years as a colleague and friend, and have long admired her abilities across every dimension of her career as a psychologist. But it is her unique combination of talents and abilities, evident everywhere in this book that contributes so much to the sensibility and tone of this research.

Sherry's interest in everything related to the scope and process of psychotherapy is longstanding. A review of her lengthy curriculum vitae is not attempted here. What is more relevant to the current project is that she is not just a talented teacher, but also a beloved one. At Fielding Graduate University, where we both serve on the faculty, Sherry is well known for her generosity in working with students to develop their interest in and love of research, scholarship, and clinical process. Her ability to nurture the skills and talents of her students is evident from her many research projects with graduate students, APA presentations, poster sessions, and talks. In that regard, this volume is only the latest iteration of her efforts to raise the next generation of scholar-practitioners in the field of psychology. She serves in a number of institutional capacities (those thankless jobs that are so essential to the running of any academic department or institution), perhaps the toughest of which is Faculty Chair, where her fair-minded and judicious manner is legendary and has earned the respect of all. Her contributions were recognized in July 2014 when she received a Certificate of Recognition for Teaching and Mentoring from Fielding Graduate University.

Hatcher has published extensively, but this book marks a particular achievement because it integrates Sherry's great interests in the psychotherapy process, the development of the psychotherapist, and the growth of students academically, professionally, and personally. In Chapter 1, Kipper-Smith outlines the investigation and the layout of the book and, in doing so, remarks on the ways she too was moved by and learned from the experience of the project:

> *Our listening carefully to these interviews, as researchers and clinicians, provided us with an overwhelming feeling of gratitude for the field we have chosen. We realized that psychologists were sharing their life experiences with their clients—even if not explicitly—and, as often happens in interview-based research, that realization in itself afforded learning, for both the interviewees and interviewers, yielding a variety of "parallel process."*

Other themes highlighted in this work are respect for clients, including their coping strategies; nonjudgment; and the relative abandonment of the fantasy that the therapist knows and needs to persuade the client of the "correct choice." Not only must we give up what Freud referred to as therapeutic ambition, but we must also be willing to examine and explore ideas that at times might appear to be nonsensical. To avoid a control struggle whose goal is compliance with the will of the therapist, we must empathically enter the world of the patient to understand the problem from his/her point of view, and maintain an open mind regarding the "correct choice." This essential nonjudgmental stance, respect for the individual, and humility of the therapist are overarching ideas that are echoed throughout the interviews with clinicians. As discussed so beautifully in Chapter 1 by Kipper-Smith and Hatcher, in Chapter 4 by West, and again in Chapters 10 and 11 by West and Hatcher, the myth of omnipotence to which all newer psychotherapists are prone—a fantasy not easily relinquished by any of us—must yield in the face of the ingenuity and courage that mark the strategies clients develop to save their psychological lives. Evelyne Schwaber's work on empathy and empathic listening in psychoanalysis reminds us that countertransference itself can be understood as a retreat from the patient's point of view (Schwaber, 1981, 1983a, 1983b). It appears that the wish that we can (or should) know better than the client or can solve problems by simple didactic instruction is not given up easily.

Although each chapter of this book focuses on a particular aspect of this special type of learning, again and again we hear in these conversations the notions of courage, on the part of both client and therapist, to engage in the therapy process; respect for the client; a nonjudgment stance; the ability to listen well and deeply; the capacity to be with another person with the desire to understand rather than try to "fix" a problem; and respect for and curiosity about cultural and individual differences as well as these universal issues that concern us all. What strikes the reader is the willingness of interviewers to ask and participants to share their experiences of the type of personal and profound learning that moves the soul and disrupts, at least momentarily, the sense of self. There are reflections on courage in Chapter 5 by Frye, Kipper-Smith, and Hatcher, and the discussion of coping in Chapter 4 by West and Hatcher also addresses this issue. Here the participants reflect not only on the admiration they have for the courage demonstrated by their clients, but also on the ways they have allowed these observations to challenge their own ways of coping, living, and understanding their lives.

One of the many strengths of this project is the illumination of the sense that "we're all in the same boatness" in terms of human experience. In Chapter 2, Waddell and Hatcher remind the reader that we all face the fundamental dilemma posed by the prospect of human relationships: relationships are "important, necessary for survival" and, at the same time, "complicated, difficult." In Chapter 6, West, Boothe, and Hatcher take up the issue of developmental/life stages, reiterating the universality of our humanness in quoting the work of Skovholt and Starkey (2010): "The human story is not reserved for clients: therapists are also fully involved in the human narrative" (p. 129). In Chapters 8 and 9, Tighe, Frye, and Hatcher ask the reader to consider cultural competence from this more relationship-centric perspective. What does culture mean? Does family or social class reflect a culture? Does consideration of cultural differences enhance stereotyping or undermine it? In Chapter 7, West, Waddell, and Hinojosa consider what is learned about the elusive constructs of personality and psychopathology, while in Chapter 3, Uhe, Boothe, and Hatcher engage the psychologists in an examination of their working understanding of ethics and resolution of ethical dilemmas. The participants have much to say about their experiences, and many of their conclusions seem congruent with one of the paradoxes of life and intimacy the concept that the more we can recognize and allow for individual difference, the greater the possibility for intimacy and deep connection. In the spirit of this long-awaited effort, I want to join the discussion, albeit in a very informal way.

* * * *

The consultation request initially appeared routine. As the attending psychologist on the consultation/liaison service of a local rehabilitation hospital, I was called on this occasion to evaluate Mr. G, a 75-year-old diabetic man who had refused consent to the therapeutic amputation of his left leg secondary to diabetic neuropathy. Over the previous few days he'd declined to discuss his decision with any of the nurses and doctors on the unit and had become, by staff report, withdrawn and incommunicative. There was a question of diminished capacity, possibly due to cognitive impairment, dementia, or depression, and the referring physician was eager to obtain a determination, as the procedure could not be postponed for long. The treatment team, although normally patient and tolerant, was becoming concerned and a little irritated with this man. After all, the procedure needed to be done and soon. Only a depressed, demented, or suicidal person would refuse a life-saving surgery. My task was clear: I was to identify the source of the patient's resistance to the necessary procedure and help eliminate the obstacle so that the right decision could be made.

When I entered the room I found a tall, handsome, gray-haired man who appeared surprisingly robust for his condition, sitting in a wheelchair near the window of his light-filled hospital room. Though I'd expected that he might not agree to speak with me, Mr. G readily allowed me to sit down next to his wheelchair. I introduced myself and explained why I was there. I started, as always, not with the issue of contention, but with an attempt to engage him in a conversation about his life and his background. He stared at me intently with a gaze I found both compelling and a little disturbing. *This man has seen something dark*, I thought.

When he spoke it was with a Slavic accent and a soft tone, but my association with his gaze was that he was speaking to me from a great depth, as if from the bottom of a deep well, pit, or grave. He asked me some questions about my training, my philosophy of life, my feelings about human beings and the possibility of change. My responses were a mix of direct answers, empathic reflections regarding his curiosity about me, and an observation that he was trying to decide whether I was worth talking to. I thought I saw him smile slightly, though I might have been mistaken about that. In the long silence that followed, I feared that he had withdrawn from the interaction. I wanted to speak, to find a way to engage him, and found my thoughts drifting to fishing, an activity about which I knew nothing. I'd only heard something about sitting still and waiting. I recalled the old psychotherapy pearl: "Don't just do something; sit there." That, at least, was something to do, something I could do. In fact, it was the only thing I seemed capable of doing, so I did that. When Mr. G spoke at last, he began to tell me the only story about his leg that really mattered.

As a young man in Eastern Europe during World War II, Mr. G had been imprisoned in a concentration camp. His entire family, his entire community, his entire world had been destroyed. Slowly, a narrative of unspeakable horrors and abuse unfolded, the murders of his family, close calls against his own life, starvation, and a courageous and harrowing escape through the woods near the camp. Mr. G described an incident that occurred as the Germans were retreating, having abandoned the camp after killing many of the remaining prisoners. Mr. G and a fellow inmate, ill, starving, almost delirious with fever, were wandering through the forest when they stumbled upon a group of Nazis. One of the men started, then grinned, drew his pistol, aimed it at Mr. G, and waited.

At this point in our conversation, my patient hesitated for the first time. His eyes narrowed and his voiced quavered. On a whim, he continued, this particular Nazi had appeared to change his mind. Perhaps he was tired at last of all the killing, Mr. G said, or had simply become bored with seeing the terrified looks on the faces of the people he was about to murder. "Who knows?" my patient shrugged, as if even the attempt to discern the motivations of such crazy and murderous behavior had long ago moved beyond what could be pondered.

The two escapees had seen the hesitation and taken the opportunity to run. Mr. G continued to relate a tale of deprivation, incredible luck, and the final achievement of safety and freedom. We had not broken eye-contact during this entire time. As I looked and listened, I felt he was trying to teach me something about his current dilemma. I started to understand that he had no intention of giving up anything else to anyone, not even to save his own life. He'd been subjected to enough, had had more than his share of both bad luck and narrow escapes, and he wasn't about to go back into those dark woods and try his luck again. He didn't have to tell me that I was a baby by comparison, an innocent who could not possibly understand what he had experienced. I could see on his face and in his expression the certain knowledge that I knew nothing of these horrors, nothing of what he'd endured. He'd also correctly sized me up as an agent of the treatment team, there to help him see the error of his current position on the matter.

There was silence in the room for what seemed like a very long time. We still looked at one another and, as we sat, I struggled with competing desires to speak, to offer what I already knew would sound like hollow platitudes and reassurances, to persuade him to "reach for life and not to let the Nazis win," and/or to say, "Okay, I get it; of course you don't want the surgery," and run from the room. In the end, the only thing I could do was sit there. The words of T.S. Eliot floated in to my mind, "I said to my soul, be still, and wait without hope. For hope would be hope for the wrong thing" (p. 28). The light in the room had become more golden and I knew our time was almost up. Finally, Mr. G spoke.

"And so now, Dr. Cramer," he said softly and without reproach, "How is it that you think you can help me?" Without breaking his gaze I tried to think, albeit a little desperately, of a response that he would find helpful, meaningful, anything that would prevent him from shutting me out, and something that would save my ebbing sense of effectiveness and growing shame at my incompetence. Finally I realized there was no escape, so I surrendered. "I don't know," I said, "but maybe you will let us continue to talk together." I left with his agreement to continue our conversation, with a clearer sense of not-knowing, deep respect for this individual for his courage and coping, greater humility, and a deeper understanding that there would be no simple answer to his dilemma.

During our subsequent conversations, Mr. G and I more fully outlined his internal fantasies about the proposed surgery: his experience of the treatment team as Nazi guards and the procedure itself as torture; his unconscious identification with the guards and their desire to murder him by finishing the job begun so many decades before; the exploration of his survivor guilt and his conviction that he had not deserved to have managed to live; his desire to torture me a bit with the breathless uncertainty about whether he would live or die; the pressure on me to "get him to make the right choice"; my desire for him to comply with the procedure conflicting with my desire to join his resistance and protect him from the team; Mr. G's understanding of this pressure and his continual testing of whether I was truly on his side or a "capo"—a representative of the oppressors' agenda, whose job it was to cajole or encourage compliance.

We struggled together to create a space in which the truth of his experience could come to life between us. This was not an ancient narrative reported from a distant land. It was equal parts high-stakes wrestling match, collaboration, and psychodrama. It was filled with life threat and profound uncertainty. I was in turn in the role of victim, perpetrator, and witness. We were in the woods, at some point, each of us feeling threatened, each of us holding the gun, each of us running away and returning. When Mr. G decided to have the surgery, we did not share the relief and joy of the treatment team. Our sojourn together had made us wiser than that. We understood that each choice brought a specific set of strengths and weaknesses, a certain constellation of gains and losses. Rather, our satisfaction seemed to come from the shared experience of having stumbled through the dark wood together, facing dangers, and feeling the precariousness of not knowing what would happen next. We'd been through something together. Mr. G even reported that he felt a bit less constrained by the catastrophes of the past. Not that anything had been resolved, or closed, or even healed especially, but rather that what had happened during the war had begun to *feel* more past. We reflected together on this as the true success, as the moment when he took a step out of the forest at last and moved into a bit more of the freedom for which he had fought so hard.

I liked and admired Mr. G very much for his feisty, angry courage, and despite the fact that it was precisely this determination that had caused him and me such difficulty in his current circumstance. He taught me that doing whatever it takes to join in with the patient, to tolerate my own discomfort, to let go of what Freud (1912) called the "therapeutic ambition" of the therapist to cure the patient, was actually what was required. We had stumbled into and out of that forest together, Mr. G leading the way. He taught me that empathic imagination and maintaining a nonjudgmental stance rather than a problem-solving one is the toughest thing in the world, both to achieve and to bring to the fight against the experiences that imprison our fellow human beings, yet that it was the only thing worth doing. Mr. G had affected me deeply, though I was a little embarrassed at the power of the experience and my attachment to this individual and the dark places we had traveled together. Mostly I wasn't sure how to understand the experience or what to make of it. Discussion in supervision was invaluable, of course, but the wisdom contained in the current volume would have provided me with the knowledge and comfort of shared experience, one of our most powerful teachers.

* * * *

While a growing body of psychotherapy outcome research tells us about the characteristics of successful treatment (Shedler, 2010; Westen, 2001), there has been little attention devoted to what therapists might gain from the process. The present volume explores what psychotherapists learn from the individuals with whom they work in treatment across a number of dimensions: life lessons, relationships, coping strategies, and ethical dilemmas. Psychotherapists report the ways they have learned more deeply about the qualities of a good relationship; relationships as sources of support; the fact that relationships are complex, difficult, and sometimes painful; the ways that one's early attachment experience and internalized expectations shape the experience of relationship; and the need to neither leave too early nor stay too long in a relationship. Therapists report that, through their work with patients, they reflect more about their own personal relationships, and have learned what not to do in them. Such knowledge has helped some therapists change their relationships with their own children or spouses. Some report feeling more tolerant of people. Some also report seeing the amount of time wasted in defensive maneuvers and the desire to avoid painful affect and, conversely, the benefit of facing pain in transforming one's life. Some report feeling less judgmental toward others and, perhaps most importantly, valuing relationships more. Again, it is important to note that theoretical orientation appears to have been irrelevant to the ability to learn from clients in these ways.

This eloquent and powerful book also examines the ways these clinicians have learned more about the impact of culture on their stance in the clinical relationship. Many psychotherapists reported feeling more aware of their own assumptions about human nature, in terms of the nature/nurture dimension, and the ways that culture defines the norms for health and pathology. There are reflections on the importance of being present in the moment with a client, what Bion (1967) called entering the therapeutic encounter, "without memory or desire."

In the final chapter, Hatcher reports on the responses to open-ended questions in which therapists report their admiration for their patients, the importance of their patients in their lives, the sense of privilege in being part of peoples' lives in this intimate and profound way, and their greater appreciation for the satisfactions of involvement in difficult work whose outcome is never guaranteed.

By tolerating ambiguity, being capable of not-knowing, maintaining a nonjudgmental stance, and having respect for the variety of individual experience, we widen the transitional space that allows patient and therapist together to discover something new. Through the practice of this challenging discipline, we have the chance to learn about the strengths and courage of our patients, understand their take on their dilemmas, and the reasons for the particular solutions that they have formulated. Without the freedom of mind and feeling created by the therapeutic space, human beings are likely not to feel free enough from concerns about compliance to consider an alternative perspective. Regardless of theory, model, or orientation, we cannot escape being squarely in the mix, unavoidably involved in a deeply human encounter. Hatcher and her team bring us closer to the depth of our attachments to our clients, and to the realization that the therapeutic relationship is no exception to this powerful meaning-making, life-changing experience of being in the moment with each other.

Margaret A. Cramer, PhD, ABPP

August 2014

References

Bion, W. (1967). Notes on memory and desire. *The Psychoanalytic Forum,2*(3), 271-280.

Ehrenberg, D.B. (1992). *The intimate edge: Extending the reach of psychoanalysis.* New York: W.W. Norton and Company.

Eliot, T. S. (1943). *Four quartets.* New York: Harcourt, Inc.

Freud, S. (1912). Recommendations to physicians practicing psycho-analysis. In J. Strachey (Ed.), *The Standard Edition of the Complete Works of Sigmund Freud, Volume XII, (1911-1913): The Case of Schreber, Papers on Technique and Other Works,* (pp. 109-120). London: Hogarth Press.

Maclaren, I. (1897). *The British Weekly,* December.

Schwaber, E. (1983a). A particular perspective on analytic listening. *Psychoanalytic Study of the Child, 38,* 519-546.

Schwaber, E. (1983b). Psychoanalytic listening and psychic reality. *International Review of Psycho-Analysis,10,* 379-392.

Shedler, J. (2010). The efficacy of psychodynamic psychotherapy. *American Psychologist, 65*(2), 98-109.

Skovholt, T. M., & Starkey, M. T. (2010).The three legs of the practitioner's learning stool: Practice, research/theory, and personal life. *Journal of Contemporary Psychotherapy, 40*, 125-130.

Westen, D. (2001). A multi-dimensional meta-analysis of treatments for depression, panic, and generalized anxiety disorder: An empirical examination of the status of empirically supported treatments. *Journal of Counseling and Clinical Psychology, 69*, 875-899.

Chapter 1

LEARNERS ABOUT LIFE AND ART

Adriana Kipper-Smith and Sherry L. Hatcher

I respect this moment of privacy and wait a while before
I draw closer
to start this conversation, which is imaginary but
perfectly possible.
I can hear an almost inaudible whisper calling me:
Come listen to the story of life. . .

(Cecilia Meireles, Brazilian poet)

Between the fall of 2008 and the spring of 2009, we interviewed 61 North American psychologists for a research project coordinated by Dr. Sherry Hatcher (Hatcher et al., 2012). With their permission, this interview process allowed us to "listen" into the lives of the therapist participants as new "windows" of understanding were opened to us. Throughout the interviews, we came to realize that our participants valued this opportunity to express their experiences in learning from their psychotherapy clients. At first we wondered if we were correctly reading their reactions but, as we were allowed to learn about their lives and gaze through their windows of observation, we concluded that the individuals whose perspectives we had the privilege to listen to very much wanted to tell us their stories.

In responding to the first question of the interview protocol ("Please give an example of some important life lesson you feel you've learned from one or more of your psychotherapy clients"), psychologists in our sample were prompted to navigate topics with which they were at times unfamiliar. As active listeners, they often realized that they were not so much listened to by others.

In a contemporaneous study by Stahl, Hill, Jacobs, Kleinman, Isenberg, and Stern (2009), trainee therapists reported feeling surprised at being asked about what they learn from their psychotherapy clients. Even considering the fact that the participants in that study were intern-level therapists, their findings highlight a lack of attention to therapist experiences in this very private line of work.

As a professional group, psychologists seem to be profoundly affected by an increasingly scientific culture of modernity in its parameters of objectivity, impersonality, and efficacy (Orlinsky et al., 2005). In that context, it is rather difficult to consider the person of the therapist, or to translate the therapeutic relationship as art rather than a science, or even equally in terms of both aspects. While, understandably, the field of psychotherapy has mostly focused on the effects therapy has on clients, its reciprocal effects on the therapist are also important to consider. Increasing emphasis on relationality, intersubjectivity, and co-constructed paradigms of psychotherapy support the notion of mutual influence in the therapy dyad (see, for example, Kahn & Fromm, 2001; Myers & Hayes, 2006; Skovholt & Rønnestad, 2003).

As Skovholt and Rønnestad (2003) have noted, the work of psychotherapists is one of the most important tasks involved in fostering positive human development. As they wrote: "Counseling and therapy can be remarkably powerful ways to reduce the severe emotional anguish and intense suffering experienced by people throughout the world-wide human community" (p. 1). In the process of helping others to alleviate their suffering and in seeking to foster positive and productive life experiences for clients, therapists are also required to address their own internal conflicts and problematic issues (Kottler, 1992). Kottler particularly suggests that therapists may serve as "models" for the potential that psychotherapy can have when psychological knowledge is applied to their own lives.

In spite of the possibility of being viewed as a model for their clients, some master therapists have agreed that they also learn from their therapy clients, in the form of acquiring new thoughts, feelings, and attitudes as a result of their professional work (Casement, 1991; Gerson, 2001; Guy, 1987; Katz, 2002; Kottler, 1993; Myers & Hayes, 2006; Orlinsky et al., 2005; Skovholt & McCarthy, 1988; Skovholt & Rønnestad, 1992; Wick, 2001; Yalom, 2000, 2002). Quite importantly, therapists have described those moments in which they feel changed by their clients as ones which represent some of the very best in their professional experiences (Kottler, 1993; Yalom, 2000; Freeman & Hayes, 2002). We believe these experiences may well depict the essence of the reciprocity in working as psychotherapists; in that role we are touched in different ways by a unique variety of people with whom we generally develop warm, collaborative, and expressive therapeutic relationships. In this connection, it is important to note that positive therapeutic gain can be associated, to some extent, with a client's becoming aware that the therapist can learn from her or him (Casement, 1991). In the study by Stahl et al. (2009) referenced earlier, this seems to be evident, as the authors suggest that even trainee therapists might consider telling their clients what they have learned from the process. That said, we note that self-disclosure on the part of therapists must be applied judiciously and only for the benefit of the client but, in fact, a great deal of what therapists may learn serves to quietly inform their work.

A handful of research-based studies on what psychotherapists learn from their clients have paved a path for more systematic research in this area. For example, Skovholt and Rønnestad (1992) interviewed 100 therapists with different levels of experience, and their findings indicate that clients are a "continuous major source of influence and serve as primary teachers" (Skovholt & Rønnestad, 1992, p. 129). Similarly, Rønnestad and Skovholt (2003) assessed the development of therapists at different experience levels, and their findings led them to propose eight phases of therapist development: a pre-training stage (the conventional helper); student phases (transition to professional training, imitation, and conditional autonomy); and post-graduate phases (exploration, integration, individuation, and integrity). Rønnestad and Skovholt maintain that professional development and growth take place when developing therapists demonstrate openness to new experiences and learning.

A later study by Orlinsky and Rønnestad (2005) focused on the complexities of therapy and its general effects on therapists' personal and professional lives. These authors collected information from nearly 5,000 psychotherapists from different specialties, theoretical orientations, nationalities, and levels of experience (i.e., from novice to senior therapists). Their findings stressed the fact that not only do therapists learn from their clients, but also that self-reflection and self-awareness are necessary ingredients for professional development. Where this study leaves off is in lacking specific discussion as to exactly what it is that therapists have learned from their clients. Nor is the focus on the effects clients may have on therapists, or the extent to which those effects may serve to change therapists' personal and professional lives.

Stahl et al. (2009) investigated what 12 intern-level psychotherapists said they had learned from their clients and reported that the lessons learned by these therapists were focused on the process of doing therapy and, further, what the therapists learned about themselves, their clients, human nature, and therapy relationships. The importance of supervision and self-awareness was also highlighted, confirming earlier research findings on these points (Orlinsky & Rønnestad, 2005; Rønnestad & Skovholt, 2003). In terms of professional development, research has suggested quite important qualitative differences between novice and experienced therapists as they conceptualize client issues and recall details of psychotherapy sessions (Cummings, Slemon, & Hallberg, 1993). In particular, Cummings et al. proposed that novice therapists tend to recall feelings and events related primarily to self-critique and self-reflection, whereas experienced therapists tend to conceptualize clients in increasingly complex ways, making thematic connections and identifying new insights. Similarly, Jennings and Skovholt (1999) stated that experienced therapists tend to recognize more subtle features of problems in their clients than do less experienced therapists. More experienced psychotherapists also seem to receive client feedback more openly and non-defensively than their less experienced colleagues (Jennings & Skovholt, 1999). These research findings suggest that greater therapist maturity affords increasingly complex learning from clients.

While previous research in this area has been quite interesting, it has not provided evidence about particular effects that clients may have on therapists at different levels of professional experience, or about the extent to which these effects may actually change therapists' personal and professional lives. The development of this area of research could enrich our knowledge about the specific kinds of effects the psychotherapy relationship and process may hold for psychotherapists as well as their clients. It is furthermore essential to bear in mind that the nature of psychologists' work can entail dealing with a great deal of human suffering. In this process, the relationship between therapist and client is not a theoretical one; the power of the therapeutic alliance accounts for much more variability in positive outcome for clients than any other aspect, including therapy technique (Messer, 2002).

Focusing on the effects of therapy on therapists, particularly on what they may learn from this process, has the potential to promote increased awareness as to how psychotherapy clients affect us as mental health practitioners. Consequently, this study may also help in the development of a sensibility that is apparently scarce in the field of psychotherapy, namely the humanization of the healing connection between the two persons engaged in the process of psychotherapy (McWilliams, 2005a).

Our Study

The collaborating authors of this study are essentially the psychologists we interviewed and those whose interview transcripts we read. Theirs are the stories we will be narrating in the following pages.

For the first and open-ended question posed to therapists in our study, participants emphasized the overall learning they accumulated in their work with psychotherapy clients, especially with regard to the impressive resilience their clients tended to show in navigating adverse life situations. Our participant therapists also emphasized that they are particularly touched by clients who may be negotiating a similar life stage as they are—or were. Therapists in our sample further emphasized the courage that their clients evidence, as well as what they had learned about being a role model, about the myth of therapist omnipotence, about relationships in general and marriage in particular, and about the importance of early experiences in the shaping of personality. These main themes—and some additional ones that occurred less frequently—will be discussed in some detail in the following pages. Table 1 presents a list of the topics and categories our participants primarily talked about in response to this first general question. The frequency of occurrences for each category is based on the 61 participants who responded. In our discussion of these occurrences, categories that overlap with one another will sometimes be grouped together.

TABLE 1: Categories and Frequencies: Lessons Learned From Clients-for Question 1 (See Appendix A for Questionnaire)

Category	Frequency
Lessons of Wisdom	33%
Lessons of Resilience	22%
Therapist as Role Model	8%
Letting Go of Control	8%
Little Insight	8%
Just Listen	7%
Early Experiences and Personality	6%
Being Nonjudgmental	6%
Sharing Similar Life Stages	5%
Hidden Nuggets	3%
Between Fear and Courage	3%
On Marriage	3%
Rare Responses	11%

Lessons of Wisdom

We called the therapists' first reactions and statements "lessons of wisdom" for several reasons. Between the first call to arrange an interview and the actual date of the interview, therapists had some time to think over the proposed topic. Our hope was that they would be inspired by the title of the research project and, in that spirit, have reviewed some general themes pertinent to the subject at hand. A frequent assumption in research—that the first question constitutes the "headlines" or ideas most important to a participant's experience—is likely a reasonable one. Though the responses to our first question were perhaps only "headlines," they also heralded more elaborated ideas to follow in the next chapters.

Our participants' first responses tended to reflect gratitude for the time in their lives spent with clients and the subsequent learning that afforded them both benefit for future clients and, at times, also for themselves. Therapists spoke of learning how to appreciate life more after sharing the experiences and setbacks in the lives of their clients, and even in learning from the moments in which they allowed their clients to challenge them. Lessons of patience, kindness, and respect for difference were also often expressed quite frequently by the therapists we interviewed.

With regard to gratitude, several psychologists noted that they are grateful for the lessons they learned by engaging in the therapy process with their clients. For example, Dr. X shared this thought:

> *Being a therapist makes one really aware. Sometimes it would be nice not to be so aware. I know that there are multiple points of view. . . so when I go down into my family, I know that mine isn't the only point of view.*

Dr. Aviva even more emphatically discussed those complex and rewarding aspects inherent in working as a psychotherapist:

> *What's profound about being a therapist is being with all that I really don't understand and that I can't hope to understand. But what I can do is try to be with people, as we together try to figure it [all] out and make some sense out of it and that's. . . the journey.*

As therapists shared their experiences and thoughts with us with regard to their clinical work, they sometimes expressed some sense of surprise in the course of applying their own academic and/or personal beliefs to clinical practice. As Dr. M stated:

> *I have shifted my thoughts about personal development and growth. I used to believe that there could be one moment in therapy or one moment in life where things get solved or things get flipped around and then life becomes easy like there is a magic moment. I've come to understand that life is a continual process; it is slowly transformed and conflicts are slowly resolved.*

Another aspect of experience emphasized by our participants relates to the importance of allowing clients to challenge the therapist's beliefs. Several reported that the respect and acceptance of such a challenge contributes to the process of change for the client—and most likely for the therapist as well. For example, Dr. Arcy shared with us that one of his client's political views were opposite to his. Through time and by allowing this client to challenge his viewpoints, Dr. Arcy courageously acknowledged that he changed some of his political beliefs. This comment reminds us of one of Yalom's (2000) narratives, detailing what he learned from his clients. Yalom's client, who spent several years in therapy with him, afforded a process that was highly transformative with regard to Yalom's emerging ideas about death, which some have described as "the ultimate insult to one's omnipotence" (Goldman, 1998). Yalom (2000) synthesized this newfound wisdom as follows:

> *In the past, I had generally put thoughts of death in the back burner of consciousness. But my work with Irene would no longer permit it. Again and again my hours with her heightened not only my sensitivity to death and my sense of life's preciousness, but also my death anxiety. . . Whoever said that therapists are overpaid?* (p. 116)

Yalom makes a good point in stating that the work of therapists is a complex task, influenced by a plethora of internal and external variables. When one considers that a therapist's task includes a fair degree of neutrality, why would we anticipate that therapists would be so intensively touched and powerfully changed by the views and experiences of their therapy clients?

Being Nonjudgmental

As might be expected, several therapists noted the importance of being nonjudgmental with therapy clients. However, as Dr. Michelle noted, most of the time we may still remain "silently" judgmental. Although it is a highly important trait for successful psychotherapy, a genuinely nonjudgmental attitude is likely only achieved through hard work, experience, and discipline. According to the psychologists we interviewed, it can be facilitated by therapeutic experience. For example,

Dr. Viola stated that his work with clients taught him that experiences may be different "but emotions are the same." He noted that regardless of socioeconomic status, ranging from homeless people living in rural areas to highly educated people living in a big city, we are all the same in terms of our wants (e.g., desire for approval from our parents, need for close relationships, and striving for meaningful work). This observation caused Dr. Viola to integrate a kind of nonjudgmental mantra into his practice to the effect that: "People are more similar than they are different across all socioeconomic categories and cultures."

Still other psychologists underscored how tricky being nonjudgmental may be. For example, Dr. Justin noted that, based on looks, stereotyping may easily occur and that it is likely unlearned only by extensive and diversified clinical experience. She further shared a vignette about a 15-year-old boy whom she first met in a detention center. Dr. Justin reported being surprised to discover, after a number of sessions that this adolescent was "a very nice boy," something she'd not expected based on context alone.

Cultural markers may lead us to anticipate things about people who dress in a certain way, or who are in a particular age range, or who reside in a certain geographical locale; more likely than not such factors influence us all. However, what is inspiring about this example is the newfound awareness on the part of a therapist who was courageous enough to acknowledge that, based on a stereotype, she had created an image of a client she eventually found to be untrue. Dr. Justin emphasized that it is essential to try to understand where each individual is coming from. Although the boy in the detention center had made a mistake, she concluded that he was not overall a delinquent person.

Another psychologist, Dr. Kristi, candidly reported a situation in which a client afforded her a profound learning opportunity. The client in this case, who was comfortable financially, had unintentionally gotten pregnant. For a variety of reasons Dr. Kristi encouraged the client to keep the pregnancy. However, although the client accepted her advice, as a new mother she realized that she was not ready to care for a child, and ultimately accused her psychologist of being judgmental. Dr. Kristi found herself in the very difficult situation in which she discovered that her actions with this client were greatly motivated by her own values: "I learned that, as a therapist, you need to keep your value system outside of therapy." Another therapist in our sample, Dr. Luke, summed up this type of scenario in stating that it is very important to acknowledge that a therapist's expectations of happiness may be quite different from those of his or her clients.

Also related to the matter of withholding judgment, Dr. Reuben spoke candidly about the recent death of one of his clients from cancer. He mentioned that the last time this client called him, she explored her wish to die after a long battle fighting her pancreatic cancer, although she decided during that conversation that she would prepare to connect with hospice care. Dr. Reuben shared how affected he was by this client, and how difficult it was to just sit with such intense feelings, summing up his role as a therapist as follows:

> There are people who trust me about being open with their wish to die. It doesn't necessarily have to be open about suicidal thoughts or ideation or wishes but rather in recognition of my knowing what dying is like and that I do not condemn people who want to die.

His eloquent report is one of combined grief, respect, and acceptance, and about not passing judgment. In regard to the impending natural death of a client, Dr. Harriet M. noted:

> I guess those kinds of clients, when you have those deeply moving attachments with something as raw and deep and as primal as facing death. . . you learn that your own death can happen at any time. . . Clients can impact you that deeply. [For example], certainly my workaholism has changed particularly in the past year.

Dealing With Client Suffering and What One Learns From It

Similar to these experiences, Dr. Pedroso talked about how difficult it is to witness clients negotiating tremendous and painful shifts in life, which "you tend to absorb through the skin." She reported learning that even those who have suffered major psychological injuries can eventually reach an "even keel," carry on, and take pleasure in the smaller things in life. However, according to Dr. Pedroso, it depends on both "the type of injury and on people's inner solidity." This therapist further noted that inner solidity has a lot to do with one's willingness to stay engaged with the world, even though an opposite route, such as withdrawing into oneself, may seem easier, and remain "a real temptation," at times.

In regard to dealing with clients who experience acute loss, Dr. Luke shared some of his experiences with refugees, including individuals who had lost family members, their identity—in his words, "everything." He said that such work has humbled him and helped him put his own life challenges in perspective. From traumatized refugees, Dr. Luke reported learning that "life goes on and that you need to gather your forces as quickly as you can to kind of rebuild and reconnect." He further stated:

> Our expectations are not tied to what is predictable in life. We tend to have blinders on in terms of these normal experiences, and when you work all the time with clients who come in with these, you come to understand that this is what life is all about. It's your ability to kind of prepare and roll with these things when they happen.

Listening to and Learning From Therapy Clients

Dr. Iris mentioned that it used to be difficult for her to work with narcissistic clients, and it was only when she started to learn about her own narcissism that she could do so. She added that she ended up learning a lot about herself in the process of addressing her clients' narcissism.

By the same token, Dr. Lucas summed up an important theme about a therapist's attitude and stance: "It is important to be kind. People come with something special about themselves." While psychologists recognize that many human emotions and aspirations are basically the same across individuals, they also note that each individual (and every new therapeutic encounter) holds something new to be learned, something that is "special."

The powerful role of truly listening was also emphasized by those therapists who participated in our study. Their descriptions closely resemble a variety of mindfulness: listening while being fully present and open. In this regard, I (first author) remember what a former professor, philosopher, and psychoanalyst used to say about listening to clients. According to him, therapists sometimes need to be present enough to listen to their clients as they would listen to music. What does the melody sound like? What kind of story or stories does the rhythm of the client's words convey, and what feelings are they awakening in themselves and their therapists?

In different ways, our participants talked about keeping their ears wide open. As Dr. Ellen said, "When people come in, I don't necessarily need to solve their problems. I can just sit with them and kind of work with them together and I don't have to be the one, I'm not the expert on anything." In another instance, Dr. McMillan, who has written a book on depression, reported once giving a copy of his book to a client who was suffering from depression. To his surprise, this client came back for the next session enraged, stating that she needed to be heard, not instructed to read a book. Other therapists, such as Dr. Mike, reported that sometimes clients are just looking for somebody to understand and hear what they have to say without criticizing, judging, recommending, or analyzing. These are lessons learned.

Many of the aforementioned accounts seem to confirm the idea that the relationship between therapist and client is not only essential in terms of its effect on therapy outcome, but that the process is, in itself, a vehicle for learning new ways to relate. Listening without filters or preconceived biases is an essential lesson reported by those in our sample. As Strupp (1996) noted, empathic listening is the most important human and technical tool in the therapist's tool box.

The Sounds of Resilience

Our participants emphasized how much they learned about human strength and resilience through their clients' extremely difficult experiences, including physical, sexual, and emotional abuse; the loss of a child; terminal illnesses; physical disability; and severe mental illnesses. It is notable how resilience is often featured as a lesson on how to approach life in creative ways that go beyond simple survival.

Dr. Goodheart, for example, stated that people can thrive in life even after terrific suffering. He shared the case of a woman who survived being horrifically beaten and stabbed, and was working toward being able to testify against the offender:

*By the end of her therapy she was preparing to go and testify
in court against him and be in the same room, facing him,
looking at him in the eyes. She not only wanted to be free
of the PTSD symptoms, but she also wanted to be able to
go into the courtroom and do a good job testifying. . . She
was not aiming to forgive him; although she thought maybe
one day that would be nice, that was not her goal. But her
goal was to be able to see him and look at him in the court
room without hating him. . .*

In a related vein, Dr. Linda shared that one of her clients who had
"awful life experiences" kept "plugging away and refusing to give up
even though [she] think[s] if [she] [were] in her shoes [she] might have."
Therapists in our study frequently reported how people are capable of
amazing strength in make difficult changes, even when their childhoods
were filled with unimaginable events. For example, Dr. Laura noted that
she learned about resilience from her clients who had major physical
problems, including chronic diseases and cancer. She expressed surprise
at how brave and persevering her clients were in the face of such great
suffering. Similarly, Dr. Odila reported learning that the things that
we see as tragic may sometimes be experienced as a great blessing. She
explained that one of her clients, who survived breast cancer and was
later diagnosed with metastatic liver cancer, amazingly reported that
"She became more herself, more whole, freer—finding more fulfillment
in her life and relationships."

Dr. Mark offered an example of a client in her fifties who had been
deaf all of her life and blind for the past seven years. Her husband had
left her and she had returned to her parents' house, having developed
a delusional psychosis. After a program of rehabilitation, she started to
function normally, secured a job and an apartment, and learned to get
around on her own despite the vision loss. Dr. Mark summed this up
as follows: "What looks like very adverse circumstances. . . there is a
possibility of quite dramatic and substantial change."

Perhaps not surprisingly, therapists tend to be very resilient people,
possibly inspired in part by their clients' strengths. Said Dr. Goodheart:

*People who become psychotherapists and are good at it
have often made use of their own suffering as children in
their families. What we do with our adult lives is shaped*

by the ways in which we suffer as children. That's part of being a creature who is dependent on big creatures who may not function at such a high level. That's nothing to be embarrassed by.

Early Experiences Impact Later Life

Therapists reported learning that early experiences often have a long-lasting influence on the way people relate psychologically, both within themselves and with others. They noted that traumatic situations can lead to emotional immaturity and even borderline states of functioning. As Dr. Ranju said:

> *Even after all these years as a therapist, I can be drawn into drama still—not just with clients but with family. There is an aspect of my personality that allows me to be drawn in if I am not careful—very, very careful.*

In a similar vein, other therapists in our sample noted that people tend to present with symptoms that can represent identifications with what they have learned from their significant others in early life. Dr. Anna contributed an apt example of this phenomenon:

> *One client I've had grew up with a very harsh religious upbringing that made her feel as if she were inherently evil. It has taken a good deal of work to, on the one hand, be respectful of her beliefs, while trying to sort out her individual good character from the tenets of the religious judgment.*

The importance of early childhood experiences in shaping personality was eloquently described by Dr. Natasha:

> *The long-term client I had, I worked with her for two years and I definitely got the feeling . . . how this exactly is played out with her. Her memories of her mother were that she was not available to her and how that affected her. How she woke up in the morning, coming down and*

*having her mother not make eye contact with her. How she
internalized that to mean "Maybe I'm not good enough,"
or "I'm not important enough," and her extreme need to
seek approval from other people as she did not get the initial
attention from her own parents.*

In observing great strength in the ways their clients often deal
with difficult upbringings, psychologists reported finding the "hidden
nuggets" that they described as pivotal in terms of mastering life
challenges. Dr. Lucas stated that if "that little nugget" can be found,
then and only then can he help his clients (and, surprisingly, also
himself) to change. And Dr. Yetty shared the following:

*No matter how bad things seem to be, there has to be a
silver lining, something where I can begin to work towards
the positive. Thinking like that makes me feel more hopeful,
even when difficult things happen in my life.*

Summing up this theme, Dr. Luke noted that most people have a
lot of hidden skills that they may not acknowledge. She added that it is
often the case that people around us also fail to recognize our hidden
nuggets of strength. It is the work of therapy to uncover the strengths
in our clients, using our own strengths as therapists to help accomplish
this goal.

Learning How to Be a Model and Mastering One's Own Life

Several participants noted that therapists sometimes needed to
better follow their own advice. This notion involves a fairly well-known
concept in the world of commerce: If you want to sell something,
you'd better believe in it or, perhaps, you sell more effectively what
you consume yourself. As applied to the therapeutic relationship, this
suggests that advice-giving only works when therapists are genuine and
consistent in that which they embrace as healthy for their own lives as
well.

In terms of self-care and maintaining a healthy lifestyle, Dr. Sarah
stated: "I can't give messages I don't believe myself." Dr. Laura noted that
it is unfair to ask clients to do something that a therapist is unwilling

to do for him or herself, such as some types of homework. Dr. Rick reported learning how to use some therapeutic techniques *along with* clients (such as stress reduction strategies). However, as Dr. Rick also noted, sometimes therapists feel overwhelmed with the stresses of life and they forget to use those techniques for their own well-being. This is an intriguing comment, given that self-care and behavioral techniques are most needed, in both therapists' and clients' lives, when the "stresses of life" abound.

Mutual learning seems to be a mechanism by which change is possible. According to Dr. Rick, "It's inspiring to see someone using that stuff that has a big positive effect emotionally." In this regard, psychologists such as Dr. Sarah emphasized the importance of a calm nervous system and self-relaxation techniques for the therapist. As she reported:

> *If I am calm and can keep myself calm, which I am pretty good at doing. . . that's one of the glories of getting old. You know how to settle down. But the impact of my calm nervous system with the folks that I work with is remarkable, just quite remarkable.*

In the same vein, Dr. Steve concluded that he likely became proficient in applying therapeutic techniques in his personal life as a result of teaching clients how to employ those techniques.

In areas that go beyond the practices of self-care, Dr. McMillan expressed his thoughts about marriage and how his work with couples has nourished his own marital relationship. He noted that marriage requires hard work and, for this reason, in teaching clients to "clean up their messes" and to be creative, he ended up teaching himself in that same spirit: "We all share this journey together. Watching couples work and love each other is inspiring and it challenges me to be a better husband and tend to my marriage better."

All of these accounts powerfully express the mutual influence of the therapeutic enterprise. However, as it turns out, this kind of learning (i.e., therapists learning from clients) seldom takes place if therapists do not relax their need for over-control. Several research participants reported learning from their clients that they cannot solve everything, and that they also need to accept their own personal limitations, including those as psychotherapists. Some psychologists indicated that, at times, even their best is not enough. As Dr. Pedroso said, "I just sort of realized this is bigger than whatever I can do. . . [that is] humility and acceptance of not being omnipotent, not being totally skilled or totally adequate."

Dr. McMillan reported a long-term professional relationship with a client from whom he learned a great deal:

> *She taught me of the importance of letting go, and she showed me how arrogant I was/I am; she taught me about my need to have the world the way I want it to be. I had to accept ambiguity and life without control, and that was a very powerful and meaningful relationship to me.*

In facing personal limitations, Dr. Justin similarly claimed that we should not take life too seriously; he observed that he has learned how to relax by not taking things personally.

Dr. McMillan, who is Caucasian, reflected on an interaction he had had with an African-American client. He candidly shared that this client taught him that people in dominant societal positions tend to be unconscious of what is going on around them because they do not need to shape themselves to fit in the way minorities often need to do. Dr. McMillan shared with some discomfort that he learned that, as a Caucasian male, he tended to take things for granted. However, this kind of revelation is one of the highlights of our research: to be deeply touched by the wisdom therapists glean from clients, often by dint of honest introspection.

It seems appropriate to end this section of Chapter 1 with the words of seasoned therapist Alvin Mahrer (1996), who stated in regard to letting go of absolute truths:

> *Therapists can breathe the heady air of new possibilities, exciting creativity, and can move in the direction of becoming better therapists by letting go of absolute truths and daring to enter a world of whole new ways of seeing what may help account for psychotherapeutic change, whole new ways of making sense of what clients are like, hole new methods of effecting changes, whole new ways of being with clients, whole new ways of becoming better therapists.*
> (p. 141)

Sharing Insight and Similar Life Stages

In this section we will discuss learning effects for psychologists that may occur by somewhat unconscious or automatic processes, rather than by intentionality. In this respect, several psychologists noted that the majority of their clients are quite often initially unaware of their problems, limitations, or even their strengths. Participants who suggested this issue also tended to emphasize the importance of becoming aware of how one's behavior affects others. For instance, psychologists in our sample often reported seeing discrepancies between the ways some clients view themselves and how others, such as co-workers, may see them. Dr. Homer noted that many of his clients, who are physicians, tend to be viewed as disruptive by others with whom they worked, whereas they instead viewed themselves as perfectionists. Similarly, Dr. Rose emphasized the importance of therapeutic work in fostering deeper insight into clients' lives. However, she noted that in order to accomplish this, it would seem necessary first to acknowledge how little insight some clients have into their own problems and how they "clearly engage in either thoughts or behaviors that really make their lives unhappy and make them unhappy."

The development of deepening insight through psychotherapy is a well-known goal of some treatment paradigms. Interestingly, essential insights can be catalyzed for clients when therapists learn along with their clients, who may be navigating similar life stages—as for example in child-rearing, negotiating middle age, or anticipating retirement. Our sample of psychologists reported learning much about themselves. As Dr. Martina stated straightforwardly, he learned about what it means to be a parent partly through his patients' experience of parenting. Dr. Martina shared that he was initially rather impatient with one client's "very hard edge" with regard to her three sons, who all had ADHD. However, after his own son was given a diagnosis of ADHD, he reportedly changed the way he listened and understood, not only with this client, but with others as well. As he said, "I have empathy for my clients when I've negotiated a similar life stage or experience." Similarly with regard to parenting, Dr. Michelle reported becoming more understanding of clients who are parents struggling to set boundaries and who are pushing their own limits of patience. As she said: "It doesn't matter how compassionate you are. . . I get fed up with my kid, too."

At times, therapists, like their clients, have to face difficult illnesses, and such experiences may serve to change the ways they work with their clients thereafter. According to Dr. Gimpenfeld, clients who are fighting a disease tend to affect their therapist's ways of coping with illness. In summarizing this dynamic, psychologist Dr. Tom noted something he has noticed throughout the years—that he is "ready to hear different things at different stages of my professional life."

Sharing similar (at times too similar) life stages with clients prompts therapists to look into their own decisions and belief systems, sometimes effecting change in their own lives, even as such change comes no more easily for them than it does for their clients. In this regard, some of our participants reported learning how to deal with their own fears through the experience of their clients' similar struggles. For example, Dr. Tom offered the following account:

> *I see that and have learned. . . not only from watching individual patients struggle to maintain their avoidance under the guise. . . of trying to protect themselves, but I have also learned it from the other end of the continuum where patients [have] solved that puzzle, which is to go through something hard. . . and to realize one's own agency or efficacy provides them with a tremendous sense of relief and [that they] can regain control of their life. I think that is probably one of the more poignant and powerful things I have learned in my current work.*

Dr. Tom offered an example of client who was a veteran, and who avoided recollecting his combat experience for over 40 years. However, in the midst of the therapeutic process, he courageously started to talk about his feelings and what was on his mind, which had the effect of greatly ameliorating his long-standing history of anxiety and depression.

Similarly, Dr. Beach reported learning that one cannot be afraid of the emotions that come out of a frightening situation, even though it takes much personal courage to face these matters. He gave the example of a husband who decided to accept his wife's infidelity because he was afraid to be alone. As Dr. Beach asserted, the answer was not to just "accept" the situation or to say "get out of the house," but to work courageously on the risks involved in analyzing where the problems really were for both parties.

So we see that witnessing courage in their clients' lives—even that which partly results from their own influence on a client's life—tends to circle back as benefit for the therapist's own sense of courage and optimism.

Relationships, After All

A few of our participants specifically talked about marriage, particularly if they worked in couples therapy. For example, Dr. Felipe reported learning from his clients that if both partners experience extremely negative feelings, it can be almost impossible to save the marriage. He offered the example of a couple in which each partner believed that the other was not trying nearly as hard as they believed they were. Dr. Trayton reporting learning that couples who endure in their marriages are not necessarily nice to each other at all times. He noted, "I learned that there are different ways to survive and thrive, and it made me more tolerant and creative."

Whether in the context of a marriage or in other forms of intense relational exchange, our participants reported learning how to be more compassionate and grateful in relation to their own lives based on what they derived from their work with clients. Their clients' struggles and significant losses were repeatedly translated into greater appreciation of their own lives. Some, such as Dr. Wilbur, reported learning how to be increasingly compassionate towards disabled people through working with a client who had suffered a serious accident. This caused Dr. Wilbur to confront the possibility that he himself might incur significant disability just as easily. As he said: "Every client affects the way I feel about mankind and about my level of empathy and compassion toward people. . . The more stories I hear, the more open hearted I am." Dr. Kristi summed up her feelings by saying that she learned to have more gratitude for the experiences she had in her personal and professional life because these prompted her to become a better psychologist: "Whatever I've been through. . . [other] people have been through worse."

Altogether, in analyzing the content of these interviews, we found a recurrent and abiding sense of therapists' gratitude toward their clients. Many of the therapists in our sample reported becoming aware of the fact that they sometimes "forget to be grateful enough." For example, Dr. Clark pointed out that we cannot take life for granted; he offered the example of one of his clients who had lost a child—a tragedy he had never faced.

Many of these accounts relate to psychologists' own developmental stages as professionals. For example, Dr. Peyton noted that therapists generally start out their practices very close to their own frames of reference but eventually segue into becoming more client-centered. This idea is corroborated by the available literature on therapist development, which associates flexibility, integration, and versatility—a kind of ". . . authentic chameleon" (Lazarus, 1996) quality—with becoming a competent psychologist (Norcross, 1996).

A Few Concluding Thoughts

After we had completed the first few interviews with the selected group of psychologists, we realized that we were frequently hearing words such as "compelling" and "moving." This reaffirmed our sense of the importance of our topic. At the same time, we observed our therapist participants thinking hard to identify examples of their learning from specific clients. For our interviewees, it seemed much more familiar to talk about what their clients go through, rather than selecting specific examples that may have affected them personally and/or professionally.

Our listening carefully to these interviews, as researchers and clinicians, provided us with an overwhelming feeling of gratitude for the field we have chosen. We realized that psychologists were sharing their life experiences with their clients—even if not explicitly—and, as often happens in interview-based research that realization in itself afforded learning, yielding for both the interviewees and interviewers a variety of "parallel process." We also came to realize how brave our participants were in verbalizing some of their fears and even identifying some of their own perceived weaknesses. Listening to these stories brought up feelings of amazement in the researchers, as if we were vicariously experiencing pieces of the therapeutic process that our participants had shared with their psychotherapy clients.

As Richardson and St. Pierre (2005) pointed out, rather than writing stories only about other people and cultures, we sometimes tend to write about ourselves. This work is indeed about ourselves, and each of us—as interviewers, psychologists, and trainee therapists—who have had the opportunity to see ourselves through the generous narratives of these inspiring psychologists.

Psychotherapy is, after all, a relationship between two (or more) individuals who believe that, if the client can trust someone with their most hidden conflicts and secrets, they can eventually grow and heal. On the other hand, perhaps the gradually increasing interest in this line of research may indicate a maturing sense of trust in our techniques. We hope the findings of this research will eventually afford greater growth and understanding of the aspects of mutuality in the therapy relationship.

The themes introduced in this chapter will be explored in more detail in each of the chapters that follow.

References

Casement, P. J. (1991). *Learning from the patient.* New York, NY: Guilford Press.

Cummings, A. L., Slemon, A. G., & Hallberg, E. T. (1993). Session evaluation and recall of important events as a function of counselor experience. *Journal of Counseling   Psychology, 40*, 156-165.

Gerson, B. (2001). *The therapist as a person.* Hillsdale, NJ: The Analytic Press.

Gilligam, C. (2004). Recovering psyche: Reflections on life-history and history. *The Annual of Psychoanalysis, 32*, 131-147.

Goldman, D. (1998). Surviving as scientist and dreamer: Winnicott and "the use of an object." *Contemporary Psychoanalysis, 34*, 359-367.

Guy, J. D. (1987). *The personal life of the psychotherapist: The impact of clinical practice on the therapist's intimate relationships and emotional well-being.* New York, NY: Wiley.

Hatcher, S. L., Kipper-Smith, A., Waddell, M., Uhe, M., West, J. S., Boothe, J. H. . . Gingras, P. (2012). What therapists learn from psychotherapy clients: Effects on personal and professional lives. *The Qualitative Report, 17*(Art. 95), 1-19. Retrieved from http://www.nova.edu/ssss/QR/QR17/hatcher.pdf

Jennings, L., & Skovholt, T. S. (1999). The cognitive, emotional, and relational characteristics of master therapists. *Journal of Counseling Psychology, 46*, 3-11.

Kahn, S., & Fromm, E. (2001). *Changes in the therapist*. Mahwah, NJ: Lawrence Erlbaum.

Katz, P. (2002). Lessons my patients taught me. In L. T. Flaherty (Ed.), *Adolescent psychiatry: Developmental and clinical studies* (Vol. 26). *Annals of the American society for adolescent psychiatry* (pp. 3-23). New York, NY: The Analytic Press/Taylor & Francis Group.

Kottler, J. A. (1992). Confronting our own hypocrisy: Being a model for our students and clients. *Journal of Counseling and Development, 70*, 475-476. In J.A. Kottler (1993), *On being a therapist*. San Francisco, CA: Jossey Bass.

Lazarus, A. A. (1996). Some reflections after 40 years of trying to be an effective psychotherapist. *Psychotherapy: Theory, Research, Practice, Training, 33*, 142-145.

Mahrer, A. R. (1996). Lessons from 40 years of learning how to do psychotherapy. *Psychotherapy: Theory, Research, Practice, Training, 33*, 139-141.

McWilliams, N. (2005). Preserving our humanity as therapists. *Psychotherapy: Theory, Research, Practice, Training, 42*, 139-151.

Meireles, C. (2001). *Poesia Completa* [Complete Poetry]. Rio de Janeiro: Nova Fronteira.

Messer, S. B. (2002). Let's face facts: Common factors are more potent than specific therapy ingredients. *Clinical Psychology: Science and Practice, 9*, 21-25.

Myers, D., & Hayes, J. A. (2006). Effects of therapist general disclosure and countertransference disclosure on ratings of therapist and session. *Psychotherapy: Theory, Research, Practice, Training, 43*, 173-185.

Norcross, J. C. (1996). The lifetime lessons of six psychologists: An introduction. *Psychotherapy: Theory, Research, Practice, Training, 33*, 129-130.

Orlinsky, D. E., Rønnestad, M. H., Gerin, P., Davis, J. D., Ambühl, H., Davis, M. L., Dazord, A. . .Schröder, T. A. (2005). The development of psychotherapists. In D. E. Orlinsky and M. H. Rønnestad (Eds.), *How Therapists Develop: A study of therapeutic work and professional growth* (pp. 3-13).Washington, DC: American Psychological Association.

Richardson, L., & St. Pierre, E. A. (2005). Writing: A method of inquiry. In N. K. Denzin & Y. S. Lincoln (Eds.), *The Sage handbook of qualitative research* (3rd ed., pp. 959-978). Thousand Oaks, CA: Sage Publications

Rønnestad, M. H., & Skovholt, T. M. (2001). Learning arenas for professional development: Retrospective accounts of senior psychotherapists. *Professional Psychology: Research and Practice, 32*, 181-187.

Rønnestad, M. H., & Skovholt, T. M. (2003). The journey of the counselor and therapist: Research findings and perspective on professional development. *Journal of Career Development, 30*, 5-44.

Skovholt, T. M., & McCarthy, P. R. (1988). Critical incidents: Catalysts for counselor   development. *Journal of Counseling and Development, 67,* 69-72.

Skovholt, T. M., & Rønnestad, M. H. (1992). Themes in therapist and counselor development.   *Journal of Counseling & Development, 70*, 505-515.

Skovholt, T. M., & Rønnestad, M. H. (2003). The hope and promise of career life-span counselor and therapist development. *Journal of Career Development, 30*, 505-515.

Stahl, J. V., Hill, C. E., Jacobs, T., Kleinman, S., Isenberg, D., & Stern, A. (2009). When the shoe is on the other foot: A qualitative study of intern-level trainees' perceived learning from clients. *Psychotherapy, Therapy, Research, Practice, Training, 46*, 376-389.

Strupp, H. H. (1996). Some salient lessons from research and practice. *Psychotherapy: Theory, Research, Practice, Training, 33*, 135-138.

Wick, E. (2001). Hearing the unspoken: From hypnotherapist to comatherapist. In S. Kahn & E. Fromm (Eds.), *Changes in the therapist*. Mahwah, NJ: Lawrence Erlbaum Associates.

Yalom, I. D. (2000). *Momma and the meaning of life: Tales of psychotherapy.* New York: Perennial Books.

Yalom, I. D. (2002). *The gift of therapy: An open letter to a new generation of therapists and their patients.* New York: Harper Collins Publishers.

Chapter 2

LEARNING ABOUT RELATIONSHIPS FROM PSYCHOTHERAPY CLIENTS

Manuela L. Waddell[1] and Sherry L. Hatcher

An interpersonal relationship may be conceptualized as an established connection between two or more human beings. It is most often a regularly shared encounter that continues over a period of time (Argyle & Henderson, 1985) and has holistic qualities that include behavioral, cognitive, and emotional components (Perlman & Vangelisti, 2003). Collins and Madden (2006) further explain that relationships involve at least two people who are interdependent in such a way that each person in the dyad affects and is affected by the other in an essential variety of ways. Relationships are essential to human beings and provide us with a meaningful existence, essential for our survival and psychological well-being.

The field of psychology has proposed multiple theories regarding interpersonal adaptation. Early on, Fairbairn (1944) stated that humans are "object" (or other-person) seeking. Bowlby (1973, 1979, 1980) famously demonstrated that we are prewired for human contact, whereas Baumeister and Leary (1995) discussed how people have an innate need to belong together with others. In particular, developmental studies have offered compelling evidence that much of an infant's innate

---

[1]   Thanks to Katherine Tighe for her early work with Manuela Waddell on the relationship data.

behaviors facilitate the baby's social interactions (see Siegel, 1999; Stern, 1973). For example, shortly after birth, infants visually follow the human face farther and longer than a different stimulus of similar complexity (Johnson, Dziurawiec, Ellis, & Morton, 1991).

Developmental psychology theorists and researchers have shown that a human's need for relationship continues throughout the lifespan: first in within-family relationships and then also in relationships outside of the family that begin to emerge as early as the second year of life. Toddlers, for example, exhibit more reciprocal interactions with preferred playmates than with those less preferred (Hartup, 1989, 2009). There is a plethora of research that discusses adolescent peer relationship quality as a strong predictor of teen and young adult well-being, competence, and adaptation (Brown, Eicher, & Petrie,1986; Meece & Laird, 2006) and these findings extend well into older adulthood (Carstensen, 1993).

In a classic study, Kliniger (1977) found that when Americans were asked what provided meaning to life they frequently mentioned close relationships with parents, children, siblings, partners, and friends. And, from a systems perspective, Gilbert (1992) noted that after food, water, and shelter, interpersonal relationships are primary determinants of life quality. In particular, relationships with family and friends are a key to happiness and mental health, whereas work relationships are central to productivity. Even among nations, relationships are central to matters of war and peace.

As we read how our study participants learned from their clients about the essential nature of relationships, we are reminded of the movie *Cast Away*, where the character played by actor Tom Hanks is stranded on a desert island with no human contact. In the service of survival, he creates a friend in the image of a volleyball that he names Wilson, which comes to represent the internalized memories of his prior human relationships, providing him with strength and support.

The Psychotherapy Relationship

Psychotherapy is a particular and unique variety of relationship (Gelso, 2014; Truscott, 2010). Based on a growing body of research, we know that it is a relationship that directly relates to positive therapy outcomes (Norcross, 2011). Almost no other life relationship affords the level of confidentiality and focus on one person in a relationship, whereby the other listens exclusively with a goal of understanding and helping the other person to problem-solve, to ameliorate presenting concerns, and aim to improve quality of life. As in any relationship, the working alliance in a therapy relationship may be temporarily compromised, such that it is essential to repair such ruptures in order to sustain the collaborative alliance. Indeed, the repair of relationship ruptures can ultimately, be quite therapeutic (Safran, Muran, & Rothman, 2006).

It is entirely plausible to propose that the psychotherapy relationship has an important effect on each of those involved in the process, including the psychotherapist. Consequently, as our clients learn from psychotherapists how to navigate relational life situations and problems, psychotherapists tell us that they have also learned from their clients about the nature of well-functioning and/or conflictual relationships.

The Research Protocol

The second question of our research protocol investigated the very important area of relationships by asking the 61 psychotherapist participants: *What have you learned from your psychotherapy clients about relationships?* Follow-up questions requested de-identified examples from the psychotherapists' practices, as well as inquiry into whether and how their learning about relationships from clients may have affected them personally and/or professionally.

All 61 psychotherapists responded to the relationship question, resulting in rich and detailed data with accompanying, illustrative examples. Ninety-five percent of the respondents indicated that they had learned something about relationships from their psychotherapy clients, while 5% indicated their work with clients reinforced what they already knew, but in some ways touched them, nonetheless. The therapists in our sample provided elaborated examples of what they had learned about relationships from their clients and they described the impact of that knowledge on their lives. All provided at least one response to the relationship question, with a large proportion offering multiple responses. The sizeable number of responses indicated to our research team both the importance and the depth of therapist learning about relationships from clients.

A summary of the major themes that emerged from the therapist narratives can be seen in Table 1 and will be discussed further in the first half of this chapter. The second half of this chapter offers specific illustrations of these themes and others offered by the therapists in our study. It is interesting to note that, while the nature of relationships was not specified in our research question, a majority of therapists focused their responses to this question in the context of romantic relationships, even as many also spoke of nuclear family, work, and friendship-type relationships.

Major thematic response categories regarding what therapists learned from clients about relationships are listed below in Table 1. Most of these will be illustrated later with examples from the therapists' narrative responses.

TABLE 1

Themes and Frequencies Re: Learning About Relationships From Clients (Respondent may have endorsed more than one category).

Theme	Frequency
Relationships are important and necessary for survival, healing, and support	30%
Relationships are complicated and difficult, even paradoxical	46%
Relationships provide learning about the therapist relationship and therapeutic technique	33%
The negative side of relationships: hurting those we care about; unkindness, loss, and endings	29%
Qualities of good relationships: communication reciprocity, trust, and love	21%
Individual personality factors: attachment, attraction, and projection	29.5%
How relationships can improve: preservation and Resilience	26%
Unrealistic expectations: assumptions/myths	7%
Different ways of being in relationships	6%

Participant Responses About the Importance of Relationships

> *"The importance of relationships, even to people who say they are not important. . . even to people who think they don't want or need relationships of whatever sort, that it is essential. It's the nature of being human. We can't be independent, even if we would like."* (Dr. Mark)

Our participants provided multiple responses indicating that they have learned— including from their work as therapists—that interpersonal relationships are truly vital to human existence. In the words of Dr. Laura, "Relationships are essential. . . it is hard to survive well without them." Similarly, Dr. Ranju emphasized how clients have taught him that "relationships are the single most critical aspect of anyone's life," whereas Dr. Steve indicated he has learned that "improving relationships is one of the major variables in improving quality of life."

As our participants explained the essential nature of relationships, they spoke of healing and supportive qualities and indicated that relationships, even those outside of psychotherapy, can have a therapeutic effect. In the words of Dr. Trayton, "non-therapy relationships can be as therapeutic as formal relationships." This psychologist noted how he applied this idea to his personal life. He told us that some aspects of his relationship with a dear friend several years his senior embodied "essentially the same things. . . that would have happened in therapy although the therapy has a certain focus. . . and certain rules of engagement. . ."

One of our respondents, who has worked with large number of immigrants, Dr. Yetty, shared a saying from her native language that sums up what she believes she learned about the healing aspects of relationships: "In my language. . . people are people's medicine." She further noted, "I think, overall, what I have learned from relationships [is that] when they are healthy, [they] are like medicine and preclude the need for treatment." Dr. Yetty placed this observation within the context of cultural differences between her immigrant clients and the broader American culture, further suggesting:

> *People from more communal cultures seem to have more time for friendships, so that you inevitably have someone to go to when you need them. It is rare to have those kinds of relationships in the U.S. but, when people do, they rarely need me.*

As will be further elaborated in Chapters 8 and 9, other therapists in our study also spoke of cultural issues that can profoundly affect human relationships. For example, Dr. Luke, in further discussing his immigrant clientele, said he learned that relationships are essential to prevent isolation: "I find that people are often painfully isolated from others. This is common for immigrants. . . and it is the most painful thing to be isolated, separated from the larger community and family. . ." Similarly, Dr. Raju stated:

> People who have lost families are at a shocking disadvantage. Torture survivors. . . who had lost their families or who had no idea where they were, were the most disadvantaged clients I have ever seen. Terrible! There was no real meaningful healing until they were connected to the world of people who provide at least some measure of support.

These quotations speak clearly and emphatically to the construct of "support" as an essential, albeit unsurprising, property of interpersonal relationships. As noted early in this chapter, there is an abundance of relationship research that provides evidence for the connection between interpersonal support and human well-being. In the words of Dr. Laura, "It is hard to change without a social support system." Dr. Eliza echoed this opinion, stating:

> Support systems are necessary. . . Those with a support system do significantly better than those who don't have one. . . more than one support system is best, but having two or three close people is better than having, say, 20 people who are not as close.

Similarly, Dr. Anna stated, "In the end this [relationship] is what people rely on." She provided an example of her experiences with patients who seemingly live day to day for work, but turn to other people for support when faced with crisis. In her words:

> If someone is diagnosed with a serious illness or other traumatic challenge, they normally draw comfort from the people close to them. This was even true of workaholic patients I've had who work to restore and renew important relationships when facing developmental or other life challenges.

Thus therapists spoke of learning that having supportive relationships encouraged clients to seek therapy and further helped them as they traversed the sometimes painful journey of self-discovery in the course of psychotherapy. For example, Dr. Antonia told us that she learned:

> *In some cases some people's relationships have been a tremendous catalyst in their improving themselves. So I can say that I have had clients who were suffering and their significant others have helped them to go through that difficult time.*

Likewise, Dr. Sarah stated she had learned that, "those who have support systems almost always heal more quickly, always have a sense of there being something out there—that they are not alone and that sense of not being alone helps them again in their recovery." Similarly, Dr. Natasha stated:

> *If people have strong relationships, I see that they bounce back quicker from a mental illness; there is more support. . . If you have strong relationships, or even one strong relationship in life, it helps them to fall back on something or be able to feel strength from it.*

Whereas Dr. Natasha and Dr. Eliza provided examples to the effect that even one relationship can be a sufficient source of support, Dr. Luke believes a variety of relationship supports is most healthy, but found this view absent, at least in some cultures. In his words, ". . . not having enough relationships or a broad range of relationships and expecting too much of the ones you have is one thing about relationships that I see as problematic in certain cultural groups."

Relationships Are Complicated and Difficult

> *"I've learned an enormous amount about complexity in relationships."* (Dr. Iris)

> *"They are difficult. . . and how complicated they are."* (Dr. Steve)

Forty-four percent of the therapists in our study indicated that they have learned something from their psychotherapy clients about the complicated, paradoxical and/or contradictory nature of relationships. In the words of Dr. Rose, "there is no perfect relationship. . . [Relationships] can be a big source of distress, but at the same time can help you survive." Dr. Martina echoed this sentiment as she reflected on her psychotherapeutic work with both student and adult populations. In her words, "They may not be 100% happy in the relationship, but there's a part of that relationship that fulfills something in their life that they are willing to negotiate and have a level of unhappiness." Similarly, Dr. Leslie stated:

> I am struck by how many people live with relationships that are at once deeply attached and limited. I'm struck with how showing generosity of spirit and the ability to think beyond one's own immediate needs [is] difficult for many people in relationships, even when the rewards of doing so are great. I've also learned that when people can think about how they might become more engaged and do take the risk of reaching out in these ways, that things can go remarkably better.

Dr. Leslie elaborated further elaborated this idea by offering an example in which a psychotherapy client, distracted by a writing block, found the need to feed and dress his son in the morning while his wife got ready for work as an intrusion on his time. With some work in therapy it occurred to the client that:

> Many people would cherish this time with their family, and that he was depriving himself and them of what could be a wonderful time together. He tried out his attitude, taking time with his son to enjoy feeding him; he thought about how much his wife needed and enjoyed the time she spent getting ready before work and, as a result, his son was lively and cheerful, and his wife felt cared for and thought about, and my client felt a lot better about himself and them.

Some of the other responses in this category touched on the complicated nature of unconscious processes in relationships. For instance, Dr. Mark noted, "there are many ghosts and shadows that inhabit relationships as well as what is obvious." And Dr. Oliver indicated that he has learned that relationships are "very difficult" because people:

> . . . bring with them a composite of inner objects that [is] greater than the sum of the parts of the individuals. And when they get together they touch on each other's inner object relationships in a way that doesn't properly mesh. Or they engage in a kind of an interaction that is opposite to what the other one needs. That's when the relationship will have its difficulty.

Some participants who discussed the difficult nature of relationships identified particular relational patterns. For instance, Dr. Carmen stated:

> I've learned they are pretty hard. . . Every relationship, be it a couple relationship or a mother daughter relationship, goes through cycles of withdraw and pursue. . . shows me that the games people play happens everywhere, happens for me also.

Learning About the Negative Aspects of Relationships

Some of our participants discussed the negative aspects of relationships as they spoke of learning how unkind people can be to one another, the hostile destructive forces in some relationships, including infidelity, and how—though painful—it is necessary for some relationships to end.

In terms of being unkind in relationships, Dr. Ellen noted, "Couples don't seem to treat each other very nicely in the sense that you would treat a friend nicely. They are just not, in some ways, polite or kind and that creates a lot of stress in the home." Similarly, Dr. Rachel said, "I've learned how much people hurt each other. . . and how sad it is and I know that it's all about survival in their own way, but some of it is so surprising to me." She provided two examples of this from her practice, both of which involved infidelity. The first involved a client whose wife experienced depression; the husband wanted her and his mistress to become friends so *his* life would be easier. The second example was of a married male client who wanted couples therapy for himself and his mistress.

Discussing the sometimes cruel nature of couples' relationships, Dr. Reuben spoke of a couple that he was seeing separately; he reported disparaging comments and continual anger from the wife, despite her noticing how caring her husband could be.

Altogether, some therapists discussed learning about clients' faulty assumptions and beliefs about their relationships, how hard it is to change those assumptions, and how such dynamics can negatively affect all those involved.

The Impact of Learning From Clients on Therapists' Personal and Professional Growth

Research has indicated that therapists do learn from their clients (see the range of such examples in Chapter 1 and throughout this volume). Indeed, the focus of this research study was to qualitatively understand what it is that therapists may have learned from their psychotherapy clients and how that learning has affected them personally and professionally.

The first half of this chapter addressed what our psychotherapist participants reported learning about relationships. In this section we will focus on what the participants told us about the impact of that knowledge as applied to their own personal and professional relationships. Though most of our respondents indicated they had been affected—even changed—by what they learned from psychotherapy clients about relationships, some respondents communicated this more directly and others more subtly.

In the category of personal growth, we found four basic themes that arose, whereby therapists discussed a) how their work with clients inspired them to reflect more on their own personal relationships; b) how their personal relationships had changed as a result of their work with clients; c) how they learned what not to do in personal relationships; and d) how they were, at times, negatively affected by what they had heard in the consulting room.

Within the category of professional growth we also found four themes: a) the ways in which therapists' learning from clients informs their work with other clients; b) that it informs how they view clients and clients' problems; c) how work with clients has affected the therapist's identity as a psychotherapist; and d) how it has affected their career paths and/or theoretical orientations.

Therapists Reflect on Their Own Relationships

Dr. Sarah's response captured the overall theme of this category when she stated that after "looking at what people do, I then get reflective about some of the relationships I have been in, and think. . . if I would have had that perspective would that have made this relationship any different?" Alternatively, Dr. Mike discussed that his learning from clients led him to reflect on and feel appreciation for his good relationships, given that he has worked "with people who often don't have those types of family relationships."

Dr. Wilbur, in observing the centrality of relationships for clients stated, "I think that relationships are the most important thing, and I think about my relationships more carefully, and more thoughtfully, and more lovingly, than I used to." Similarly, Dr. Jack indicated how his work led him to reflect upon his own relationships and realize what he longed for or thought about what was missing in his personal relationships. He said, "I have been moved to tears in a session when a couple connects. . . you know part of me goes to a place that I want more of that in my own relationships." And, as Dr. Eliza discussed regarding the construct of attachment, and that aspect of reoccurring patterns in relationships:

> I don't view myself as different from anyone I work with and I certainly have patterns in my own life. . . I look at those and how they were established. I look at "Do I have balance in the relationship?". . . I'm pretty much analyzing my own relationships all the time now to keep a check on them.

Learning from the tragic effects that enmeshment had for a client who was frequently hospitalized, Dr. Linda shared the following observation:

> . . . I start to look at my own life. I can't help it. What role
> will the people around me play? In my own development,
> how are people holding me back or how are they helping
> me move forward. . . We don't realize that [our clients]
> are mirroring in a way some aspect of our own lives. . . I
> couldn't help but look at my own family. Have I moved
> forward or backwards, depending on who I was with,
> including my friends and my co-workers? You start to look
> at what role are you playing around them. . .

Similarly, Dr. Carmen discussed how her learning about the push and pull of relationships for client couples caused her to reflect upon her own relationships in terms of "being able to see how couples withdraw and pursue each other. Just seeing those models helps me to look at my own relationships and when I may be pursuing or withdrawing. . . looking at those things."

Dr. Luke, who reflected upon the constructs of empathy and love, offered an example that occurred during his training, something he has carried with him ever since. He spoke of being amazed at the loving empathetic relationship between a mother and her child after the mother learned that her daughter had been sexually abused. He indicated amazement that the mother-daughter relationship grew stronger from this tragedy and that the mother tried to support her child—as well as evidencing self-care—despite her own strong emotions. This promoted reflection by the therapist on own relationships:

> . . . You see other people interact and you take that away
> and go to your own daily life and. . . if you can look at
> these people and see how they embrace each other, and
> you're not in such a difficult situation and they're in much
> more crisis, then why as human beings can't we do the
> same thing when we're not even in the same situation?. . .
> That enabled me to walk away and realize. . . whatever
> I think is bad in my life can't really even relate to such a
> thing [as] that.

Therapist's Personal Relationships Are Influenced by Work With Their Clients

Several of the therapists in our study indicated behavior changes in their patterns of relating, and that their own relationships had changed as a result of working with their clients. "I think all my work with couples and just individuals has really influenced my relationship with my husband in a really positive way. . . a really, really, positive way," said Dr. Rachel. And Dr. Anil suggested how he applied his work with clients to his own parenting in saying, "My knowledge helps me in dealing with my children."

Dr. Harriet M., who thought about the positive aspects of relationship preservation—despite relationships being imperfect—said, "I am more tolerant of people I want to keep in my life. That doesn't mean that I put up with people. . . I don't want in my life, but of the ones closer to me I am probably less [complaining]." Dr. Michele shared that she had not been married long and spoke of learning about perseverance from a client who had been married for 30 years:

> I haven't been married nearly that long [and] learned from [my client]. . . that in relationships, sometimes people hurt you, and sometimes they disappoint you and. . . you just have to keep going back to the drawing board and seeing what you can do to figure it out and improve it.

Alternatively, Dr. Lewis reflected upon the importance of equitable relationships from his work with clients, applying this to other relationships in his life:

> In all my business relationships, my relationships with students and parents, and my family relationships, I have tried to maintain equity, where you give and get, because if you are always getting and not giving, then the relationship is eventually going to end up in turmoil.

And Dr. Luke, who reported learning patience both in forming relationships and empathy for differences among his clients, stated:

I'm not so quick to make judgments about people. I'm not so quick to stereotype or label. I think therapy is also a study of patience, because if you're working with people you have to be patient. . . it's impossible to not bring some of this stuff that you learn in session outside because you're dealing with people, you're dealing with relationships. And how could you be a true genuine person and form relationships with others in the office and then turn it off when you're outside the office?. . . How it's helped in [my] relationships? It's made me more patient.

Dr. Rick spoke of applying his work on relationship preservation to his own life in the following way:

As far as what I take from that for my own life would be, I think, I am first of all aware in my own relationships that if a relationship is not going well, that it can be improved many times, that it is not too far gone if we apply specific techniques to try to improve things. And as well I think it has made me more aware at a very gut level [of] what would be the thing that I need to do to improve my relationship. . . I will think, "Well, what's going on in this part of the relationship as far as what needs attention?" based on the same kind of things that I would talk about with clients, and I would try to address those things.

Learning What Not to Do in Relationships

Dr. Cody provided an example of what not to do in relationships when he said, "When you see how much wasted time and energy goes into hurting each other, you think 'That is not what I want for my own personal life.'" And Dr. Rachel, who discussed observing the ill effects of harsh verbal communication from her therapy clients, elaborated on how she is more vigilant now:

In my own relationships I give it a lot of attention and I demand a lot of attention within my relationship with my husband. . . When [clients] come in and use sarcasm or criticism. . . I am so aware that I don't want that in my house. . . so I really work hard at not having it and. . . if it comes up, to address it.

Dr. Ellen discussed learning from couples who are nasty and disrespectful to one another that one needs to keep a perspective on the whole relationship and to pick one's battles, as opposed to focusing on all the little things. She shared how she applies this to her own marriage when it is in conflict:

. . . with me and my husband, I'll get really pissed at him for something, but then I'll think, I'll say "Well, look at all the good things that he's done for me.". . . So I think before I snap or before I decide that I'm going to get mad or something. I think that this is really. . . not worth that. You have to look at the whole picture, not just one incident.

Dr. Tevin, who worked with a client on the harmful effects of assuming the role of victim rather than focusing on the "50% they bring" to the relationship shared that, "It helps me in my own life try to focus when things aren't going right. 'What am I doing to contribute to the situation?' rather than focusing on 'How am I getting shafted?'" Whereas Dr. Raju indicated that work with couples has holistically changed his view of marriage and that he appreciates that for some people it is better to remain single. He further utilizes this knowledge in his role as a grandparent:

. . . I have learned that couple relationships are less important than I used to think. [There are] so many terrible marriages, especially in some. . . immigrant families—much violence. Watching women in violent relationships—or not violent but demeaning or just simply unhappy—it is so much better to be alone. . . a single person with friends and family is a worthwhile goal. I don't pressure my granddaughters to get married. Now I say, "Stay in school, support yourself." I'm a very different person because of what I have seen and experienced.

Similarly, Dr. Jeremey spoke of working with couples as like "a springboard to begin to look at your own relationships." He elaborated:

> *It's as if something will occur to me that I'm either hearing from them or telling them and [then] ask myself—are you willing to make the same kinds of changes or to risk the same kinds of things in your own relationship? And if the answer is no, not right now. . . whoa, that in itself is an important kind of awareness.*

Dr. Jeremey also provided an example of a couple where both partners engaged in triangulation as they developed outside relationships, ostensibly to have their needs met. He shared this that this experience inspired him to take a closer look at how his own "primary relationships were being diverted into other relationships" and "how to kind of rearrange those priorities."

A few participants reported feeling negatively affected by what they had learned from psychotherapy clients. As one psychologist said, "Being a therapist makes one really aware; sometimes it would be nice not to be so aware." And, as Dr. Rachel stated, "Because of my work, I think my view of couples and relationships has become very skewed. . . I'm getting a really warped view of what normal is."

Professional Growth and Change

Psychologists reported that what they have learned from their clients has informed their subsequent work with other clients, as well as affecting them in such a way that they were moved to change or refine the therapy process, their theoretical orientation, or even their career path.

Informing Work With Subsequent Clients

Several of the therapists we interviewed indicated that the knowledge they had gained from their psychotherapy clients usefully informed future work with subsequent clients. Dr. Tom summed up this result by stating:

This sounds a little general, but I think that there are always slight little things that we take away from each completed therapy or each failed therapy. You go back in reference to it and see if [what is happening in a current therapy] is something else you went through with somebody else. Intuitively it seems to be a body of knowledge about people and different types of peoples' relationships. And me, with certain types of people. . . I am sure it has an effect on the way I work.

Dr. Homer discussed learning to self-monitor closely so as to not cause fragile clients to decompensate. He provided the following example of how this knowledge was derived from working with a psychotic client:

I think of a client that has impacted me significantly. . . and I think part of that has been the recognition of the power that patients give to therapists over their lives. And I never violate that confidence while I'm trying to build her own confidence and power within herself and her own capabilities. But I've come to recognize that my behavior would have more than the usual impact on her, so if I'm having a bad day, she's highly sensitive. I have to be very careful to keep that in check so I don't do or say something that's likely to destabilize [this] pretty fragile individual, so I've learned to self-monitor carefully in all of my therapy.

Dr. Mike, in thinking about the complexity of relationships and how they are, at once, "primary, troublesome, poisonous, hard work, incredibly rewarding, and needed," indicated that he promotes relationship perseverance in his practice. He discussed his work with a client with a long history of strained relationships who struggled especially around the holidays and concluded, "I encourage people to persist in relationships with their family members," as opposed to "suggesting [for clients] to distance themselves from negative family relationships."

Reflecting upon client reports of attachment insecurity and the power of fond friendships, Dr. Arcy stated, "I have over the years become warmer and less interpretive and [less] intellectual with my clients." He further noted that he has had some recent "health challenges," such that when clients noticed his tiredness and inquired about his well-being he was more "willing to disclose a little bit." Said Dr. Arcy, "I have found that it actually seems to improve the alliance and help them be more comfortable talking about their own issues." This is similar to what psychiatrist Dr. Ralph Greenson reported in a lecture following the much-publicized suicide of his client, Marilyn Monroe. Greenson had to decide whether to see his other clients that same week, all of whom had read in newspapers about this unfortunate happening, including that he had been Ms. Monroe's current psychotherapist. He ultimately decided that if he expected his clients to be resilient in the face of adversity, he needed to demonstrate his willingness to do the same— even if he did so with tears in his eyes (Greenson, 1968).

Relationship Challenges Inform Therapists' Views of Client Problems and Progress

Our participants told us about how their experiences with their clients' relationship challenges informed their view of both problems and progress in the work of the therapy. For example, Dr. Mai discussed how learning about communication problems from his clients impacted his subsequent work. He spoke of the frustration that members of a dyad can feel when they misunderstand each other because they don't ask questions that could potentially clarify such misunderstandings. He indicated that he now believes, "even if there is something that I don't want to say, don't want to ask [the client], it's easier, it's better to ask."

In further consideration of therapy problems and progress, Dr. Viola noted that it's hard for clients to break out of recurring self-destructive relational patterns. They seem to change in therapy, but sometimes, when in a different relationship, the same destructive behaviors may occur. Dr. Viola observed that her interpretation of these patterns is not as important as the client's view of the problem and his or her desire to change it:

> It's not about what I want for them, it's about what they
> want. . . I can see a pattern and I can view it as a negative
> pattern and hurtful. . . [However], it really only matters
> what they are needing out of their relationships and how
> they see their patterns.

Another example is apparent in Dr. Rick's narrative, where he indicates that client progress is dependent upon the quality of the therapeutic relationship; this is entirely consistent with findings in the psychotherapy research literature (e.g., Norcross, 2007). As Dr. Rick said, "If you want to make progress in an endeavor, having a good relationship is going to be fundamental and essential. . . [For] any client who has made progress, we had a good relationship."

As an example of "transfer of learning," Dr. Jeremey discussed how his appreciation for the struggles of "coupling" brought increased empathy and genuineness to his work with individual psychotherapy clients who were experiencing couple relational difficulties. He reported:

> *It allows me to bring a kind of empathy to the [consulting room and to say] "You're right, this is a struggle, these are challenges, and yet if you don't address them, this is what happens in relationships. That is what is happening in your relationship now.". . . It's a combination of being realistic with them as well as empathetic with regard to how easy it can be to slide away from people, and these are the kinds of decisions that you have to make in order to get closer.*

Therapist Identity and Role

Some psychologists discussed how their self-perceptions and their identity as psychotherapists had changed based on their relational experiences with clients. For example, Dr. Raju, who believed work with clients brought about an overall change in his worldview stated, "I am a very different person [now] because of what I have seen and experienced [with clients]." Dr. Trayton said the following about his identity as a psychotherapist: "Every piece of clinical work I do and have done for many years now, makes me a better therapist. . . if you want to become an expert in something you have to do it ten thousand times." Perhaps Dr. Trayton is in some sense speaking to the Jennings, Skovholt, Goh, and Lian (2013) concept of the master therapist and how one develops a view of self as a master therapist over time.

Then there is Dr. Iris, who indicated she had learned from clients that not all relationships can be fixed and that she has further realized it is not her role to "fix" her clients:

> *I'm not the one to fix them, they need to fix themselves. . .*
> *I serve as a mirror, as a commenter, as a person who is*
> *walking along with them as they get this done and somebody*
> *who can point some things out periodically that they may*
> *not be able to see.*

Similarly, Dr. Luke spoke of learning that it is a painful to realize one's work is sometimes ineffective and that, despite all conscientious efforts, the therapist cannot help all types of clients. He further indicated feeling an ethical responsibility "to know when to let them go."

Modifications to Theoretical Orientations or Clinical Specialty Areas

A small number of therapists indicated new interests and areas of expertise as a result of what they reported learning from work with their psychotherapy clients. For instance, Dr. Muhomba, a cognitive behavioral psychotherapist with no prior interest in hypnosis, solution-focused therapy, or systems theory, explained that he had developed an interest, and subsequent career specialty, in all of the above after considering the power of relationship reciprocity. As an example of this shift in his practice, Dr. Muhomba spoke of a teenage male patient who was incredibly enmeshed in a perfectionistic family and who utilized self-induced paralysis as a symptomatic coping mechanism. It was only after the client was allowed to teach Dr. Muhomba about the experience of being paralyzed that this therapist was able to truly understand and help the client.

In a similar vein, Dr. Antonia reported modifying her theoretical orientation after learning from clients that "childhood experiences with significant others really affect their relationships." As she said:

> *I have a cognitive behavioral orientation when it comes*
> *to understanding people, [but] what I can do is a little*
> *bit psychodynamic in me as far as how people's initial*
> *relationships have evolved and how they have shaped how*
> *they can relate to people.*

Conclusions

Conventional wisdom suggests an image of the psychotherapist who teaches his or her clients about life and, in particular, about relationships. To a great extent that is true. However, the degree of reciprocity in the therapy relationship itself is dramatically present in the responses we gained from our sample of experienced psychotherapists. That they themselves reflect and learn from the pros and cons of relationship connections from the reported experiences of their clients is an essential part of the process, both for helping those in their care and apparently also for benefit in reflecting on their own lives. Being a psychotherapist involves a life-long learning process, and the care that psychotherapists offer to their clients can only improve if the therapists, too, reflect on their own relationship plusses and minuses—including in the context of the therapy relationship itself.

References

Argyle, M., & Henderson, M. (1984). The rules of friendship. *Journal of Social and Personal Relationships, 1*, 211-237.

Baumeister, R. F., & Leary, M. R. (1995). The need to belong: Desire for interpersonal attachments as a fundamental human motivation. *Psychological Bulletin, 117*, 497-529.

Bowlby, J. (1969). *Attachment and loss.* New York: Basic Books.

Bowlby, J. (1973). *Attachment and loss: Separation, anxiety, and anger.* New York: Basic Books.

Bowlby, J. (1980). *Attachment and Loss: Loss, sadness, and depression.* New York: Basic Books.

Bowlby, J. (1988). *A secure base: Parent child attachment and healthy human development.* New York: Basic Books.

Brown, B., Eicher, S. A., & Petrie, S. (1986). The importance of peer group ("crowd") affiliation in adolescence. *Journal of Adolescence, 9*, 73-96.

Carstensen, L. (1993). Motivation for social contact across the life span: A theory of socioemotional selectivity. In J. E. Jacobs (Ed.), *Nebraska Symposium on Motivation, 1992: Developmental perspectives on motivation. Current theory and research in motivation, 40* (pp. 209-154). Lincoln, NE: University of Nebraska Press.

Collins, A.W., & Madsen, S. D. (2006). Personal relationships in adolescence and early adulthood. In A. L. Vangelisti and D. Perlman (Eds.), *The Cambridge handbook of personal relationships,* (pp. 191-210). New York, NY: Cambridge University Press.

Gelso, C. (2024). A tripartite model of the therapeutic relationship: Theory, research, and practice. *Psychotherapy Research, 24,* 117-131.

Greenson, R. (1968). *Mistakes and errors in psychotherapy and psychoanalysis* (audiotape). Presented at the Medical Center of the University of Michigan, Ann Arbor, MI.

Hartup, W. W. (1989). Social relationships and their developmental significance. *American Psychologist, 44,* 1120-126.

Hartup, W. W. (2009). Critical issues and theoretical viewpoints. In K. R. Rubin, W. M. Burkwski, & B. Laursen (Eds.), *Handbook of peer interactions, relationships, and groups* (pp.121-142). New York, NY: Guilford Press.

Jennings, L., Skovholt, T. M., Goh, M., & Lian F. (2013). Master therapists: Explorations of expertise. In M. H. Rønnestad & T. M. Skovholt (Eds.), *The developing practitioner: Growth and stagnation of therapists and counselors.* New York, NY: Routledge.

Johnson, M. H., Dziurawiec, S., Ellis, H., & Morton, J. (1991). Newborns' preferential tracking of face-like stimuli and its subsequent decline. *Cognition, 40*(1-2), 1-19.

Meece, D., & Laird, R. D. (2006). The importance of peers. In F. A. Villarruel & T. Luster (Eds.), *The crisis in youth mental health: Critical issues and effective programs, Vol. 2: Disorders in adolescence* (pp. 283-311). Westport, CT: Praeger Publishers.

Norcross, J. C. (Ed.). (2011). *Psychotherapy relationships that work: Evidence-based responsiveness* (2nd ed.). New York, NY: Oxford University Press.

Perlman, D. (2007). The best of times, the worst of times: The place of close relationships in psychology and our daily lives. *Canadian Psychology, 48*, 7-18.

Siegel, D. J. (1999). *The developing mind.* New York, NY: Guilford Press.

Safran, J. D., Muran, J. C., & Rothman, M. (2006). The therapeutic alliance: cultivating and negotiating the therapeutic relationship. In W. O'Donohue, N. A. Cummings, & J. L. Cummings (Eds.), *Clinical strategies for becoming a master psychotherapist* (pp. 37-54). Amsterdam, Netherlands: Elsevier.

Stern, D. (1973). *The interpersonal world of the infant.* New York: Basic Books.

Truscott, D. (2010). Person-centered. In *Becoming an effective psychotherapist: Adopting a theory of psychotherapy that's right for you and your client* (pp. 67-81). Washington, DC: American Psychological Association.

Vangelisti, A. L. & Perlman, D. (Eds.) (2006). *The Cambridge handbook of personal relationships.* New York, NY: Cambridge University Press.

Willerton, J. (2010). *The psychology of relationships.* New York, NY: St. Martin's Press.

Chapter 3

ETHICAL DILEMMAS: PERSONAL GROWTH AND PROFESSIONAL RESPONSIBILITY

Mechtild Uhe, Jason H. Boothe and Sherry L. Hatcher

"This is one of the toughest things to deal with because my experience has been that we all fall on a different place on that moral/ethical spectrum." (Dr. Sunny)

In the course of their psychotherapeutic work with clients, most psychologists experience situations that challenge their professional and/or personal ethical and moral beliefs. Thus, the need for ethical and moral decision-making can arise from a conflict presented by clients in psychotherapy, and such issues can be both complex and various. Clients' questions and problems cannot always be resolved by "one-size-fits-all" solutions and, at times, psychologists can be left questioning their ethical and moral responsibilities as well as their personal beliefs.

Although much has been written in the literature about ethical decision-making, moral dilemmas, and boundary violations, there is a scarcity of research concerning the internal struggle of psychologists with regard to their psychotherapy clients, particularly when faced with an ethically challenging situation. How this struggle might influence a psychologist's professional practice and personal values is an important question. For example, Rogerson, Gottlieb, Handelsman, Knapp, and

Younggren (2011) cited numerous personal and interpersonal factors that influence ethical decision-making for mental health professionals.

We proposed the following research question: *"What have you learned from psychotherapy clients about resolving moral or ethical dilemmas?"* We invited participating psychologists to share their personal experiences in this connection, in order to gain insight into their ethical decision-making processes. Participants used the opportunity to explore ethical conflicts experienced by or generated by their clients, along with explaining their own thoughts and emotions when guiding their clients through difficult decision-making processes. Occasionally those in our sample shared their awareness of some unanticipated ethical infractions.

Inevitably, psychologists deal with the complexity of human behavior and use their knowledge and expertise to support their psychotherapy clients' growth and development. Through the training psychologists receive in graduate school and through clinical supervision, it is expected that psychologists will act in a responsible, wise, thoughtful, caring, and consistently ethical manner in order to assure the best outcome for their clients. The profession of clinical psychology is devoted to assisting clients, to doing no harm, and, above all, to acting in an ethically consistent and thoughtful manner. However, occasionally psychologists become unwittingly entangled in difficult and multifaceted ethical dilemmas.

The difficulty and challenge in dealing with ethical and moral dilemmas is expressed in Dr. Ranju's statement, "Nothing you learn in graduate school ethics class can prepare you for the real problems of the world. Every day you are questioning yourself about what to do." The guidelines and codes of ethical conduct established by professional organizations such as the American Psychological Association (APA) and Canadian Psychological Association (CPA) are the binding rules for psychologists. These guides provide tools for difficult decision-making, and ensure the welfare of clients by setting standards of practice even as "gray areas" inevitably exist in the course of honorable and ethical decision-making (APA, 2002; APA, 2010; CPA, 2000).

Psychologists frequently deal with ethical and moral dilemmas in their profession, which is reflected in the number of books and articles that have been written on this topic (e.g., Kitchener, 1984; Pope & Vasquez, 2011; Stout, 1993, to name just a very few of these resources). One also cannot doubt the importance of or the occasional difficulty involved in reliable, ethical decision-making. The aim of the published literature on ethics in clinical psychology practice has been to share experiences, propose decision-making models, provide guidelines, and discuss the difficulties encountered within the professional and the legal system, while offering strategies for successfully dealing with critical ethics issues (e.g., Kitchener, 1984; Koocher & Keith-Spiegel, 1998; Pope & Vasquez, 2007; Pope & Keith-Spiegel, 2008; Tjeltveit & Gottlieb, 2010).

Kitchener (1984) wrote an influential paper on decision-making in ethics in which she discussed the importance of evaluating ethical principles and the fact that "neither the identification of ethical principles nor accepting them as *prima facie* valid relieves the psychologist from the burden of decision-making in ethical dilemmas" (p. 53). She proposed that the process of moral reasoning occurs on two levels, namely the immediate intuitive level and the critical evaluative level (Kitchener, 1984, 2000). The intuitive level reflects processes based on one's own moral beliefs. However, moral intuition is not always sufficient to result in appropriate professional, ethical decision-making. In this study, we attempted to explore these processes—both the intuitive as well as the ethical reasoning processes for psychologists in our sample.

Bearing in mind that psychotherapeutic processes encourage the exploration of deep-rooted conflicts that are brought forward in sessions, psychologists are entrusted with their clients' innermost emotions and quests for problem-solving. Therefore, appropriate ethical decision-making is essential to this process. From the beginning of their training, psychologists are made aware that they carry ethical and moral responsibilities in the context of their work with clients. However, being aware of and even knowing the relevant ethics codes and guidelines does not necessarily make it easier to decide what to do in arising situations. The application of codes and guidelines in clinical practice is not always straightforward, but rather it is unique to each individual situation, and influenced by multiple factors.

Pope and Keith-Spiegel (2008) point out that constant alertness on the part of psychologists to potential ethics issues entails an active process of self-awareness, personal responsibility, and vigilance to client needs. Responsiveness to and knowledge of ethics codes and standards is just one aspect of a psychologist's decision-making process. Codes and standards for the profession of psychologists cannot substitute for critical thinking processes; nor do they guarantee appropriate and successful solutions for any given ethical dilemma. Rather, the written guidelines for professional conduct are further influenced by the psychologist's personal values, theoretical orientation, and culture as well as relevant legal statutes. It might be interesting to note the research by Lutosky (2005), who found that knowledge of the APA Ethics Code was a better predictor of psychologists' ethical behavior than performance on a test of moral reasoning.

Methodological Considerations

Each of the 61 participating psychologists in this study responded in a detailed manner to the question *"What have you learned from your psychotherapy clients about resolving moral or ethical dilemmas?"* Participants provided examples of their own professional learning about ethical and moral dilemmas in considering the challenges posed by their clients. They further discussed how dealing with ethics dilemmas in a psychotherapeutic setting also influenced their personal lives, values, and decision-making processes. The underlying tenor of the responses to this question was one of empathy, understanding, concern, and respect. This was also the context of a state ethics committee on which the (third) author of this chapter served for many years. Good ethical decision-making is inevitably paired with fairness, kindness, and thoughtfulness.

Participants in our study offered a rich variety of examples of their professional and personal experiences with ethics issues, which are reflected in the 10 main themes that emerged from their responses. The psychologists elaborated on their clients' ethical dilemmas along with their own professional and personal values in the context of ethical decision-making. In their narratives, psychologists frequently outlined scenarios in which they described how some of their clients struggled with problems such as infidelity and feelings of betrayal, conflict with religious values, and sexual identity, while other client narratives described guilt and shame related to such issues as war crimes. When referring to themselves, psychologists reported on their own decision-making role in relation to their clients' ethical decision-making process and the mutual influences that sometimes ensued. The following key themes emerged from responses to this topic:

- Clients who try to do the right thing
- Psychologists contemplating the interpretation and nuances of professional guidelines
- Contextual issues occur in resolving ethical/moral dilemmas
- How to resolve ethical/moral dilemmas involving gray areas
- Solving ethical/moral dilemmas as a process, over time
- Ethical and moral dilemmas as learning experiences
- Maintaining professional boundaries
- Emotions that arise in resolving ethical/moral dilemmas
- Ethics in the professional and personal lives of psychologists
- The role of psychologists in helping clients resolving moral/ethical dilemmas

Clients Who Try to Do the Right Thing

"I've learned how honest and ethical most people are, and how often they try to do the right thing." (Dr. Leslie)

One theme that emerged from the narratives was the psychologists' appreciation for the efforts of clients to resolve the ethical and moral struggles that they bring to therapy. Psychologists viewed the efforts of their clients as, generally, attempts to make the right decisions in their lives in an effort to resolve arising moral issues. "It has been very rare that I found a client that didn't really want to be a good person, a better person," said Dr. Steve. In responses relevant to this theme, the genuine positive regard in which psychologists hold their clients was evident, perhaps reflecting a basic humanistic principle, as in Dr. Laura's comment: "Given enough time, attention, and seriousness, most people come to their own center, to their own good place about ethical decisions, most of them." Dr. Kristi echoed this response by noting, "[The client] is a good person; they don't mean to be doing bad things, but they have a problem."

Psychologists Contemplating the Interpretation and Nuances of Professional Guidelines

> *"While you are maintaining one ethical principle, almost by definition you are in some degree breaking another."*
> (Dr. Vincent)

Research shows that the majority of psychologists take the ethical obligations of their profession seriously, and they uphold these guidelines even when doing so may be challenging (Pope, Tabachnick, & Keith-Spiegel, 1987). Across responses, our participants communicated their knowledge of the relevant ethics and legal codes governing their professional behavior as well as their awareness of ethical decision-making processes. For instance, Dr. Antonia discussed her dealing with a case of child neglect and her need to comply with professional ethical requirements, even when the client may have disapproved of her doing so:

> *[It] was important to me that I was doing the right thing as a professional and it does not matter if the client is upset with me or not because I have to do what I have to do and take care of those kids regardless of whether the client thinks I am doing the right thing or not.*

Fortunately, only a minority of psychologists reported possibly violating their governing ethical guidelines. For instance, Dr. Reuben, who acted as a consultant for a psychologist who had committed an ethics violation, openly discussed his decision to act on personal morality rather than professional mandate:

> *What I learned was that I sometimes, and this was an instance, will not yield to ethical principles as they are declared by the authority in our professional life. I know that I am supposed to, but this is where ethics and morality perhaps interact for me. I see it as a more important moral obligation to protect this person, and not do what I am supposed to, which is to report him.*

Dr. Reuben is a long-practicing psychologist, and the research reflects that most ethics breaches are committed by older, longer-practicing psychologists (Borys & Pope, 1989; Rodolfa, Hall, Holms, Davena, Komatz, Antunez, & Hall, 1994). Rodolfa et al. (1994) observed that as a therapist ages and accrues more experience in practice, he or she may disregard professional standards of practice in favor of "moral considerations," as was the case with Dr. Reuben.

Another respondent, Dr. McMillan, acknowledged that he viewed ethical guidelines as irrelevant to his practice: "I think that a lot of the ethical rules in our profession are really self-serving. . . I just think that it is a self-serving, sort of academic exercise when your clients would be better served without them." Dr. Pedroso provided a similar perspective when he stated, "Your ethics are determined by what the court asks, not by what the college asks—and not really anything else." The candor of these rare responses highlights the commitment of participants in our study to provide an authentic depiction of themselves as individuals who sometimes struggle mightily with the conundrums of ethical decision-making.

Still other respondents reported that they based their ethical decision-making on the guidelines governing their practice, but that they do so in combination with their own clinical judgment. This is evident in Dr. Ranju's response, "What I have learned is that different situations call for different actions. Being rigid just to stick to the rules is silly. . ." Here, Dr. Ranju seems to express respect for the ethics code and the recognition that ethical decision-making takes place within a complex contextual reality that psychologists have an obligation to consider. For example, this combination of responsiveness to ethical guidelines and clinical judgment has been endorsed by Pope and Keith-Spiegel (2008) as a responsibility facing all psychologists.

Contextual Issues Occur in Resolving Ethical/Moral Dilemmas

"What I have learned. . . is you have to really look at that individual's culture, life history, personal beliefs and help them just explore those beliefs and . . . explore the feelings around those beliefs and where they come from."
(Dr. Rose)

Participants in our study observed the importance of viewing clients' exploration of ethical and moral dilemmas within the context of their particular cultural/religious realities. Responses on this theme reflected an understanding of the importance of psychologists' ability to respond to all client populations with the goal of culturally competent practice. For instance, as Mr. Michael said, "One of the things that I have learned is that most of my clients have a moral or an ethical or a religious base, a place they come from in making those decisions."

This perspective aligns with the APA's *Guidelines for Providers of Psychological Services to Ethnic, Linguistic, and Culturally Diverse Populations* (1990), which calls on psychologists to incorporate an understanding of the ethnic and cultural realities in their clients' lives. Only psychotherapeutic work that is based on this kind of contextual understanding of culture can allow psychologists to truly comprehend the ethical and moral struggles of their clients (Pope & Keith-Spiegel, 2008). This point is reflected in one response from Dr. Ricky: "I think what I have learned is that is important to be patient and tolerant of people's various ideas about what ethics are and what morals are. . ."

Dr. Luke reflected on clients with worldviews different from those of Western society and how that can complicate the application of APA ethical standards. He reminds us that caution is needed when dealing with a diverse clinical clientele, stating that, "Especially when dealing with people who come from a different worldview. . . you need to be very cautious about applying standards of morality to individuals who come from a world that we can't even relate to." He further explained, "It's really important to suspend judgment [in] dealing with people who come from cultures where survival is the basis for rules. . ."

Resolving Ethical/Moral Dilemmas Involving Gray Areas

> *"[There] are usually no easy answers. . . as soon as you start trying to put black and white solutions onto moral/ethical issues, I think you put yourself in a draconian sort of bind and it doesn't usually work."* (Dr. Wilbur)

Many of the responses from psychologists in our sample referenced the fact that there are often no definitive right or wrong answers to ethical and/or moral dilemmas. For instance, Dr. Rose observed:

> *. . . Certainly a process that I am still in is seeing that moral and ethical dilemmas are often not nearly as cut and dry or black and white as I may have originally thought when I was younger. That there is a lot of gray area in terms of what constitutes moral behavior or ethical behavior.*

This statement seems to reflect the perspective of the wider North American psychological community. For example, Pope, Tabachnick, and Keith-Spiegel (1987) found that a majority of psychologists would deem certain acts as clearly ethical or unethical. However, when surveyed, most psychologists reported that some behaviors in which they may engage in with clients fall somewhere in between these two points. That reality, along with aspirational rather than prescriptive ethics codes, necessitates that psychologists constantly critically evaluate their behavior from an ethical reasoning perspective. Narratives on this theme involved describing the complexity of making ethical/moral decisions. As Dr. Jeremey shared:

> *There is a lot of complexity. . . and there is blurring, kind of grayness about most issues. And I think I have learned from people how important it is to visit each side of that polarity and then, ultimately, make decisions regarding how to move on.*

Dr. Carmen echoed this response, providing her view: "What I learned from [ethical and moral dilemmas] is that in many of these things there is no clear answer. It's pretty muddy and there's just no right or wrong."

Solving Ethical/Moral Dilemmas Over Time

> "*I have learned that people's standards are very different and they vary and they are inconsistent and they change and evolve over time. Somebody's ethics today may not be that somebody's ethics tomorrow.*" (Dr. Ricky)

The psychologists' responses reflected that most of them try always to respect their clients' prerogative to make ethical/moral decisions based on their individual needs, time constraints, and belief systems. However, due to the ambiguity of some moral and ethical dilemmas, resolution may require a methodically based decision-making process. Several such paradigms exist in the literature and can be shared with clients to aid them with their ethical reasoning processes (CPA, 2000; Koocher & Keith-Spiegel, 1998; Welfel, 2002).

Ethical decision-making models offer help by suggesting practice-based processes (e.g., Cottone, 2001; Hansen & Goldberg, 1999; Pope & Keith-Spiegel, 2008). Often these models feature details for specifically addressing situations such as cultural competence (Hansen & Goldberg). Overall, ethical decision-making models encourage the clinician to review appropriate professional guidelines and ethics codes, consider all relevant laws, rules, and regulations, and advise engaging supervision or consultation—or even legal guidance—while always having the client's welfare front and center.

Dr. Tom, who treated war veterans, summarized his learning experience about ethical decision-making processes:

> *What I have learned is that there is a way in which people come to their knowledge of what it is that is the right action for them and that it may keep them just enough under the radar so that they are not getting into trouble. That works a heck of a lot better rather than my trying to preach something to them that is not really going to penetrate their kinds of structure. I think what I have learned is that it is important to be patient and tolerant. . .*

Dr. Laura echoed the observation that clients may need time to resolve ethical/moral dilemmas: "Given enough time, attention, and seriousness, most people come to their own center, to their own good place about ethical decisions—most of them."

Ethical and Moral Dilemmas as Learning Experiences

> *"I would say that as I listen to other people grapple with things like difficult decisions, I've learned to ask the question: 'What is this person trying to teach himself?' Just like I've learned to ask myself the question. . . let me step*

back from the situation enough to try to see. . . what am I trying to teach myself?" (Dr. Odila)

Psychologists described how working through the resolution of ethical and moral dilemmas with clients has informed their ability to do the same in their own lives and that it has further offered them the opportunity to deepen their knowledge about themselves and human nature. Street, Douglas, Geiger, and Martinko (2001) argue that the "level of cognitive expenditure" (p. 265) invested in the decision-making process is central to the recognition of the ethical dilemma. It may be that the greater the cognitive investment, the greater the potential for learning to take place. On this theme, Dr. Ricky said, "[Clients] have taught me the importance of living one's truth, being honest to one's heart; those are the principles that I learned from my clients." Similarly, Dr. Trayton stated, "I think I have learned. . . that there is no magic way out of [ethical and moral dilemmas]; at some point [the client] has to bite the bullet and it is always upsetting." And Dr. Goodheart observed as follows:

> *Sometimes I realize that I cannot always be objective if a moral and ethical dilemma comes into play with some of my values and I have to step back a little bit and that is where I might learn a little bit [about] myself.*

Finally, Dr. Linda observed that learning for ethical decision-making began during the training phase of her career when dealing with a difficult psychotherapy client:

> *I had two totally different opinions from my two supervisors. I had to go against one of them in the end, which wasn't pretty, but I had to go with my instincts or my sense of what I should do. I think that was a lesson for me personally— not to go against my moral or ethical instincts.*

Maintaining Professional Boundaries

"Clients expect you to bend backwards for them in many areas and boundaries are an issue as to how much they can push the boundary and ask you to do things." (Dr. Antonia)

The maintenance of professional boundaries is central to ethical psychological practice and can constitute a daily challenge for some practitioners. Simon and Shuman (2007) report that therapists have the responsibility to maintain appropriate boundaries regardless of the difficulty involved. Pope and Keith-Spiegel (2008) offer a nine-step decision-making model regarding boundary issues that encourages psychologists to evaluate whether a boundary crossing will be helpful or harmful to the client or to the therapeutic process.

Many of the psychologists who participated in this study alluded to the fact that they pondered ethical codes and standards related to boundary issues to "take care to do no harm" as established in the first principle in the APA guidelines (2002). Gutheil and Gabbard (1993) discuss in detail the concept of nonsexual boundaries in psychotherapy and the difficulties with boundary crossing and boundary violations. They note that while many clinicians have an intuitive understanding of the concept of boundaries, they often struggle with this concept when they have to explain it to others or apply it in practice (p. 188).

Several factors are seen as instrumental for avoiding harmful boundary crossings and possible liability issues. These factors include clinical judgment, adequate discussions, exploration of the issues, and good record keeping, each of which is emphasized in psychological training programs and continuing education courses. The extensive literature on this topic is not only an indication of its importance, but it also acknowledges the complexity of factors involved in boundary crossings or violations as well as the potential uniqueness of each situation. As Pope and Vasquez (2011) point out:

. . . Awareness of the ethics codes is crucial to competence in the area of ethics, but the formal standards are not a substitute for an active, deliberative, and creative approach to fulfilling our ethical responsibilities. Codes prompt, guide, and inform our ethical consideration; they do not shut it down or replace it. (p. 3)

The deliberations reported by our participants in this connection testify to the importance of this statement. As another example, Dr. Iris noted:

> *Learning what boundaries are and how to effectively put them in place without putting people at a distance in a therapy relationship has been a real learning over time and that has directly to do with moral and ethical process.*

Dr. Mai discussed time constrains and the inability to charge for certain services such as phone calls:

> *Those things were really difficult for me to maneuver through morally and ethically when I wanted to do the best for the clients but [there were] external constraints and internal constraints of what would actually be the best boundaries to set for these clients.*

Dr. McMillan reminded us that setting and maintaining client–therapist boundaries is a continuously evolving process that requires constant awareness in therapeutic work: "I keep bumping up against the fact that there are boundaries in our [client–therapist] relationship and there need to be."

Emotions That Surface in the Course of Resolving Ethical/Moral Dilemmas

> *"People feel guilt even when they don't know they're feeling guilt."* (Dr. Goodheart)

Participants in our study talked about emotional issues when dealing with ethical/moral dilemmas. This relates to how Betan and Stanton (1999) examined the role of emotions in ethical decision-making among 258 clinical psychology students. These authors found that their participants were likely to actualize inadequate ethical behavior when pulled by emotions, such as anxiety, that compromised their ethical judgment. Psychologists guiding clients through ethical and moral decision-making processes often reported fatigue and discomfort. Dr.

Rachel noted the emotional toll of her work with clients: "I get really tired of it. I am getting tired of the dishonesty. I get tired of the lack of moral courage in people. . . It does drag me down and wears me down. . ."

Respondents in our study also reported observing their clients struggling with emotions, which sometimes made it difficult to problem-solve. The feeling of guilt is mentioned repeatedly and appears to be especially difficult to negotiate in therapy. Guilt often hampers a client's decision-making process and can impede the change process. As Dr. Felipe noted, "I see a lot of patients who struggle with excessive guilt that makes it hard for them to resolve moral and ethical dilemmas." Dr. Leslie went a step further, indicating that problems related to guilt are often present for many years in a client's life: "I am not sure that people guilty about betrayal ever resolve the issue really. . . guilt and shame seem to remain on the back burner for years."

Dr. Anna provided insight into the emotional turmoil of a self-punitive client as follows:

> One man I saw who was open to people of all cultures harbored great guilt because his great grandfather was part of an abusive European regime. One of the great challenges in doing therapy with such clients is to [help them to] be a) kinder to themselves and b) evolve a sense of more flexible moral judgment. . . this person felt guilt by association, guilt with ancestors, as opposed to the fact that he has nothing to feel guilty about.

Ethics in the Professional and Personal Lives of Psychologists

> "I think. . . this job is very much about behaving in an ethical manner with your clients and. . . I have the benefit of carrying it over into my life in terms of making ethics be more second nature..." (Dr. Rick)

Considering the recurrent confrontation with ethical and moral dilemmas in psychotherapeutic practice, it is not surprising to find that psychologists talked about the impact of their work on managing ethical and moral dilemmas in their personal lives. Dr. Sunny provided an example of how changes in ethical perspectives occur for her as a private or professional person:

> *Something that me—the mom, the wife, the daughter—*
> *sees as ethical or unethical doesn't necessarily fit in with*
> *the spectrum of me as the psychologist or the advocate for*
> *my client. So, that's a hard line sometimes for me to walk.*

Dr. Sarah expressed similar sentiments on the intertwining nature of professional and personal values when she stated:

> *Sometimes I realize that I cannot always be objective if a*
> *moral and ethical dilemma comes into play with some of*
> *my values and I have to step back a little bit and that is*
> *where I might learn a little bit [about] myself.*

Applying a complex ethical standard for himself, Dr. Wilbur reported, "I tend to be pretty critical and judgmental of myself and don't have the same compassion for myself than I do for others." An alternative response was provided by Dr. Harriet M., a senior psychologist, who described the impact of her work on her personal life, "I have become less defensive and trying to live at a higher standard. . . I live by my values and not by rationalizations or convenience." On the other hand, Dr. Felipe, another senior psychologist, emphasized the difficulty in determining the relative contributions of his learning about ethics:

> *It's so hard to separate what you have learned and what*
> *I've done for 40 or 50 hours a week for over half of my life.*
> *I have also been in personal psychotherapy for almost 30*
> *years. . . it's hard to tease out what I have learned where.*

The Role of Psychologists in Helping Clients Resolve Their Moral and Ethical Dilemmas

"It is not my role to judge; my role is to create a safe haven."
(Dr. Trayton)

One theme that emerged frequently was about the psychologist's role in helping their clients resolve ethical and moral dilemmas. In this context, participants revealed that they approached this challenge from a nonjudgmental perspective and by respecting their clients' autonomy. As Koocher and Keith-Spiegel (1998) observed, "Psychologists can be helpful, caring, empathic human beings *and* maintain professional parameters with which they effectively relate to clients, students, or other service consumers" (p. 197). This theme is exemplified by Dr. Sarah's comment: ". . . it is not my job to judge [the clients] and nobody who has not walked in their shoes can understand the situation they are in . . . I am not here to place judgment on them and their decisions." A similar sentiment is echoed in Dr. Oliver's response:

> *The therapist's job is really to assume an absolutely neutral and amoral position. . . The therapist's job is not to be in an ethical and moral position. It is to interpret and help the patient understand so he or she can make decisions for him or herself.*

On the other hand, Dr. Ellen elaborated on the difficulties in staying unbiased and being nonjudgmental in her work with couples. Her approach in these situations is to ". . . tell them up front that I'm sort of biased, I try to keep couples together." She further says: "I can't say I'm not judgmental, but I try really hard not to come across as judgmental." These statements are an indication of psychologists' self-awareness and self-perception of their, at times, difficult position. It is also an indication of their thoughtfulness in how to position and handle complex clinical encounters without judging their clients.

Final Thoughts

The discussion of ethical and moral dilemmas is perhaps one of the more controversial topics in this book. Participants in our study demonstrated various levels of awareness of ethical principles, the interpretation and use of codes, and interpretations of their local legal guidelines.

Each of the participants in our study elaborated on our question related to learning from psychotherapy clients about ethical and moral dilemmas. This question, in itself, offers the opportunity to consider the topic from various perspectives. Respondents discussed both their clients' struggles when trying to resolve moral or ethical dilemmas and how, as psychologists, they deal with these struggles—both in a professional context and in their personal lives.

The importance of ethical awareness and practicing according to ethical guidelines is illustrated by the numerous examples provided by these psychologists, who also described the difficulty of sometimes working quite literally within the scope of these guidelines. Interestingly, when asked for permission to publish their anonymous responses to this question, several psychologists asked that parts of their answers be redacted from their transcript, and this was done. These psychologists cited the need to assure the anonymity of their clients as the motivation for this request. However, others requested that some part of their transcript be removed for fear of being judged by others for their interpretation of ethical and professional guidelines. This may reflect a climate within the field in which psychologists feel hindered in their ability to discuss ethical struggles with complete freedom. On the other hand, it may reflect a desire to behave outside of the scrutiny of their peers.

Stout (1999) conducted a study using oral history. He interviewed psychologists and psychiatrists using a set of specific questions about adherence behavior to ethical principles such as insurance issues, nonsexual and sexual boundaries, and liability issues. While the purpose and methodology of Stout's study differs from our research, his results also included reports of decision-making that span a spectrum ranging from strict adherence to ethical guidelines, to ambivalence about the guidelines, to justification for potential misconduct. These findings once again indicate that ethical and moral dilemmas require complex analysis with regard to specific client situations, and that various levels of interpretation and application of the guidelines are sometimes in effect.

One final observation is that, given the statistics on the crossing of sexual boundaries between clinicians and clients, we expected, according to a national survey by Pope and Vetter (1992), that approximately 4% of participants might have reported violations of this nature. However, in our study, only a single respondent referred to having knowledge of such an ethical violation, and no respondents reported sexual behavior about clients that could have necessitated ethical evaluation. It is possible that the data-gathering format of this study (i.e., face-to-face interviewing by doctoral psychology students) may also have disinhibited such disclosures, even though we assume such behavior is rare and that most psychologists follow their prescribed ethics guidelines—as our participants clearly strove to do.

In sum, the underlying tenor of the responses to our question about ethics indicated high regard and honest concern for the welfare of the client as well as a constant striving to adhere to professional guidelines. The responses of our participants demonstrated how psychologists actively process any struggles to resolve ethical dilemmas in a manner consistent with ethical guidelines and in tandem with their own morals and values. Indeed, as is noted within the actual ethics guidelines, psychologists are mandated to engage in this kind of struggle, as it defines the very nature of ethical practice. Dr. Sarah summarized psychologists' often delicate ethical decision-making processes when she stated:

> One thing that I have learned is that the client can never be compromised as you are dealing with moral or ethical issues. You always have to put their needs first. . . they challenge us to make sure we do the right things even at a personal loss to ourselves. We have to be able to put them first. We learn a lot about ourselves. We also learn a lot about our lives as we see them stuck in a moral and ethical dilemma and they come to us often wanting our approval or forgiveness if they have done something wrong.

References

American Psychological Association. (1993). Guidelines for providers of psychological services to ethnic, linguistic, and culturally diverse populations. *American Psychologist, 48,* 45-48.

American Psychological Association. (2002). Ethical principles of psychologists and code of conduct. *American Psychologist, 57,* 1060-1073.

American Psychological Association. (2010). 2010 Amendments to the 2002 "Ethical principles of psychologists and code of conduct." *American Psychologist, 65,* 493.

Betan, E. J., & Stanton, A. L. (1999). Fostering ethical willingness: Integrating emotional and contextual awareness with rational analysis. *Professional Psychology: Research and Practice, 30,* 295-301.

Borys, D., & Pope, K. (1989). Dual relationships between therapist and client: A national study of psychologists, psychiatrists, and social workers. *Professional Psychology: Research and Practice, 20,* 283-293.

Canadian Psychological Association. (2000). *Canadian code of ethics for psychologists* (3rd ed.). Ottawa, Canada: Author. Retrieved from http://www.cpa.ca/docs/File/Ethics/cpa_code_2000_eng_jp_jan2014.pdf

Cottone, R. R. (2001). A social constructivism model of ethical decision-making in counseling. *Journal of Counseling and Development, 79,* 39–45.

Garcia, J. G., Cartwright, B., Winston, S. M., & Borzuckowska, B. (2003). A transcultural integrative model for ethical decision making in counseling. *Journal of Counseling and Development, 81,* 268-291.

Gutheil, T.G., & Gabbard, G. O. (1993). The concept of boundaries in clinical practice: Theoretical and risk- management dimensions. *American Journal of Psychiatry, 150,* 188-196.

Hansen, M., & Goldberg, I. (1993). Therapist perceptions of family violence. In M. Hansen and M. Harway (Eds.), *Battering and family therapy: A feminist perspective* (pp. 42-53). London: Sage.

Kitchener, K. S. (1984). Intuition, critical evaluation and ethical principles: The foundation for ethical decisions in counseling psychology. *The Counseling Psychologists, 12,* 43-55.

Kitchener, K. S. (2000). *Foundations of ethical practice in research and teaching in psychology.* Mahwah, NJ: Erlbaum.

Koocher, G., & Keith-Spiegel, P. (1998). *Ethics in psychology: Professional standards & cases* (2nd ed.). New York, NY: Oxford.

Lutosky, C. A. (2005). *Managing non-sexual dual relationships in small and rural communities: Does moral reasoning help?* (Unpublished doctoral dissertation). Fielding Graduate University, Santa Barbara, CA.

Pope, K. S., & Keith-Spiegel, P. (2008). A practical approach to boundaries in psychotherapy: making decisions, bypassing blunders, and mending fences. *Journal of Clinical Psychology, 64,* 638-652.

Pope, K. S., Tabachnick, B. G., & Keith-Spiegel, P. (1987). Ethics of practice: The beliefs and behaviors of psychologists as therapists. *American Psychologist, 42,* 993-1006.

Pope, K. S., & Vasquez, M.J.T. (Eds.). (2011). *Ethics in psychotherapy and counseling: A practical guide* (4th ed.). Hoboken, NJ: John Wiley and Sons, Inc.

Pope, K. S., & Vetter, V. A. (1992). Ethical dilemmas encountered by members of the American Psychological Association. *American Psychologist, 47,* 397-411.

Rodolfa, E., Hall, T., Holms, V., Davena, A., Komatz, D., Antunez, M., et al. (1994). The management of sexual feelings in therapy. *Professional Psychology: Research and Practice, 25,* 168-172.

Rogerson, M. D., Gottlieb, M. C., Handelsman, M. M., Knapp, S., & Younggren, J. (2011). Nonrational processes in ethical decision making. *American Psychologist, 66,* 614-623.

Simon, R. I. (1999). Therapist-patient sex: From boundary violations to sexual misconduct. *Forensic Psychiatry, 22,* 31-47.

Simon, R., & Shuman, D. (2007). *Clinical manual of psychiatry & law.* Washington, DC: American Psychiatric Publishing.

Stout, C. E. (1993). *From the other side of the couch: Candid conversations with psychiatrists and psychologists.* Westport, CT: Greenwood Press.

Street, M., Douglas, S. C., Geiger, S.W., & Martinko, M. J. (2001). The impact of cognitive expenditure on the ethical decision-making process: The cognitive elaboration model. *Organizational Behavior and Human Decision Processes, 86*(2), 256-277.

Tjeltveit, A. C., & Gottlieb, M. C. (2010). Avoiding the road to ethical disaster: Overcoming vulnerabilities and developing resilience. *Psychotherapy: Theory, Research, Practice, Training, 47,* 98-110.

Welfel, E. R. (2002). *Ethics in counseling and psychotherapy: Standards, research, and emerging issues* (2nd ed.). Pacific Grove, CA: Brooks/Cole.

Chapter 4

WHAT THERAPISTS LEARN FROM THEIR PSYCHOTHERAPY CLIENTS ABOUT COPING

Joanne S. West and Sherry L. Hatcher

"The greatest gift clinically that my clients have given me is what I have learned from them, what has worked for them and their self-discovery, not what I have done for them." (Dr. Felipe)

The psychologists who generously participated in our study also shared their reflections on the various ways in which their clients cope with adversity. While several key themes were in response to the question of what the psychologists had learned from their clients about coping, the overall tenor of the responses reflected respect for the resourcefulness with which those seeking psychological assistance were able to meet difficult challenges with impressive resilience. In this chapter, the central themes that emerged from the narratives on what therapists learned from their clients about coping will also be presented in the context of relevant psychological research and theory.

The central themes that emerged from the coping question include: 1) the influence of psychologists' theoretical orientation on their perceptions of different coping strategies; 2) how individuals vary in their abilities to cope; 3) that people are generally resilient; 4) that coping is influenced by what is meaningful to the individual; 5) that coping skills can be taught; 6) that there is a need for therapists to be nonjudgmental in relation to clients' preferred coping mechanisms; 7) that coping varies with life stages; and 8) the impact on the therapists' own coping mechanisms when they work therapeutically with individuals learning to cope with adversity.

Prior to presenting illustrative material on the themes that arose, it will be useful to explore some of the ways in which coping is conceptualized within the field of psychology.

Some of the Psychology Literature on Coping

The many ways in which individuals cope with adverse events have long been a consideration across the practice of clinical psychology. Coping can be defined as those thoughts, emotional states, and/or behaviors employed to tolerate, mitigate, avoid, master, or resolve problems or stressful events (Folkman & Lazarus, 1987). It is a dynamic process, involving an interaction among characteristics that include an individual's personality, values, and the nature of the problems that arise as difficult life events.

Theories of coping strategies identify both active coping, characterized by the conscious implementation of problem-solving strategies such as seeking social support (Compas et al., 2001), and emotion-focused coping, which examines the regulation of the emotional consequences of stressful, adverse experiences (Eisenberg et al., 1997). The latter group of researchers argues that all coping is a form of emotion regulation, and that these phenomena (coping and emotion regulation) can be considered as synonymous (Eisenberg et al., 1997). Research indicates that an individual may employ either or both forms of coping and that an ability to be flexible in one's coping style is the most effective strategy (Lazarus & Folkman 1984).

Coping mechanisms can be further categorized as either engaging or disengaging approaches. Engaging coping mechanisms are those aimed at actively dealing with the stressor in either a problem-solving or emotion-processing manner. Coping of this type can take the form of support-seeking, emotion regulation, and/or cognitive restructuring (Carver & Connor-Smith, 2010). Disengaging coping often takes the form of denial or avoidance (Carver & Connor-Smith). It should be noted that both engaging and disengaging forms of coping can be either adaptive or maladaptive. As an example of maladaptive coping, an individual may engage in self-harm as a form of active emotion regulation, or in substance abuse as a means of avoidance.

Theme One: The influence of theoretical orientation

Examination of the ways in which people deal with the challenges they face has long been of interest to psychology. Various psychological theories conceptualize coping differently, and interventions employed to enhance client coping are guided by these theoretical perspectives. The influence of our participants' theory orientations on what they have learned from clients regarding coping is the first theme to be identified from the data, and appears when psychologists described the wide variety of coping mechanisms in which their clients engage.

Psychodynamic theory

Psychodynamic approaches to treatment have focused on unconscious means of coping with stressors, including the individual's defense mechanisms. According to this perspective, defense mechanisms can distance an individual from the cognitive and emotional impact of difficult experiences, serving a protective function until such time as the individual is better prepared to deal with this material (Cramer, 2000). Whereas some defense mechanisms are frequently adaptive, such as sublimation or moderated intellectualization, others, such as regression, can be quite fragile and pathological. Vaillant (2011) observed that the concept of individual coping mechanisms seems to have replaced that of "ego mechanisms of defense" in common usage.

It should be emphasized again that defense mechanisms may be adaptive or maladaptive, depending on their nature and how they are utilized. Research has illuminated how clients' use of coping defenses can shape the psychotherapeutic relationship. For example, Hilsenroth et al. (2005) found that therapists responded to clients who used maladaptive coping mechanisms (acting out, dissociation, projection) by making particular use of psychodynamic interventions such as interpretation, exploration, and encouraging in-session emotional expression.

A number of narrative responses from our psychologists seem to illustrate the ways in which theoretical orientation shaped their learning from clients about coping. Some participants reflected psychodynamic ways of understanding about coping. For instance, Dr. Mark observed that "defense mechanisms also are the mechanisms by which people manage to cope with their difficult things in life," reflecting the psychodynamic perspective that coping can take the form of implementing unconscious defense mechanisms. Dr. Jeremey, too, used this paradigm to characterize what he learned from clients regarding coping, stating, "Defense mechanisms, I think, are much more automatic; they're much more—I guess we can say—unconscious. . . And I think that's where coping mechanisms come in."

Another psychologist, Dr. Vincent, related the coping he had observed in his clients to a hierarchy of coping mechanisms discussed in the psychoanalytic literature: "I think this psychoanalytic literature hasn't done enough in pushing the notion of mature defenses versus the immature or the psychotic or neurotic defenses. . . . I really believe in the mature defenses." This idea seems to suggest that Dr. Vincent may have learned that clients who are able to implement mature defenses when coping with stressful life events are better able to adapt to stress than those who tend to employ more primitive defense mechanisms.

Cognitive-behavioral theory

Cognitive perspectives on coping tend to define coping as conscious, intentional, goal-directed responses to the specific demands of a stressor, with the objective of restoring equilibrium (Lazarus & Folkman, 1987). By this theory, coping responses emerge from an interaction between an individual's resources and the demands of the context in which they occur. An individual brings his or her characteristic coping style to a challenging life situation, and the nature of that situation serves to shape the coping response that person employs (Skinner & Zimmer-Gembeck, 2007). Cognitive appraisal influences one's ability to cope, such that if an individual perceives him- or herself as able to cope with a stressor, then effective coping strategies tend to prevail; however, if personal resources are inadequate, then that person is more apt to react in maladaptive ways (Wei, Heppner, & Mallinckrodt, 2003).

Therefore, cognitive-behavioral approaches concentrate on the restructuring of negative thoughts related to self-efficacy and seek to aid clients in substituting adaptive methods of coping for maladaptive ones. "Third wave" cognitive behavioral approaches specifically teach clients coping skills. For instance, dialectic behavioral therapy (DBT) places central importance on aiding clients to develop adaptive coping skills as a means of consciously managing emotional affect through the substitution of high-level skills for less-adaptive ones (Linehan, 1993). For example, self-harm, dissociation, and impulsivity are to be replaced with self-soothing, mindfulness, radical acceptance, and weighing the pros and cons of choosing adaptive choices (Linehan, 1993).

The cognitive behavioral perspective makes an appearance in relation to what some of our participants reported learning from clients about ways of coping. Several psychologists shared that they learned about the role that changing cognitive appraisals plays in relation to coping. For instance, as Dr. Clark said: ". . . the various automatic thoughts that come up and things you can tell yourself to get out of that head space can be helpful." Similarly, Dr. Natasha said:

> . . . people can come to some acceptance, but only after the cognitive work. You know, seeing things differently, knowing their situations don't change but that you can look at it in a different way. I feel that if a person can really . . . get that feeling, then that is another way of coping.

Mindfulness as an adaptive, teachable coping mechanism is also central to a number of third-wave cognitive behavioral approaches. In addition to DBT, acceptance and commitment therapy (ACT) uses mindfulness as a way to enable coping by addressing both cognition and the affective dysfunction resulting from maladaptive appraisal of stressful situations (Hayes et al., 1999). Similarly, mindfulness is also a central coping mechanism taught in mindfulness-based stress reduction therapy (MBSR) (Kabat-Zinn, 2013). As Dr. Goodheart said about what he had learned from clients about the use of mindfulness, "What goes under the nickname 'mindfulness' these days, being present in the here and now, is a fabulous and really powerful coping mechanism and people who can anchor themselves to the present moment have a huge resource."

Theme Two: Coping mechanisms are unique and varied

A second theme that emerged from the narratives provided by our participants about what they learned from clients is that coping mechanisms are unique to each individual, such that there are variations across individuals' strategies in coping with adversity. Although similar behaviors—adaptive or maladaptive—may be observed across individuals, each person's coping is an interactive process between their internal characteristics and those of the environment. As a result, the various ways in which an individual may attempt to cope with adversity are numerous and unique. When Skinner, Edge, Altman, and Sherwood (2003) attempted to organize all possible means of coping, they succeeded in generating a list of more than 400 different categories!

The observation that there are seemingly endless ways in which people respond to adversity is reflected in the statement of psychologist Dr. Juan, who said, "What I have learned is that there may be as many coping mechanisms as there are people who are in a place of needing to contend with difficulty." He illustrated this by referring to the various means of coping he has observed that clients utilize:

> . . . most clients cope best when they become involved in something that has in the past resulted in feeling better emotionally, physically, spiritually. It may be listening to music, reading poetry, doing physical exercise, or collecting stamps which may be. . . a way of distracting themselves.

Many of our interviewees emphasized the importance of exercise as a coping mechanism. For example, Dr. Ellen said: "We talk about coping mechanisms a lot, especially because I have people come in stressed all the time; it's one of the big things. Right now, I'm a firm believer in exercise."

Part of what our participant psychologists reporting learning was also the uniqueness or individuality of the coping mechanisms employed by their clients. For example, Dr. Tom commented on the singularity in a way a particular client coped:

> He learned some specific things that were unique to him that helped him to identify when it was happening and then he began to practice this. . . when he would start to feel this kind of arousal toward anger he would say some things to himself that really had some poignancy.

Similarly, Dr. Justin observed:

> *I've learned that everybody's got different ways of resolving situations, and I think everybody's got different ways of kind of dealing within, and you've got to find out what works for that individual and then you can use that as that kind of mechanism.*

In this same vein, Dr. Anna shared her view that:

> *People cope with the most unimaginable difficult life situations in a variety of adaptive and courageous ways using everything from religion to psychotherapy to exercise to creative work to confiding in friends and/or journals and/or some combination of these.*

> Referring to her learning about means of coping, Dr. Linda said, "Some of them are. . . unique to the individual and some are the real basic ones that we hear about daily."

Research into these differing coping strategies has revealed various factors that contribute to the manner in which a person copes with stressful life events. For example, personality factors have been linked to coping style (Carver & Connor-Smith, 2010) and are thought to predispose one to a particular coping style. Personality has been shown to determine levels of stress exposure, such that neuroticism has been associated with higher stress exposure (Grant & Langan-Fox 2007), while conscientiousness predicts lower stress exposure (Lee-Baggley et al., 2005). In addition, the personality characteristics of conscientiousness, extraversion, and openness shape an individual's appraisal of events, allowing that person to perceive stressors as challenges to be overcome rather than threats to survival; these qualities also connect with an individual's ability to positively self-appraise his or her internal coping resources (Penley & Tomaka, 2002). In this connection, Dr. Oliver observed, "Some people are better equipped. Some people are lesser equipped. [It] has to do with the way people are made up."

The relatively stable ranges of coping strategies employed by individuals in response to stressful events are also predicted by people's level of social support. When individuals perceive themselves to be valued and cared for by others, psychological distress is lowered, and they are better able to cope with differing stressful conditions (Taylor, 2007). Dr. Antonia reflected on the importance of turning to others for social support in order to cope, noting that this seems to be difficult for some clients:

> *I have seen people from different cultures have probably better coping skills because they seek out family; family support is there for them to help them go through a difficult times. In Western, individualized society. . . people [do not] find a very productive way of coping with their stress.*

When people perceive themselves as having adequate internal resources to deal with adverse life events, they are better able to cope (Taylor & Stanton, 2007). A number of our participants noted that they had learned about the effectiveness of using forms of artistic expression as a means of coping that enhances self-efficacy. As Dr. Yetty observed:

> *I had a couple of clients . . . one did short stories, one did poetry, and you listen to the poem and it's just so gripping and it's amazing also how [comforting] it is for them. . . by sharing their poems—and sometimes they share them, sometimes they don't—but it's such a release for them.*

Dr. Laura also shared an example of a client using creativity to cope:

> *I've got one client who struggles with very severe bipolar depression and a lot of medical problems on top of that. And one of the things that she does to cope and can really pull herself out of a deep dark cold is painting. She inspires me.*

Theme Three: Learning people are resilient

> *"Well, I do know that people are resilient that and that no matter how bad things seem to be they can turn things around that sometimes just small changes over time can result in long-term changes."* (Dr. Cody)

A theme prominent among the responses of the psychologists in our sample was their learning about the degree to which people can be resilient. Psychologists shared that they had learned from their clients about having the strength to face adversities that might have been expected to overwhelm them, but where they rose to the challenges of coping through great difficulty. As Dr. Sarah remarked, "Resilience of the human spirit. It is amazing. The kind of horrible things that people can experience and continue to live their life and keep going." Similarly, Dr. Cody noted: "I do know that people are resilient, and that no matter how bad things seem to be they can turn things around."

Resilience has been defined as an interactive process between an individual's inner resources and the environment in which adversity is to be overcome (Rutter, 2006). It is a dynamic process of positive adaptation in the face of significant adversity (Luthar, Cicchetti, & Becker, 2000). This definition is reflected in the response of Dr. Cash: "People's ability to adapt and recover is much greater than we ever expected," and in what Dr. Maya said: "People really are surprising, are capable of things that you would not expect them to be capable of amazing strength. . . I am learning that people can be pretty powerful within their own lives. . . powerful, capable of change, strong."

The psychologists in our study expressed respect and awe for the manner in which their clients rose to meet the challenges before them. As Dr. Doral said, "I am astonished at people's ability to cope," and Dr. Mai said he "learned a lot about how people find dignity in distress and take the pain that comes into them and transform into fertilizer for the future and for growth." Particularly poignant was Dr. Anna's reflection on what she learned from clients who have lost a child: "Over time, each has shown more courage than I could imagine for myself in such a situation by moving on, by remembering and honoring the lost child and by devoting themselves to other children in the family."

Theme Four: Coping mechanisms can be taught

As previously described, different psychological orientations suggest alternative approaches to the role of therapists in aiding their clients in coping with adversity. Specifically, psychodynamically informed psychotherapy may focus on helping clients to accrue insight into how their past history informs the present and to shift from immature to more mature defense mechanisms as one way to help clients develop self-understanding and effective means for coping with adversity. Cognitive-behavioral practitioners focus on bringing about change in the perception of events and, therefore, one's capacity to cope with challenging situations. For example, Dr. Kristi shared a cognitive-behavioral perspective on teaching clients about adaptive means of coping:

> . . . *That's a big part of what we do as therapists, you know, give them coping mechanisms. I guess this cognitive-behavioral work is so helpful. . . teaching them to focus on what they can control. . . which allows them to be more accepting of what they cannot control.*

Across theoretical approaches, all of the psychologists in our sample spoke of learning that coping mechanisms can be taught, and they reflected on the role they could play in helping clients learn news ways of adaptive coping.

It is interesting to note that when asked what they had learned from their clients about coping, our participants tended instead to share experiences about what they had taught their clients about coping. It may be that the therapists were more conscious of their teaching experiences in this connection, such that those types of examples came most readily to mind. Or it may be that they felt most comfortable in the role of teacher, rather than learner, on this topic most particularly. As Dr. Ricky said, "I have learned that people need to be taught how to cope; people need to teach others how to treat them." Similarly, Dr. Eliza said: "I think you can teach coping skills and I think that can make a difference." Dr. Mark also noted that "helping people see a way of coping through an issue, when they didn't see it in the beginning, is really rewarding." And Dr. Yetty reported, "My job is to help people to get back in touch with positive coping stuff." In a slightly different vein, Dr. Tevin observed that his ability to help clients learn to cope is particularly important for those who come to therapy with few coping mechanisms of their own. He stated, "What I have learned from my patients about coping mechanisms is that. . . if it was never modeled through parenting, then it's very difficult to learn from word on the street or from other dysfunctional people."

Psychologists observed their need to help clients use new coping mechanisms in a flexible way—to respond to a range of situations and employ a variety of coping approaches in the service of problem-solving. In this spirit, Dr. Muhomba said, "Stop the things that only work up to a point but don't get them any further and start training them and exposing them to patterns of possibility that allow them to get much further than their current coping mechanisms." Dr. Ricky spoke of the hazards of reacting to stressful life events in a singular manner, saying "People don't have specified coping mechanisms. That's kind of hazardous, so I've learned that people need to be taught how to cope. . . I learned that from my clients." Similarly, Dr. Iris shared her thoughts on the need for a variety of ways to cope with adversity:

> . . . what is a coping mechanism in one circumstance is not a coping mechanism in another. And that is another thing about working with people, is to teach them flexibilities, and to work with them to see the flexibilities and the effective placement of a coping mechanism in any situation so that they don't trip over themselves or use something in one place that was effective but is not effective in another place.

Dr. Luke reported learning that some clients may not have their own means of coping, and may want assistance beyond being taught techniques by their therapist:

> Some people, you will try to teach them about breathing and so forth and they want something bigger. They don't want you to teach them the technique. They don't want something that depends entirely on themselves. They are not there yet. They want something more external.

In a similar vein, Dr. Tom discussed learning that therapists must provide clients with something more than just technique, and that they must inspire clients to real-world change in their coping with adverse events. He observed:

> We can give them didactics, but I think what I have learned over time in doing these kinds of manualized applications of coping strategies and different self-management strategies is that people learn things not only in unique individualized ways, but they learn things through practice, trial, and error.

Theme Five: Coping is influenced by what is meaningful to the individual

"Coping mechanisms are largely decided or determined by the client on the basis of whatever works for him or her. . ."
(Dr. Juan)

A theme that appeared in a number of the responses we received from our participants in relation to their learning from clients about coping is that many people cope with adversity by making meaning of the event. According to the meaning-making model of coping, a traumatic event shakes previously held beliefs as to the predictability or controllability of the world (Park, 2010). "Meaning-making coping" is defined as the conscious identification or the appraisal one makes of a challenging situation or event, followed by the implementation of intentional problem-solving strategies that may involve a revision of one's goals that is meaningful to the individual (Folkman, 1997). Dr. Linda shared an illustration of this form of meaning-making when she described a client who used found a personal way of managing her anxiety:

> *She took out a rock that she had used as grounding. I always knew the grounding stuff was there, but her rock— she had rubbed it so much over the years. . . she told me she had it for over 10-15 years— you could actually see the imprint of her thumb in it from rubbing it.*

Such a meaning-making process can be automatic or unconscious (Creamer, Burgess, & Pattison, 1992). For some this process may involve spiritual beliefs and experiences, but it may also be that individuals activate a broad range of effortful coping activities that draw on their beliefs and values directed at finding meaning—even including benefits that can accrue from negotiating stressful experiences (Tennen & Affleck, 2002). Dr. Tom referred to this form of coping on the part of one of his clients who had experienced adversity: "It was something from his own mind and it stopped him in his tracks. It was very powerful."

Meaning-focused coping may be characterized by accommodating the changes that challenging events bring to one's life, and/or reappraising the impact of those events in light of one's capacity to deal with them, or even in re-examining one's priorities (Park, Edmondson, & Blank,

2009). These kinds of meaning-making approaches to coping seem most likely to occur when an individual experiences stressful events as located outside of his or her control (Folkman, 2008). Research has indicated that when individuals engage in these kinds of meaning-making reactions in order to deal with adverse life events, they can experience positive growth (Park, Edmondson, & Blank, 2009).

In this connection, Dr. Jeremey shared what he had learned from a client who appeared to engage in this form of coping:

> *For example, I've got this one client who . . . it's both for her own self-esteem, but it's also for an invitation for her to move to a more forgiving position. And so what she does is. . . she has several kind of affirmations, or/and statements out of a book or something that have to do with forgiveness. And so she puts them in various places—like one in her billfold, one near her computer, one maybe on her mirror or something, so that a number of times per day she's reminding herself. And so to me that is a coping strategy.*

A cognitive processing model of meaning-making coping has been suggested by Park and Folkman (1997). According to this model, individuals possess a global meaning system that underlies their interpretation of events and experiences. When a person encounters a challenging or stressful event, the extent to which his/her appraisal of the event challenges the global system of meaning is the extent to which it causes them distress (Park & Folkman, 1997). Therefore, the individual engages in meaning-making in order to reduce a discrepancy between the appraisal of a situation and its global meaning in order to restore, or establish, a sense of meaningful existence. The outcome of a successful integration of an event with an individual's ability to make meaning about it can result in improved personal adjustment thereafter (Park & Folkman, 1997).

Psychologists' learning regarding their clients' meaning-making in the face of adverse events appears to reflect some of the above conceptualizations in terms of how making meaning is central to an individual's coping with difficult life experiences. For instance, Dr. Tom shared the following:

When I think about this, what I have really learned about coping from patients is that, in order for it to be effective, it has to be meaningful to them and it has to have a direct and immediate payoff or they are not going to practice it, or endorse it, or try to repeat it.

He then went on to say:

I don't think we can give those things to people. I think we need to help them find it and establish a foothold and expand on it, but it has to come from some kind of internal structure rather than from an external knowledge base.

Dr. Ranju also talked about learning that the therapist must help clients develop ways of coping that are meaningful to them, saying, "If you are working with someone to change a bad coping mechanism, you have to be ready to help them replace it with something more positive that is personal for the person."

Theme Six: Maintaining a nonjudgmental stance toward clients' coping

"It's about letting go of control and what you think the person should be doing." (Dr. Ranju)

The next theme identified in response to the question about learning from clients regarding coping mechanisms is that one must be open-minded when evaluating the effectiveness of coping mechanisms that clients may choose to implement. In particular, psychologists noted they had learned about the need to maintain a nonjudgmental stance when evaluating clients' ways of coping with adversity. For instance, Dr. Wilbur said:

I tend to be more open-minded about defense mechanisms and coping skills and try not to. . . use some kind of personal code of ethics or some moral compass that I think is arbitrarily right to determine whether somebody is doing a good job managing their life, or not.

So, psychologists reported that they had learned the need to be accepting of both clients' adaptive and maladaptive means of coping, recognizing that clients typically exert their best efforts to manage the impact of difficult experiences. They also typically say that one useful means that clients report for coping with stresses is co-created between client and therapist. As Dr. Muhomba said, the therapist needs to have "respect for coping mechanisms, looking at the positives and negatives of the current coping mechanisms, examining patterns of possibility that could be more adaptive to the current context." The respect for their clients' individuality that psychologists reported reflects their recognition of the legitimate autonomy to which clients are entitled, and that the personal coping style of each person is the ultimate determinant of how they will deal with adverse life events.

The psychologists we interviewed also reported that learning to respect their clients' best efforts at coping, even when it appeared as though the means employed were maladaptive, was sometimes a challenge. As Dr. Luke said:

> *I think that people. . . when they are under great stress, there is a tendency to cope but to cope in a very maladaptive way, and it's important to identify those maladaptive ways as their coping mechanisms, just not very effective ones— whether isolation or drinking, whatever. They could be things that just are working for them.*

Along with their acceptance of clients' various means of coping was the authentic concern that some ways of coping were, however, likely not so healthy. For example, Dr. Anil said along these lines: "For some I have appreciation on how can they do that, on the other hand, I think I have some kind of disgust, how come they cannot do that [more adaptive thing]?" Another respondent, Dr. Ricky, appeared to judge coping, in itself, as a less than optimal way to respond to adversity:

> *I learned that coping is a lower level of living—you know, when one copes that's the difference between surviving and thriving. Surviving people cope, thriving people don't look at it like they are coping; they just find a way to thrive no matter what life throws at them, even cancer. You can thrive during a cancer treatment. So I think the whole coping thing is really overrated.*

Mr. Mike shared his learning that clients coping with adversity in maladaptive ways may be negatively perceived by others: ". . . people looking at them think angry, spoiled, mean little kid who very often is just a real sensitive anxious kid underneath that but whose coping mechanism is really not effective for him."

However, the majority of the psychologists we interviewed believe that clients may implement both positive and negative ways of getting through difficult times, and expressed their nonjudgmental appreciation of that continuum. For instance, Dr. Sarah reflected on the sequelae of trauma and how that can lead clients to use both adaptive and maladaptive ways of coping. She reported learning not to judge such efforts on the part of the client:

> *They have so much shame and guilt and responsibility and blame. . . how incredible they were at finding a way to survive their abuse to use a skill that kept them safe and to repress the memory so that they would not harm themselves. Even if they did have to harm themselves, it was a coping tool to stay alive and to deal with the overpowering influence of the trauma.*

Similarly, Dr. Harriet M. said, "I guess I have learned not to be judgmental when people use less functional coping strategies— avoidance or anger—or they are smoking marijuana to avoid doing something they hate." And Dr. Luke reminds us to understand an individual's way of coping as reflective of the scope of their capabilities, by saying ". . . you need to think about what is going to work for this individual, and I think what you really need to explore is what is in the repertoire of that individual."

Theme Seven: Coping mechanisms vary across life stages

Earlier in this chapter we discussed the idea that individuals possess a repertoire or range of ways in which they typically respond to challenging life situations. Various factors including personality, and various life experiences including learning that alternative coping mechanisms, through the therapeutic process, can bring about an expansion in an adaptive range of coping responses and behaviors, shape this repertoire. Many of the stage models of lifespan development identify what constitutes a successful transition from one developmental stage to the next, as predicated on resolving the challenges of the earlier stages in order to successfully cope with the next stages. In this way, some developmental models seem to identify positive coping as a factor that is necessary for normative life development.

The psychologists we interviewed seemed to reflect the view that coping strategies may change over the lifespan. They shared with us their observations that what may have been an effective means of coping at one stage is no longer adaptive at a later stage of development, and vice versa. For instance, Dr. Iris observed: "Sometimes what looks like a block at this age was a very effective coping mechanism at a much earlier stage in life." And Dr. Odila shared her thoughts on this topic, describing the internal monologue of a client reflecting on coping at different life stages:

> . . . "safety strategies" that I think are taking care of me—because maybe when I was five they did and they were adaptive—but now that I'm 50 or however old I am, they're really causing me to suffer, and they're causing my life to be limited, and they're causing me to repeat falling in the same hole over and over again.

Dr. Jack expanded on this theme, saying:

> One theme that reappears time and time again is about how in youth we develop coping mechanisms that get us through our youth, and they serve us well to get us through sometimes dramatic childhoods. And then it seems like the coping mechanisms begin to take on a different shape as the person enters into their late 30s. . . these coping mechanisms seem to turn around on themselves. . . now they almost become this person's enemy, and begin to cause this person all kinds of problems in relationships and dealing with emotion. . . that seems to be a pretty consistent theme that I see in people that I've worked with.

The responses we received from psychologists seem to suggest that their clients' acquisition of wisdom during each life stage is either positively or negatively affected by the ways in which earlier adverse experiences impacted them and/or by their ability or inability to expand their range of coping responses as they progress through life.

Theme Eight: Learning from clients impacts a clinician's own coping

> *"I have certainly had clients who can do things that I couldn't do."* (Dr. Anna)

One of the serendipitous privileges that therapists accrue from working with individuals who allow us to join on their journeys from dysfunction to health is the possibility of drawing on their wisdom to effect change in their own lives. In our study, psychologists were frank about the ways in which watching their clients rise to face the challenges that confront them has often been instructive and inspirational. Dr. Linda's assertion embodies this theme: "I think just thinking about our clients when we are in dire straits is a coping mechanism, because we can see that if they do it so can we." And Dr. Rick said that seeing clients successfully cope inspires him in the following ways:

> *It is one thing to say, yeah, I should use coping mechanisms in my life, but it's another to really be motivated to do it. And I think seeing how quickly they can have good positive effects, [observing] coping mechanisms from working with clients, makes me more motivated to use them.*

Dr. Julia shared the recognition that she did not always implement the same adaptive ways of coping that she advised clients to use:

> *Sometimes I question when I don't practice what I preach, you know? But to witness someone putting some coping mechanisms into practice is always cool—to watch how it works. A lot of times it renovates me; I want to try.*

And Dr. Mai said that he had learned from clients a need to be accepting of each one's particular efforts to cope, even when that behavior might be seen as maladaptive or non-productive:

> *Seeing how clients use those negative coping mechanisms and reflecting back on what I do and seeing my own patterns . . . sometimes you just have to use the negative coping mechanisms. I drink when I am frustrated sometimes—nothing like a glass of wine. I avoid things that I don't like at times and to some degree that works for me. And when it becomes a problem and prevents me from things I want to do then I try to change. But, you know, to some degree, those negative coping mechanisms they teach you about in school? Don't underestimate them, because they often work and it's okay.*

Psychologist Dr. Jack noted that seeing clients cope at different stages in their lives has caused him to reflect on how his ways of coping have changed over the course of his own life:

> *It makes me wonder about my own coping mechanisms in childhood and how I brought those into adult life and into my marriage, into my life as a father and how I parent my children. And I think it kind of stimulates some part me that wants to work on myself.*

And Dr. Homer shared that his work in aiding clients to develop effective coping skills has translated into positive effects with his own children:

> *I think that has made me sensitive within my own family constellation—my children as they were growing up—to try to sort of unofficially, informally try to get them to think about coping mechanisms and dealing with situations without using those terms and words, but getting them to think strategically about problem solving.*

Finally, one psychologist noted that she was quite personally impacted professionally by her work with clients who struggled to find ways to cope with life challenges. Dr. Harriet observed that learning from her clients' struggles helped her better work with future clients:

> *I guess because you are talking about coping with your clients all the time every day, I guess we get the benefit of their knowledge to see for ourselves as well as the next client who walks in the door as to what works/doesn't work, and a broad range of ideas. . . . We learn more from our clients as the years roll on and more from the next client to pass on.*

Concluding Thoughts

Across the themes regarding what psychologists learned about coping from their psychotherapy clients, it was evident that having therapeutic contact with individuals struggling to cope with life's adversities has had a significant impact on the clinicians themselves. They repeatedly noted that, through these therapeutic relationships, they learned to appreciate the many shapes that coping can take, and that the various ways in which people cope will inevitably vary across one's lifespan. Psychologists also told us that they learned not to judge the ways in which others choose to cope. They also reported learning that, while they have a role to play in shaping the coping strategies of their clients, doing so will only be successful if the methods of coping align with the values and psychologies of each individual. As in their responses to most of the other questions we posed in this study, psychologists reported learning tremendous respect for human resilience and their client's noble efforts at coping with adversity. Further, they discovered that they had been impacted personally and professionally by their clients' often remarkable resilience in the face of trauma and conflict. All of the above is evidence that the therapeutic relationship is bidirectional in nature, capable of affecting and even changing both client and therapist.

References

Carver, C., & Connor-Smith, J. (2010). Personality and coping. *Annual Review of Psychology, 61,* 679-704.

Compas, B. E., Connor-Smith, J. K., Saltzman, H., Thomsen, A. H., & Wadsworth, M. E. (2001). Coping with stress during childhood and adolescence: problems, progress, and potential in theory and research. *Psychological Bulletin, 127,* 87-127.

Cramer, P. (2000). Defense mechanism in psychology today: Further processes for adaptation. *American Psychologist, 55,* 637-646.

Creamer, M., Burgess, P., & Pattison, P. (1992). Reaction to trauma: A cognitive processing model. *Journal of Abnormal Psychology, 101,* 452-459.

Folkman, S. (1997). Positive psychological states and coping with severe stress. *Social Science & Medicine, 45,* 1207-1221.

Folkman, S. (2008). The case for positive emotions in the stress process. *Anxiety, Stress & Coping: An International Journal, 21,* 3-14.

Hayes, S. C., Strosahl, K., & Wilson, K. (1999). *Acceptance and commitment therapy: an experiential approach to behavior change.* New York, NY: Guilford Press.

Hilsenroth, M., Blagys, M., Ackerman, S., Bonge, D., & Blais, M. (2005). Measuring psychodynamic-interpersonal and cognitive-behavioral techniques: development of the comparative psychotherapy process Scale. *Psychotherapy: Theory, Research, Practice, Training, 42,* 340-356.

Kabat-Zinn, J. (2013). *Full catastrophe living: using the wisdom of your body and mind to face stress, pain, and illness.* New York, NY: Bantam Dell Books.

Lazarus, R. S., & Folkman, S. (1987). Current states of transactional theory and research on emotion and coping. In L. Laux & G. Vossel (Eds.), *Personality in biographical stress and coping research, 1,* 141-169.

Linehan, M. (1993). *Cognitive behavioral therapy of borderline personality disorder.* New York, NY: Guilford Press.

Meléndez, J. C., Mayordomo, T., Sancho, P., & Tomás, J. M. (2012). Coping strategies: gender differences and development throughout the life span. *The Spanish Journal of Psychology, 15,* 1089-1098.

Park, C. (2010). Making sense of the meaning literature: an integrative review of meaning making and its effects on adjustment to stressful life events. *Psychological Bulletin, 136,* 257-301.

Park, C. L., Edmondson, D., & Blank, T. O. (2009). Religious and non-religious pathways to stress-related growth in cancer survivors. *Applied Psychology: Health & Well-Being, 1,* 321-335.

Park, C. L., & Folkman, S. (1997). Meaning in the context of stress and coping. *Review of General Psychology, 1,* 115-144.

Penley, J. A., & Tomaka, J. (2002). Associations among the Big Five, emotional responses, and coping with acute stress. *Personality and Individual Differences, 32,* 1215-28.

Rutter, M. (2006). Implications of resilience concepts for scientific understanding. *Annals of the New York Academy of Sciences. 1094,* 1-12.

Skinner, E. A., Edge, K., Altman, J., & Sherwood, H. (2003). Searching for the structure of coping: A review and critique of category systems for classifying ways of coping. *Psychological Bulletin, 129,* 216-69.

Skinner, E. A., & Zimmer-Gembeck, M. J. (2007). The development of coping. *Annual Review of Psychology, 58,* 119-144.

Taylor, S. E. (2007). Social support. In H. S. Friedman & R. C. Silver (Eds.), *Foundations of Health Psychology* (pp. 145-71). New York: Oxford University Press.

Taylor, S. E., & Stanton, A. (2007). Coping resources, coping processes, and mental health. *Annual Review of Clinical Psychology, 3,* 377-401.

Tennen, H., & Affleck, G. (2002). The challenge of capturing daily processes at the interface of social and clinical psychology. *Journal of Social and Clinical Psychology, 21,* 610-627.

Vaillant, G. E. (2011). Involuntary coping mechanisms: a psychodynamic perspective. *Dialogues in Clinical Neuroscience, 13,* 366-70.

Wei, M., Heppner, P., & Mallinckrodt, B. (2003). Perceived coping as a mediator between attachment and psychological distress: a structural equation modeling approach. *Journal of Counseling Psychology 50,* 438-447.

Chapter 5

COURAGE: A MASTER KEY
TO PSYCHOTHERAPY

Joan M. Frye, Adriana Kipper-Smith, and Sherry L. Hatcher

"Life shrinks or expands in proportion to one's courage."
— Anais Nin

When I first received this assignment, I (first author) had a very strong emotional response. After much reflection, I realized my strong feelings emanated from the fact that my father, a WWII veteran, had participated in the liberation of hundreds of Jewish victims from the German concentration camps. Having been exposed to such horrific experiences, my father instilled a very strong ideal of courage in my personal psychological makeup. The result of this conceptualization of courage often left me feeling less than courageous and, as such, I experienced some degree of ambivalence in considering the topic of what therapists learn about their clients' courage. Nonetheless, I found myself eager to learn about and gain a better understanding of ways in which other people demonstrate and perceive courage in their lives.

The interviews with the psychologists in our study are fascinating and instructive. Interestingly, I believe that I have been personally influenced by studying their moving responses, especially as they described experiences with courageous clients. In general, our participants responded to our questions in conveying that they have learned much about courage from their clients and that this learning process has influenced them in many ways, both professionally and personally. More specifically, psychologists reported have learning to be more courageous themselves in participating with their clients, who often faced tremendous adversity in their daily lives.

One frequent response from therapists was that engaging in the process of psychotherapy itself requires courage on the part of both participants. Many of our respondents remarked that everyone has the potential to be courageous, and that therapy can help clients to develop their courage and to become increasingly courageous over time. Notably, many therapists in our sample were emotionally moved when relating examples of the courage they had witnessed in their clients and, overall, they felt very privileged to have been allowed to join with their clients in impactful, life-changing experiences. For many, vicariously participating in the process as their clients progressed in successfully employing courage to face their adversities became a key reason for continuing work in a field that offers hope but does not guarantee success.

As noted in previous chapters, although there are anecdotal records of the ways in which clients influence psychotherapists, there is a paucity of research in regard to what therapists learn from their clients (Farber, 1983). In their 2002 article, Freeman and Hayes found that clients actually serve as a source of critical teaching in the development of counselors. The authors' conclusions reflect the earlier findings by Skovholt and Rønnestad (1992) that interpersonal experiences have more influence on therapists than do impersonal data. Working with clients was cited as the most important influence on the psychologists' development as counselors. Specifically, in this study participants indicated that their clients act as a continuous source of feedback to the counselor—as a person, and with regard to the counseling interventions. Other research studies report similar findings (Orlinsky, Botermans, & Rønnestad, 2001). Freeman and Hayes (2002) illustrate the important learning they have received from clients: "My values, beliefs, and ethics have changed due to my encounter. . . I am more accepting and tolerant of differences" (p. 20). One of these authors particularly notes how the courage of a very distressed client had a significant impact on him: "Facing my own fears made me more courageous, ethical and compassionate" (p. 20). The authors go on to say that profound experiences with clients, especially in the context of adversity, may be therapeutic for both the client and the therapist. They state that "Counselors do seem to be changed by their clients' stories and experiences. . . Courageous clients may teach counselors a great deal about the change process and assist professional helpers throughout their careers" (pp. 20-21). Another study of 100 experienced therapists (Rønnestad & Skovholt, 2003) found that experienced psychotherapists report considerable learning from their thousands of hours of direct interaction with clients, in that they abstract and generalize the knowledge acquired from one client to another. The authors also found that clients who report particularly profound experiences, or whose therapy was remarkably successful or unsuccessful, have the most significant impact on therapists. Importantly, Rønnestad and Skovholt note that the therapists' professional learning in therapy can be transferred to their private lives.

In a more recent study on what beginning therapists learn from their clients (Stahl, Hill, Jacobs, Kleinman, Isenberg, & Stern, 2009) 12 graduate psychology interns responded to questions regarding "what therapists learn from clients" (p. 376). The results of this research indicated that these novice therapists learned important lessons from participating in psychotherapy with clients. More specifically, they learned about themselves, about their clients, about human nature, and about the therapy relationship.

Research on Courage

Courage is a concept with which we are all very familiar. We frequently read and hear about people displaying courage in many diverse situations: a person diving into a river to save the life of a child; a mother facing intractable cancer with grace and dignity; or a young soldier bravely leading troops into battle. As I (first author) was preparing for this chapter, I often found the word "courage" prominently featured in the titles of newspaper and magazine articles describing the inspiring journeys of individuals or groups as they face myriad problems and adversities. Articles proclaim the courage of soldiers returning from the battlefront to deal with mental and/or physical difficulties. Journalists call for congressmen to display courage as they make decisions that may significantly affect citizens during difficult economic times. The common use of the word "courage" implies that we have a shared understanding of its meaning.

Courage has been discussed by philosophers and writers for hundreds of years, dating back at least to the time of Aristotle (Putman, 2010). More recently, proponents of the positive psychology movement (Seligman & Peterson, 2000) have proposed that courage is one of the six positive "virtues" or human strengths that add meaning to one's life. Specifically, "the strengths and virtues buffer against misfortune and against the psychological disorders, and they may be the key to building resilience" (Seligman & Peterson, 2003, p. 306). In fact, Seligman and Peterson (2003) addressed the role of courage in the therapeutic process. They describe courage as one of the primary, key personal strengths, finding it to be a basic requirement in order for therapy to be beneficial to a client. Dick-Niederhauser (2009) commented specifically on the way in which such personal strength in courage can be built: ". . . the important intrapsychic resource of courage can increase only by taking risks. It is not possible to build up courage without facing challenges squarely," (p. 197). Our participants' responses echoed a similar belief.

Since courage appears to be a familiar construct, in fact described as a "universal virtue" by positive psychology researchers (Greitemeyer, Osswald, Fischer, & Frey, 2007, p. 117), one might think that there was a vast body of research literature on courage. However, the opposite is the case. As I began looking into the research on courage in order to assimilate the many meanings our participants ascribed to the concept of courage, I found that much of the literature is anecdotal in nature. For example, Bugental (1991) notes that his clients have taught him lessons that are simple, yet profound. He cites one such lesson as being "there is always more, that courage, persistence and determination can open possibilities where none seemed to exist" (p. 29). Related to the lack of research on the psychological construct of courage in general, there is a corresponding paucity of research on the role of courage in psychotherapy (Pury & Lopez, 2010, p. 3). However, on a promising note, due to the burgeoning interest in positive psychology (Seligman & Peterson, 2000), a small body of research on courage is accruing. In this chapter we will discuss our findings on what therapists learn from their clients about courage, as well as the research regarding the construct of courage in general. We will see how our study of what therapists learn from their clients both supports and deviates from past and current research on this topic.

Courage as a Psychological Strength

Before we venture further into our exploration of the role of courage in psychotherapy as described by the participants in our study, we should spend some time developing an understanding of the psychological strength known as courage. As with most concepts discussed in the field of psychology, there is no consensus as to a precise definition (Woodard & Pury, 2007). In fact, one investigator found 41 different definitions for the construct of courage (Rate, 2010). To add to the complexity of defining courage, researchers note that there are several types of courage. Three types of courage that are especially relevant to our discussion are physical, moral, and vital (or psychological) courage. Physical courage includes action taken in the context of physical risk, moral courage includes authenticity and integrity in expressing personal views and values in spite of risk, and vital courage is displayed when a person faces a threat to his or her psychological or physical health and well-being (Greitemeyer et al., 2007). We will see that the responses of our participants touch on all three types of courage, with a special emphasis on vital courage.

Rate et al. (2007) focused their research on establishing an empirical definition of courage in order to facilitate further research on the topic (Rate, 2008). In his 2010 article, Rate indicated that recent research studies on the construct of courage appeared to support ideas presented by Peterson and Seligman (2004) and Peterson (2006) that courage can be conceptualized as:

> . . . (a) a willful, intentional act, (b) executed after mindful deliberation, (c) involving objective substantial risk to the actor, (d) primarily motivated to bring about a noble good or worthy end, (e) despite, perhaps, the presence of the emotion of fear. (p. 95)

Importantly, Rate reported that experiencing fear may not be necessary for an individual to have courage. These authors concur in seeing courage as including such strengths as "bravery, persistence, integrity, and vitality" (Seligman, 2004, p. 199). However, a definition of courage that may be more attuned to our endeavor in discovering what psychotherapists learn from their clients about courage is one proffered by Jerome Gans (2005). He states that courage is "a mental act that involves a decision to face and deal with emotional pain as honestly as possible without any guarantee of a positive outcome" (p. 576). Gans goes on to say that courage is not absolute but "arises out of a particular context, one that is often spontaneous and unanticipated as well as co-constructed, rooted in the history of the individual. . . .and . . . culture" (p. 576).

Our Research Study

Sherry Hatcher and nine graduate students commenced this research project in the summer of 2008. As a long-time practicing psychologist, Dr. Hatcher indicated that she became increasingly interested in what other psychologists also learned from their psychotherapy clients. In reviewing related professional literature, she noted that the focus of research on psychotherapy has largely centered on learning and change as experienced by the client, with much less research reported on the impact of psychotherapy on the psychotherapist's personal and professional life (Hatcher et al., 2012).

The nine graduate students each interviewed from five to 10 practicing psychologists in various regions of the United States and Canada about what they may have learned about courage from their clients. In many cases, our respondents seemed emotionally moved by reporting their experiences with courageous clients and what they had learned both personally and professionally in that regard. Responses to this question were grouped into seven categories. The following table lists the categories and frequencies of the responses.

TABLE 1

Categories and Frequencies—Learning About Courage

Category	Frequency
1. Definitions of Courage	75%
a. Perseverance	33%
b. Facing fears	26%
c. Empowering strategies	16%
2. Beliefs About Courage	95%
a. Incredible courage comes from within	56%
b. Individual differences	25%
c. Connections to others	15%
3. Courage and Psychotherapy	41%
a. Courage can be learned or increased	23%
b. Therapists help clients be courageous	18%
4. The Therapeutic Process Requires Courage	80%
a. Clients are courageous	48%
b. Courage to face oneself	18%
c. Courage in therapy is a paradox	7%
d. Change is difficult	9%
5. Therapists Are Courageous	15%
6. Therapists Gain Much From Courageous Clients	43%
a. Learning to be courageous	15%
b. Inspiration	28%
c. Hope	7%
d. Satisfaction with therapeutic work	8%
7. Infrequent Responses	10%
a. Courage is rare	3%
b. Courage requires a strong faith	5%
c. Miscellaneous	2%

Implicit Definitions of Courage

Seventy-five percent of the psychologists in this sample offered a personal definition of what courage means to them. Courage was defined by 33% of the participants as perseverance, or putting one foot in front of the other no matter what life's difficulties. A second definition of courage (26%) was facing one's problems by walking toward the fear, being afraid but taking action anyway. Other participants defined courage as various empowering strategies that clients use to face difficulties (16%). This latter group viewed courage as dependent on a particular person and the context of a situation. Specifically, these participants indicated that it is not always easy to determine what the courageous response might be with regard to any given situation. In fact, while a response may not appear courageous to observers, it may involve significant courage on the part of the particular individual.

Courage as Perseverance

The majority of our participants described courage as perseverance, or continuing to put one foot in front of the other no matter what difficulties arose in life. This is a private view of courage, though one which is recognized in the literature (Rate et al., 2007). It does, however, take courage out of the realm of those who are likely to be recognized publicly as courageous, and perhaps even rewarded for their bravery— such as police officers, firemen, and EMTs. It is also distinct from individual heroic acts such as rescuing a drowning child at significant peril to the individual's own well-being. While the people who perform these acts are certainly courageous and deserve the honors bestowed upon them, in at least one of our participants' view of courage it was clear that clients may demonstrate courage quietly, on a daily basis, and within their own lives.

Following are some examples from our participants of specific client circumstances reflective of courage as perseverance. As Dr. Gimpenfeld stated, "So much of courage is perseverance. . . that's maybe the most courageous thing. When people are successful it's mostly because they just keep putting one foot in front of the other." Another participant, Dr. Linda, discussing her work with clients suffering from obsessive-compulsive disorder (OCD), noted:

When I think of the clients . . . that are severely OCD, I think of courage. While they look terrified, and they are, it must take a lot of courage to just put one foot in front of the other every day, especially if they are germ phobic and do not want to touch anything. They are convinced that if they do, they will die, and yet every day they do it.

Dr. Jeremey summarized this viewpoint as follows:

Courage is, in addition to events that have a lot of impact. . . kind of suiting up every day in life and making good faith efforts to be the . . . best kind of person that they can be given that we all do it imperfectly.

Facing One's Fears

Therapists we interviewed described courage as not just persevering but also taking a very active position by walking toward the fear, being afraid, and doing what is necessary in spite of the fear. This definition taps into a controversy in the literature regarding whether experiencing fear is a necessary component of courage or not (Rate et al., 2007; Rate, 2010; Woodward & Pury, 2007). For these therapists, their clients clearly experienced fear and yet often were able to take effective, positive action. We do not know whether these psychologists see their clients who do not experience fear as not being courageous, but clearly experiencing fear is an important component of courage to these respondents (Rank, 2008). Following are some illustrative scenarios and quotations related to this second definition of courage. As Dr. Goodheart succinctly stated, "Courage involves fear and actually feeling afraid." Another participant, Dr. Harriet M., commented:

Courage is not about an absence of fear. It is about trying to muddle through life's difficult times and, in fact, being fearful of it but still trying to go forward. . . .Courage is kind of doing it anyway, even when you have fear.

Dr. Harriet M. clearly spells out, as many of our respondents imply, that courage is not the opposite of fear, but can coexist along with fear.

And yet another respondent, Dr. McMillan, described his perspective on courage with these words:

> ...*it is courage to walk toward the fear and move into it instead of away from it and take that wisdom that fear gives you because sometimes there are very good reasons to be afraid and if you learn from your fear and keep going, that's great, that's as good as any of us can do.*

Facing fears was also noted by some of our participants in the context that courage is observed when clients suffer traumatic events in the course of their everyday lives. As one example of this, the psychology literature cites examples of individuals demonstrating courage when faced with serious illness. This type of courage may be called psychological or vital courage or "fighting for life" (Putman, 2010, p, 25) because it has to do with a potential fear for one's life. Dr. Ricky described such a case in his work with very ill clients fighting cancer. He observed, "Through my very sick clients I learned that when people have to, they find the inner resources, they find greater courage through trauma than they do just through everyday life." In describing a vivid example of a husband and wife who were dealing with the wife's breast cancer, Dr. Ricky also noted, "To sit in the middle of the night and panic attack at three in the morning and talk about life and death issues. Before cancer, they never had to talk about that. . . I think you have to talk about that."

Interestingly, Dr. Natasha related a personal experience regarding what she had learned about courage through her work with clients. She explained that she regularly worked with her clients on developing courage to face their fears. Dr. Natasha reported she herself was fearful of running group therapy sessions and had avoided doing so. Once she realized that she had to face her own fears, she committed to running a group. Dr. Natasha now shares this experience with her clients at the initiation of a new group. In summary, she remarked, "I committed myself to do it, and I faced it, and it makes a difference."

Finally, Dr. Goodheart summarized this issue quite elegantly:

> *Courage may be one of the master keys to life or psychotherapy in the sense that when you do what you're afraid of, as opposed to avoiding what you are afraid of, that may be the heart of anything that's empowering at all.*

Empowering Strategies

Sixteen percent of our sample described courage in terms of empowering strategies for facing life's difficulties. This particular perception of courage is not directly addressed in the literature and seems somewhat akin to adaptive coping mechanisms. In the literature, Hannah, Sweeney, and Lester (2010) describe the relationship between courage and coping mechanisms They state:

> *Coping allows a host of adaptive and maladaptive responses, such as denial or defense mechanisms that may direct one's energy away from addressing the source of threat. We hold that courage is by definition an adaptive process whereby one summons the internal and external resources to confront a threat, overcome fear, and reduce that threat.* (p.126)

Therapists in our sample provided examples of empowering strategies that may fall more into the category of defense mechanisms. Dr. Pedroso described the process of being able to deal with losses through changing one's narrative, making up a story, "so that you can own it and it is part of you." Another example was provided by Dr. Reuben who stated, "Sometimes it takes courage to be a coward and not to confront an aggressor." And yet another therapist held that there is courage in approaching fear by being still and not doing. As Dr. Goodheart described:

> *A surprise that I have seen in patients' lives regarding courage is how frightened some or many people are to be still and be in the present moment and pay attention to what is happening. There are some people who are so frightened of that for their own personal story reasons that they are going, going, going all the time and can't be still. . . .People can be frightened of being still and sometimes the courage involved in that can be a big step.*

The definitions of courage that our respondents offered do not incorporate all of the construct components that implicit theories of courage include. For example, volitional action that is conducted after consideration, which involves substantial risk to the actor, is primarily motivated for a noble purpose, even with the possible presence of fear (Rate et al., 2007). However, this may be due to the fact that we solicited examples of courage from the experiences of psychotherapists as seen in their clinical practices. If we had asked for examples of courage that were from any aspect of life, we may have obtained implicit definitions that were more in line with those of Rate (2008) and Rate et al. (2007).

Beliefs About Courage

Therapists espoused several beliefs about courage garnered from work with their therapy clients. Over half, (56%), expressed the belief that their clients are capable of incredible amounts of courage when facing adversity. In addition, many felt that people have an internal predisposition to be courageous, although allowing for individual differences (25%) in the way courage is expressed. Some (15%) also noted courage may involve connections to other people as at times, their clients acted especially courageously because of their commitments to significant others such as a spouse or children.

Clearly, most therapists (56%) observed their clients displaying incredible amounts of courage as they struggle through adversity even, if they are unaware of this trait in themselves. That observation led to psychologists reporting great admiration and respect for their clients' endurance through life's hardships.

What Therapists Said

Although there were numerous enthusiastic comments regarding how courageous many clients were, space limitations allow for presentation of only a sampling of these poignant reflections. Altogether, in reading through these comments, we found ourselves very touched by the tragic and heart-breaking life events these clients had endured with incredible courage.

Surely therapists are in the position to see their clients when they are at some of their lowest but, perhaps, also at some of their greatest moments. Dr. Yetty made the striking comment, "It just really, really shocks me and amazes me the amount of limitless courage that people have; sometimes we think that great adversities can crush them and it's to the contrary."

Another therapist, Dr. Sarah, described her experiences with people who had survived severe trauma and made the following comment:

> *I have seen people who have endured some of the worst forms of sadistic sexual abuse, torture, murder, homicide of their children, their siblings, multiple homicides within their own family. I have seen incredible courage to stay alive, to find a new meaning in their life, to use their trauma to help others in the sense of using their posttraumatic growth . . . they find something good . . . out of these horrific circumstances.*

With tear-filled eyes, Dr. Sarah also described the situation of a particular client, a grandmother who had witnessed her son-in-law murder her daughter and two grandchildren. This client had the extraordinary courage to write to her son-in-law in prison to tell him that she forgave him. Another participant, Dr. Michelle, remarked:

> *I had a patient who was raped when she was eight years old and I remember thinking, like, how do you survive that? How do you live in a world with that buried inside of you because she never told anyone. . . The things my patients have gone through and survived; it's just amazing.*

While therapists did not indicate that courage is necessarily a personality trait, they suggest that everyone has the *potential* to develop courage, or at least a predisposition to gain courage. This view as to potential courage is supported by several authors and researchers such as Peterson & Seligman (2004). These authors describe the dispositional nature of courage as consisting of such character strengths as "persistence, integrity, and vitality" (also Rate et al., 2007, p. 84). Rachman (2010) stated, based on his series of research projects with military personnel, that courage can be increased through study and training. He believes that all people are capable of courage and that extreme fear is not necessarily pathological; in his opinion, fear and courage exist on a continuum. Taking a similar perspective, that courage is a state rather than a trait, some proponents of positive psychology believe our society is in need of augmented courage. Rate (2010) articulates his viewpoint that we need courage to face unknown, future life challenges.

Reflective of the stance of researchers on the construct of courage, one of our participants, Dr. Reuben, commented, "Courage is in the repertoire of everyone." Dr. Rachel elaborated on the idea that courage is an internal predisposition in remarking, "So they've learned a lot about the life force and that we all have it inside of us to function better. And to tap that gives so much courage, that they have that courage." And Dr. Sunny said, "The folks I work with amaze me every single day. Every single one of them is courageous and resilient and just so much stronger than any of them knows." Finally, Dr. Mark noted:

> *That people can summon courage where it is not automatically there, maybe that's the lesson. It's not like some people have it and some people don't. I wouldn't necessarily see it or they wouldn't see it in themselves; [but it]. . . can be worked on or developed to surface.*

As suggested above, even though psychologists believe clients have potential to experience courage, some of our respondents (25%) specified there are individual differences in the ways courage is expressed. Dr. Anna noted one person's fear may be another person's strength. This psychologist went on to explain how she knew a trauma physician who was not made afraid by the numerous traumas that her patients experienced but she was personally afraid of spiders. As Dr. Anna said:

> *Therefore, what I have learned is not to make assumptions about what is difficult for someone or what is hard to talk about, what is a defense, even on the basis of my own experience. A thing that is easy for me may be difficult for them.*

Particularly with regard to individual differences in the amount of courage an individual may be able to muster in facing adversity, Dr. Steve suggested, "courage is very individual; some have too little, some have too much" and "too much courage can be dangerous; not necessarily a good thing." This same psychologist noted, "Too little courage is dangerous, not doing what one wants to do. You have to have courage to change." Dr. Steve also remarked that some clients have too much courage, they take too many risks. He stated they have to learn "when you jump off the cliff, remember to take your parachute." Interestingly, comments about clients having too much courage were typically made by psychologists who work with clients that have addiction problems. In this sense, being a risk-taker may not be so much having too much courage as acting in a self-injurious manner. As noted previously, some components in the definition of courage include thoughtful choices and a noble purposes, elements not likely evident for those who struggle with unremitting addiction. In summary, speaking to individual differences in courage, Dr. Vincent expressed that a balance is needed in courage, not too much, not too little, especially if one wants to make changes. He stated:

> *To say, you know, whatever I am doing, I am doing with a purpose and I believe in it. And giving up, and I will be giving up something, and I will be gaining something. And I feel somewhat sad and I will be somewhat happy at the same time.*

The Role of Others

A third notable belief about courage, as cited by some of our participants was the role that others play in an individual's ability to act courageously. Some of our participants (15%) stated that courage requires connections to other human beings. Dr. Harriet M. expressed this belief upon commenting:

> *Every client that has gone successfully through personal hardship or difficulty has had to connect or knit with other people regardless of how independent they might be or how isolative they might be. They have needed other people to get through things.*

However, the relatively low frequency of this theme was surprising. Perhaps in our culture we view courage as a personal, individualistic strength. Perhaps we do not see being courageous as encompassing the need for others. This perspective illuminates one of the paradoxical qualities of courage –individual strength combined with a need for others. In relation to this theme, several of our participants reflected the belief that connections to other people may make one more courageous. Similarly, Rate et al. (2007) indicated that one of the common conceptualizations of courage includes a sense of selfless, sacrifice for the good of others. Dr. Sarah expressed this idea in her comment:

> *I found that people who have children tended to use their courage. . . their children give them their courage, they give them meaning. They will fight through this, will endure this, because of [their] children. "I cannot leave them alone. I do not want to leave them."*

Courage and Psychotherapy

Since the focus of the question asked of our participants was, *"What have you learned from your psychotherapy clients about courage?"* therapists often formulated their responses in relation to the psychotherapy process. There were several key themes within their multifaceted responses. One theme that, identified by 39% of our participants, was that the therapeutic process can enable clients to be courageous, by tapping into their personal reservoir of courage. Dr. McMillan expressed this view in this comment: "It's great seeing people. . . [be courageous] and I help them do that, but I had to learn before I could help them do that." Dr. Steve, indicated, "Just by trying to find in their repertoire that they have been courageous and to emphasize that and reward them has been extremely effective." And, Dr. Jeremey remarked, ". . . the courage to try something differently; the courage that people have when they come in and say: 'you know, I never would have seen myself do this, but I went ahead and did this anyway.'" Dr. Justin illustrated a common tenet of psychotherapy, that is, if a client can have a new kind of interpersonal relationship, a corrective emotional experience in therapy (Teyber, 2000), then he or she may be able to have different relationships outside of therapy:

> *If they can meet an unknown person, then start to get to know that person and work on things, then it shouldn't*

be that difficult for them in the outside world to be able to establish different kinds of relationships too. So I think they can transfer things from the inside relationship to the outside relationship. That's an example of how to build up their courage.

Whereas Dr. Sarah, described the situation of a client who had been sexually abused from the ages of 8 to 18 by a family member and the role therapy played in her courageous survival:

. . . it was sadistic sexual abuse in which she was tied up for days on end by her family member and tortured and raped—the courage that she used to stay alive as a teenager and she was not allowed to tell her story because he threatened everybody in her life. She came to therapy to me for two years without speaking a word. She sat in my office; I would probe yes/no answers about school or basic things. She just sat there. The courage for her to come, I thought I was doing nothing with her until she handed me her journal one day and said "The only thing that keeps me alive is coming to your office for my appointments." I did not know.

Finally, Dr. Antonia summed up this theme, stating "Clients have the courage to tackle their problems but sometimes they just need direction and guidance and support to face their difficulties."

Another important theme that emerged from our participants' responses is that psychotherapy is empowering and can give clients hope. Dr. Goodheart made several comments in this vein. He stated, "When [clients] exercise courage, the reward to them is unbelievably empowering" and "It is its own self-fulfilling thing, to be courageous makes you more courageous." Adding to this theme, Dr. Julia commented:

I have all my past history of my work with other clients. . . with courage, that I can share – not share their stories – but it helps me to give my clients hope that they can get through this process, it's possible. And knowing that, having witnessed that, I can convey a sense of hope which, in turn, can help them to have enough courage to face whatever it is, or stay in therapy.

The Therapeutic Process Requires Courage

Forty-eight percent of our respondents commented that their clients evidence courage simply by engaging in psychotherapy. This theme is also described by physician and therapist, Jerome Gans (2005) in the following statement:

> *The human condition is itself a battlefield. Any number of feelings and impulses contend within us, causing us great fear, anger, anguish, shame, sadness, and disgust. . . .It is only fitting as our profession begins to honor human strength and resilience that we pay more attention to our patients' courage.* (p. 591)

Other themes that emerged from our research regarding the participants' learning about courage and psychotherapy include the idea that it takes courage to face what is difficult about oneself. Therapists noted that change is difficult and it requires courage to change one's environment and/or the ways in which one copes. Some therapists also described courage in psychotherapy as paradoxical. They noted it takes courage for a client to be vulnerable in the therapeutic relationship. In this context, courage implies a degree of personal strength coupled with the ability to be open, sensitive, and somewhat undefended with another, trusted person.

As is clear from the above, nearly one half of our participants indicated their belief that clients display courage just by choosing to enter and tolerate the psychotherapy process. As Dr. Sarah stated:

> *I think most people who come to therapy are extremely courageous. . . [a client] said something about it is still pretty scary to come in and see you and I just said 'thank you so much for reminding me of that because you are so brave to let yourself do that. . . "Good for you for letting yourself make that call."*

Dr. Iris echoed this idea, "I think anyone who undertakes the psychotherapy process and change, particularly the longer term stuff, has to have courage to do it." And Dr. Anna reinforced the theme in saying:

I think it is courageous to come to therapy and deal with things that are so personal and something that they have avoided for a long time. I think that person has to be in a certain amount of pain to take that step of courage to come in and talk to a stranger and hope that it will help.

Dr. Rachel described the courage of a client with a severe phobia for bridges and someone who lived in an area that had more than 40 bridges. This client was unable to walk, drive, or even ride over a bridge and her life was thus severely impaired. Dr. Rachel discussed the courage in going through visual imagery exposure to reduce her fear of bridges, even though it was terrifying for the client. Dr. Rachel's example echoes research findings that exposure as a therapeutic intervention may activate curative processes in the client which include an increase in the client's "courage and personal strength" (Dick-Niederhauser, 2009, p.192). Norton and Weiss (2009), describing their research on the role of courage in in exposure therapy, noted that "by definition, exposure connotes courageous behavior – approaching a feared or anxiety producing stimulus" (p. 213). The authors propose that dropouts from exposure therapy for anxiety disorders may be exhibiting avoidance behaviors or a "perceived inability to confront one's fears – lower courage to confront one's fears" (p. 213.) Dr. Justin summed it with one of our personal favorite quotations about courage and psychotherapy in stating his belief that, "the whole therapeutic process is courage."

A related theme noted by our therapists in our sample is the courage it takes for a psychotherapy client to look at what is difficult to accept about oneself, to look at their own issues. For example Dr. Pines, illustrated how it can be difficult to look at one's problems, stating that a client wanted to address her depression and described the client's experience:

[She]spent the week before coming in just up all night, worried about the session, worried about talking about emotions, worried about how I would react to her and convinced that I would be rejecting of her. She spent the entire session sort of shaking. . . I just remember at the end of that session . . . thinking that it took an incredible amount of courage on her end to even come in and talk about these really upsetting events in her life.

Similarly, Dr. Juan noted:

> *A lot of therapy is helping [clients] be courageous and face what they don't want to face. Sometimes they get locked into a pattern of behavior that they are not happy with and then therapy, of course, helps them. . . to break that, and that takes courage on their part.*

Another client who had a substance abuse problem was asked by participant Dr. Clark to look at how she had been in the beginning, where she was at the end of therapy, and how change had happened. In response, the client had the "courage to say that 'Maybe there is something I have to look at,' and made major steps in terms of stopping her substance use. . . the courage to face it and do something about it."

Similar to this example, many therapists expressed a related theme with regard to clients undergoing psychotherapy. Specifically, they noted that it takes courage for clients to change themselves, their environment, and the way they cope. Oftentimes, the changes that clients make as a result of therapy include becoming at least somewhat more of a "risk-taker." Dr. Clark illustrated this in describing his client who had a substance abuse problem:

> *Honestly, there are many clients where it (substance abuse) was such an integral part of their life and coping. In AA they talk about the bottle being a friend. There is a way in which you can see that this was their solace, this was their friend, and the courage for them to say goodbye to that friend and make a shift in life takes a lot of courage.*

Similarly, Dr. Steve summarized that helping a client to become courageous enough to change coping mechanisms and to become more of a risk-taker can be powerful in improving a life. In a related example, Dr. Cody said, in describing a client with an abusive spouse who was trying to determine whether to leave or stay with him:

> *Sometimes you tell people that this is a problem you are not going to solve. You just hope that they have enough resources to be able to follow through in this because a lot of times it would be easy just to turn back and not make the change that is needed.*

Another example of a client's courage in changing her life was offered by Dr. Tevin. He described a client who had been told by her mother that she would never get married because she "walked funny." Dr. Tevin explained that the client kept saying, "I'll never walk down the aisle." The therapist remarked that the client was seeing the world through her mother's eyes and, once she began to see the world through her own eyes, "she had the courage to keep on looking until she found a man who would accept her as she was." In a related example, Dr. Eliza described a client presenting with a dependent personality disorder. She noted that this client:

> . . . has recently just stepped out of her safety zone and . . . has started volunteering, which is something she has never done before. . . and her whole outlook has completely changed and she is excited. . . it's just apparent that she is happy and she has taken a step of courage.

A very interesting theme that emerged from therapists' responses is that the construct of courage is viewed by many as a paradox. To illustrate with something Dr. Rose said:

> Courage. . . I think that it is very courageous for people to continue to open themselves up to me in therapy and tell me things that they may be ashamed of, embarrassed of, because it is certainly hard for me to do that in therapy or do that with other people. . . I think that shows that many people can have great courage by showing vulnerability. . . Courage often means being able to be vulnerable. So that's a nice kind of paradoxical truth that I see with a lot of people.

In another context, Dr. Tom talked about experiences with clients in the military. He discussed a specific definition of courage that individuals in the military—who are trained to go into combat and to kill—tend to embody: "You don't show emotion. You do your mission. You protect your life and your buddy's life and if it means that you have to give up yours for him, you do that." He went on to comment regarding the depth of courage displayed by individuals in the military who subsequently enter therapy:

I am always amazed at how. . . the real courage comes from being able to sit down and talk about what it means and how they feel about it. This is the hardest kind of gap to bridge and many of them say that. It kind of works against everything they have learned about being male, everything they have learned about being strong and courageous and what it is like to be vulnerable, to talk about emotions, to cry. . . I think there is also something about that internal strength and that fortitude to be vulnerable and to share something about one's experience that can be very courageous.

It seems this paradoxical view of courage may be specific to the context of psychotherapy, as standard definitions of courage do not include being vulnerable to others (Rate, 2008). Clearly, given the unique nature of the therapeutic relationship, our participants see their clients as both strong and vulnerable during psychotherapy sessions.

Therapists Are Courageous

Some of our participants (15%) stated that therapists must also have courage in order to engage in psychotherapy with their clients. For example, Dr. Iris expressed this view as follows:

It also means that the therapist has to have courage. . . there is a lot of stuff that crops up in a therapy context that is not pleasant to experience. It took me a long, long time to be able to deal with anger and not be terrified by it. It took me a long time to recognize my own power in a circumstance and to learn to pair it well with compassion, so that it was a balanced process. And that, I think, takes courage on the part of the therapist.

Another psychologist, Dr. Jeremey, explained:

It is an act of courage for anyone in the mental health business to work with people in this way, to be willing to sit down and be privy to other people's secrets. So it's a reminder to me of the courage that it takes. . . to work with people.

Dr. McMillan remarked:

> *I have a tendency to deny fear and pretend that it isn't there, to cover it up with anger or some sort of other intense emotion, and learning not to do that and just hanging with [the] ambiguity that fear gives us [to] see if I can learn with this, that's great.*

Mr. Michael expressed his viewpoint as follows:

> *Sure, sometimes I'll be frustrated with people who don't seem to be moving or wanting to move or make things happen. And then sometimes I have to sit down and have a little talk with myself and say, Well, maybe I'm the one that's not moving or making anything happen, and maybe I need to change it up a little bit or try something different rather than just sitting here waiting for it to happen. Maybe I need to work as hard as they do. . .*

In considering the literature on this point, Shapiro and Gans (2008) offered their view on the courage of the psychotherapist. They wrote, "We as. . . therapists may need to take risks, to display courage in order that we meet an internally set standard of the good-enough therapist for our patients" (p. 348).

Therapists Are Affected by Working With Clients

Perhaps some of the most moving and interesting responses to the question, *"What have you learned about courage from your psychotherapy clients?"* were the statements that directly reflected how therapists were themselves personally and professionally affected by working with courageous clients. Therapists (15%) stated that they have learned to be more courageous from witnessing the courage displayed by their clients. Twenty-eight percent of our participants indicated that they are very inspired by their clients and that the work of psychotherapy gives them hope for other clients in particular, and hope for humanity more generally. Many of the therapists we interviewed stated that it is going through adversity with clients and observing their courage that gives them special pleasure in their work. A number noted that if they did not have the opportunity to witness the strength and courage of their clients, they might not be working in the field.

Several therapists stated that they have themselves learned to be increasingly courageous from watching their clients display courage. As Dr. Trayton said, "You know, I think that [a client] has given me some courage; the notion that it's possible not only to survive but thrive under very adverse circumstances." Whereas Dr. Linda noted, "If I think of some of these clients, then it certainly does affect me. I will certainly get my back up, walk a straighter line, and be more daring. I feel like if they can, I can do it." And Dr. Jeremey illustrated how he has learned about courage from his clients by stating:

> I also need to be aware of those small moments [of courage] for myself that I encourage [clients] to look at and appreciate—that I need to be able to do that for myself as well and for those that are near and dear to me.

These comments from our interviewees are generally supportive of other research results in which therapists expressed that "therapeutic work can result in. . . heightened personal feelings of self-assurance, assertiveness, and self-reliance" (Farber, 1983, p.181).

Altogether the therapists we interviewed reported feeling inspired by working with courageous clients. In previously published literature, Freeman and Hayes (2002) confirmed what our participants said about how they are inspired by working with courageous clients. These authors commented that, by entering the client's worldview and encountering their suffering and courage, the therapist vicariously enjoys being able to witness a self-healing process as it unfolds. There are several moving quotations from our participants reflective of this same theme. As Dr. Sunny said, "The folks I work with amaze me every day. . . My clients have shown me that you can face anything." Another psychologist, Dr. Rick, elaborated on this theme by commenting about a psychotherapy client who confronted her boss about abuse at work:

> I don't feel like I have courage to do something but I can get inspired by my clients and . . . she was really apprehensive and she took that step to do it, so you should be able to do it too because she could do that.

One of our participants, Dr. Luke, movingly stated, "I'm just inspired by clients, by the courage of clients to overcome unbelievable obstacles in life, unfairness, injustice in life. And fight on. . . I've seen amazing examples of courage." Dr. Linda commented about how inspired she is by saying "At times I sort of think 'Oh, poor me!' I think of them [clients] and you go 'I have nothing to really whine about'. . . I feel like if they can do it, it serves to lift me up."

Therapists often discussed how their work with courageous clients gives them hope for other therapy clients. Dr. Wilbur succinctly noted, "I feel . . . hopeful about therapy and people's ability to hang in there. I love what I do." Dr. Laura expressed hope for humanity in stating:

> *Specific examples [of courage] would be the cancer patients that I worked with. To see people struggle with these kinds of issues and do well gives me hope in humanity and on the strength they show. It is a real privilege being with them.*

Finally, Dr. Viola discussed a client's courage and her own courage:

> *. . . it's great when you see that people can remember they've had [courage] before and help them get to a place where they feel like they have it again. And it's those moments, I think, that keep you being in this job, you know? Sometimes, it is the courage to have hope.*

Pury and Kowalski (2007) expressed similar beliefs in a conclusion to their study on human strengths and courageous actions. They stated that "courage may be a key virtue for expressing hope and, in many instances, kindness" (p. 128). In an article on the courage displayed by group psychotherapy leaders, Shapiro and Gans (2008) stated ". . . not only does a hopeful outlook facilitate courage; courageous responses produce hopefulness" (p. 359).

Those in the present study commented on how important their work with courageous clients is to their personal satisfaction in their work, and that this is one important reason they continue to practice. As Orlinsky et al. (2005) wrote, "...for most therapists, doing psychotherapy is not only a job but also a calling, or vocation, a worthy profession that is chosen at least in part to provide a sense of meaningful activity and personal fulfillment" (p. 11). It indeed seems to be that making the journey through life's difficulties together with one's clients—being fellow travelers, as described by Yalom (2002)—provides therapists with inspiration and helps them to enjoy what can be difficult work at times. Several of our participants expressed this idea quite passionately. For example, Dr. Viola stated, "I think if I couldn't see that in people or believe that people couldn't get to that courage or couldn't in some way collaborate with them to get to that, I don't think I would be in this job." Another psychologist, Dr. Wilbur, replied to our question, "It makes me interested almost every hour almost every day in what is going to happen, and where somebody is in their progress, and it just always feels vital and alive." And Dr. Sarah stated, "I think courage is what keeps me doing my work. It is that indomitable will of the human spirit."

Infrequent Responses

Some of the infrequent responses to our question about courage were surprising, as they seemed to be part of what we implicitly understand as courage. Others may be unique perspectives on courage. Even though over half of our respondents stated that they believe everyone has a predisposition for courage, there was one dissenter in therapist Dr. Lewis, who said that, in his experience, courage is a rare commodity, a trait that few possess. He works with clients who have problems with addiction and he believes that his clients often do not show the courage to quit the addiction:

> *Most of the people I have met in psychotherapy actually lacked courage. . . Probably people that I have seen are involved in substance abuse of one form or another. I believe it is a lack of courage that allows people to avoid facing up to their problems.*

Dr. Lewis believes that the individual's lack of courage is not malicious, but rather that it was due to a lack of adaptive coping mechanisms, or a failure to adequately manage anxiety. It appears that therapists in our sample who work with clients with addiction issues tended to view courage somewhat differently from the other therapists.

A second infrequent response we received was that courage relates to having a strong faith. Sometimes in our society, we hear people say they are placing their problems in the hands of a higher power from which they derive courage. In support of that perspective on courage, Haitch (1995) describes how both Tillich, a theologian, and Kohut, a psychologist, believed that "rather than being a sign of weakness, belief in a power greater than the self can paradoxically become the self's greatest source of strength" (p. 96).

Conclusions

Our 61 participants offered us rich and insightful responses to our questions about what they have learned from their psychotherapy clients about courage. Their responses to this question were both moving and inspiring. Their collective views of courage were both supportive of and divergent from what the current literature says about courage. It would seem that therapists see courage as facing one's fears, persevering in the face of adversity, and employing empowering strategies in the face of difficulties. In addition, they see their clients as having the courage to enter therapy and make changes in their lives even as such change is very difficult to effect. The interview material clearly reflects the personal and professional impact of psychotherapy clients' courage on therapists. These therapists noted that, as they witness their clients displaying courage, they, too become more courageous, and that they have hope for others in therapy, and hope for humanity overall. They also clearly indicated pleasure in being party to the healing process and in collaborating with courageous clients. Seeing their clients act with courage, and vicariously entering into this experience, helps therapists working in a difficult profession to stay motivated.

Working on this project has made a personal impact on me (first author) as well. This research has offered me, a novice therapist, a unique window into the minds and hearts of experienced psychotherapists. I have gained wisdom about the relationship between therapists and their clients and the incredible differences these relationships have made in the lives of the professionals. When I started working on this project I had not experienced working with clients of my own. Since then, I have worked with clients in multiple settings, and appreciate even more deeply the kind of insight and wisdom so eloquently expressed by the therapists we interviewed. The comments of this group of psychologists often come to mind when I am working with a client, and they help to make me more courageous and hopeful in my own work.

References[2]

Bugental, J. F. (1991). Lessons clients teach therapists. *Journal of Humanistic Psychology, 31,* 28-32.

Dick-Niederhauser, A. (2009). Therapeutic change and the experience of joy: Toward a theory of curative processes. *Journal of Psychotherapy Integration, 19,* 187-211.

Farber, B. A. (1983). The effects of psychotherapeutic practice upon psychotherapists. *Psychotherapy: Theory, Research, and Practice, 20,* 174-182.

Freeman, M. S., & Hayes, G. B. (2002). Clients changing counselors: An inspirational journey. *Counseling and Values, 47,* 13-21.

Gans, J. S. (2005). A plea for greater recognition and appreciation of our group members' courage. *International Journal of Group Psychotherapy, 55*(4), 575-593.

Greitemeyer, T., Osswald, S., Fischer, P., & Frey, D. (2007). Civil courage: implicit theories, related concepts, and measurement. *The Journal of Positive Psychology, 2,* 115-119.

Haitch, R. (1995). How Tillich and Kohut both find courage in faith. *Pastoral Psychology, 44,* 83-97.

Hatcher, S. L., Kipper-Smith, A., Waddell, M., Uhe, M., West, J. S., Boothe, J. H. . . Gingras, P. (2012). What therapists learn from psychotherapy clients: Effects on personal and professional lives.

---

2   I would like to thank Dr. Sherry Hatcher, Adriana Kipper Smith, and my co-researchers for the opportunity to work with them on this project. And thank you to all of the courageous psychologists who participated in the study and gave so freely of themselves (Dr. Joan Frye).

The Qualitative Report, 17(Art. 95), 1-19. Retrieved from http://www.nova.edu/ssss/QR/QR17/hatcher.pdf

Heard, K. (May 5-June 7, 2007). The courage found in faith. *Miami Times*. Retrieved from: http://proquest.umi.com.ezproxy.fielding.edu/pqdlink?Ver=1&Exp=05-13-2016&FMT=7&DID=1295895581&RQT=309

Norton, P. J., & Weiss, B. J. (2009). The role of courage on behavioral approach in a fear- eliciting situation: A proof-of-concept pilot study. *Journal of Anxiety Disorders, 23*, 212-217.

Orlinsky, D. E., Botermans, J.-F., Rønnestad, M. H., & the SPR Collaborative Research Network (2001). Towards an empirically grounded model of psychotherapy training: four thousand therapists rate influences on their development. *Australian Psychologist, 36*, 139-148.

Orlinsky, D. E., Rønnestad, M. H., Gerin, P., Davis, J. D., Ambuhl, H., Davis, M. L. . . Schroder, T. A. (2005). The development of psychotherapists. In D. E. Orlinsky and M. H. Rønnestad, (Eds.), *How therapists develop: A study of therapeutic work and professional growth* (pp. 3-13). Washington, DC: American Psychological Association.

Peterson, C. (2006). *A primer in positive psychology*. New York: Oxford University Press.

Peterson, C. & Seligman, M.E.P. (2004). *Character strengths and virtues: A handbook and classification*. New York: Oxford University Press.

Pury, C. L., & Kowalski, R. M. (2007). Human strengths, courageous actions, and general and personal courage. *The Journal of Positive Psychology, 2*, 120-128.

Putman, D. (2010). Philosophical roots of the concept of courage. In C. L. Pury & S. L. Lopez (Eds.), *The psychology of courage: Modern research on an ancient virtue* (pp. 9-22). Washington DC: American Psychological Association.

Rachman, S. J. (2010). Courage: A psychological perspective. In C. L. Pury & S. L. Lopez (Eds.), *The psychology of courage: Modern research on an ancient virtue* (pp. 47-66). Washington DC: American Psychological Association.

Rate, C. R. (2008) What is courage? A search for meaning. Ph.D. dissertation, Yale University,

Retrieved June 9, 2010, from ProQuest Psychology Journals (Publication No. AAT 3293368).

Rate, C. R. (2010). Defining the features of courage: A search for meaning. In C. L. Pury & S.   L. Lopez (Eds.), *The psychology of courage: Modern research on an ancient virtue* (pp.   47-66). Washington DC: American Psychological Association.

Rate, C. R., Clarke, J. A., Lindsay, D. R., & Sternberg, R. J. (2007). Implicit theories of courage. *The Journal of Positive Psychology, 2*, 80-98.

Rønnestad, M. H., & Skovholt, T. M. (2003). The journey of the counselor and therapist:

Research findings and perspective on professional development. *Journal of Career Development, 30*, 5-44.

Seligman, M.E.P. & Peterson, C. (2003). Positive clinical psychology. In L. G. Aspinwall, & U. M. Staudinger (Eds.), *A psychology of human strengths: Fundamental questions and future directions for a positive psychology* (pp. 305-317). Washington, DC: American Psychological Association.

Shapiro, E. L., & Gans, J. S. (2008). The courage of the group therapist. *International Journal of Group Psychotherapy, 58*, 345-361.

Skovholt, T. M. & Rønnestad, M. H. (1992). Themes in therapist and counselor development. *Journal of Counseling and Development, 70*, 505-515.

Stahl, J. V., Hill, C. E., Jacobs, T., Kleinman, S., Isenberg, D., & Stern, A. (2009). When the shoe is on the other foot: A qualitative study of intern-level trainees' perceived learning from clients. *Psychotherapy: Theory, Research, Practice, Training, 46*, 376-389.

Teyber, E. (2000). *Interpersonal process in psychotherapy: A relational approach* (4th ed.). Stamford, CT: Wadsworth/Thompson Learning.

Woodard, C. R., & Pury, C. L. (2007). The construct of courage: categorization and measurement. *Consulting Psychology Journal: Practice and Research, 59*, 135-147.

Chapter 6

WHAT THERAPISTS REPORT LEARNING ABOUT LIFE STAGES

Joanne S. West, Jason H. Boothe, and Sherry L. Hatcher

Almost all therapy calls upon psychotherapists to help others in negotiating life transitions. Psychotherapy training has often focused on providing practitioners with models of normative development as a framework for understanding their clients' stages of growth. However, psychotherapists also learn a great deal about developmental trajectories directly from their clients. From the 58 responses to the question of what they had learned from their clients about life stages, a total of nine themes emerged:

Chronological age may not fit the life stage

- Classic stage models of development are open to questioning
- Clients' and therapists' life stages can influence therapeutic processes
- Current life stages may indicate what to expect from future life stages
- Life stages both pose challenges and provide opportunities
- Trauma can have an impact on the transition through life stages
- Life stage impacts coping
- Culture can influence life stages
- Gender can influence life stages

In the field of psychology there are a number of developmental models, some of which describe the stages individuals are presumed to negotiate across the lifespan. For example, Erik Erikson's (1950) model describes development from birth to death, while others focus primarily on a single time period, such as Freud's emphasis on early life stages or Marcia's stages of adolescence and young adulthood. Still others map out development in one area, as for instance Piaget's (1959) cognitive model, or Kohlberg's stage theory of moral development (Power, Higgins, & Kohlberg, 1989.). Each of the foregoing models conceptualizes development as a step-wise progression in which an individual gains knowledge and skills, growing in wisdom over time. The participants in our study expressed familiarity with these stage models of development in their responses to our question regarding life stages. For instance, as Dr. Arcy observed: "Erikson had a lot right. . . stages have universal applicability." Whereas Dr. Jack said, "Carl Jung talks a lot about this second half of life and it isn't just some kind of a theory that some psychologist wrote down. I witness it and I experience it in conversations with clients."

Similarly, Dr. McMillan noted:

> I learned that there are life stages. I have a theory about that. I have nine stages. They are the same as with people; they follow Erikson's stages, and it has been amazing to see how people move through those and how the life journey is the same for all of us. And we are not alone [in] this; we are not unique [in] this.

Others reported using the stage models of development as a guide. For example, Dr. Mai said, "They seem to go through the stages in a different way than the theorists talk about. People kind of more or less go along the path the theorists describe, but it isn't predictable." Dr. Sarah noted that, while she maintains a healthy skepticism about developmental theory, she sees her clients grow over time and this allows her to "trust my own understanding of this process of psychological growth throughout life and how it isn't just a theory developed by somebody."

Rønnestad and Skovholt (2003) assert that clients play a crucial role in therapists' professional development in a number of ways. These authors observed that a commitment to learning fuels therapists' development, and that clients serve as therapists' primary teachers (Rønnestad & Skovholt). They further tell us that it is through interaction with clients that therapists develop experientially-based knowledge and skills. Further, these skills are shaped by the in-session behaviors and reactions of clients to the therapist's interventions, continually shifting and developing throughout the therapy process (Rønnestad & Skovholt, 2003). These authors concluded that, while clients are an important source of learning for therapists at all levels of experience, it is the novice therapist who is likely most receptive—and vulnerable—to client feedback (Rønnestad & Skovholt, 2003). In this way, what and how therapists learn from their clients may be affected by the therapist's life stage.

Theme 1: Chronological age may not fit the stage

The most common theme among therapist responses to this question was that their clients had taught them that chronological age may not necessarily align with an individual's developmental stage. Thirty-five percent of participants provided responses suggesting this conclusion. Indeed, much of psychologists' therapeutic work involves aiding clients in adjusting to life transitions. Working with individuals who are having difficulty moving through the challenges associated with various life stages may account for the prevalence of responses that noted at least some degree of dissonance between chronological age and stage of development. In this vein, Dr. Iris said, "I've learned that people get stuck at stages. . . it can be enlightening to the therapy process, and to the expectations of what one needs to get done in a therapy process." Related to this, Dr. Julia observed, "We can grow up to be adults and we can be very childish in our heads and emotions, and that is one thing I have learned from patients." Similarly, Dr. Ricky shared that:

> . . . there are very specific developmental stages. I learned that you can get stuck in various life stages and then. . . you get stuck in life stages. Then when you get older you still have to go back and understand that there are life stages, and how did you get stuck? All my clients are developmentally stuck in prior life stages.

Related to this theme, there were also a number of responses that suggested incongruence between a client's developmental stage and their behavior in relationships. Therapists noted having learned from their clients that failing to develop at the rate typically expected in North America may contribute to impaired interpersonal functioning. An example of this observation came from Dr. Arcy, who said, "The age may not fit the stage. You see it in identity/relationships. . . For example, a client who can't develop relationships because he hasn't figured out who he is yet." Similarly, Dr. Rose noted that "a particular client may be in their mid-40s chronologically, but really the issues that are being discussed in therapy are more appropriate for somebody in their early 20s." Dr. Doral gave an example of this phenomenon: "A young woman who has dated a lot may have more life experience than an older woman who has been married most of her life, in terms of navigating a life stage." In a similar vein, Dr. Justin said:

> *Even though I'm working with an eight-year-old, an eight-year-old may. . . have the mentality of a 15-year-old. So I've learned that age really is. . . just a number. . . So I think that life stage is to me is not childhood, adolescence, adulthood; it's more kind of where you are within your life and how you can build yourself up to get further in life.*

Theme 2: Classic stage models of development are open to questioning

> *"I think [I learned] humility [from my clients] because. . . I remember feeling confident and proud of my ability to survey the landscape of adult stages of life when I was in my 20s. The reality is that the knowledge that's available. . . is just so wafer-thin compared to what it's like to actually live through different decades."* (Dr. Goodheart)

Many of our respondents noted that they had learned to question the stage models that have been among the mainstays of teaching lifespan development in the field of psychology, though some participants indicated that stage models had a certain utility. For example, Dr. Lewis stated that he believed that while stage models of development offer a framework for understanding clients' experience, individuals must be understood as each charting his/her own life course:

> I have learned that the concept of life stages was sort of very theoretical. In Erikson's work, he said you know you are going to do all of these different life stages as you go through life. . . but then you begin to think about it and you see that some people may have a uniqueness to their life [in that] that they never had an opportunity to address some form of the life stage.

However, other psychologists described what they saw as the shortcomings of stage models. "Life stages are not as predictable as the theorists say," said Dr. Kristi. And Dr. Luke reflected that current stage models fail to account for the impact external forces can have on shaping development across life stages:

> I think a lot of those models need to be flexible in the way that they look at the populations we are dealing with today. The hard and fast rules about how. . . you haven't gone through this stage or you haven't worked this stage through or whatever, you know, it can be useful to some degree but I think that it's not as clear as it used to be in a more linear world and a more linear life development. I think we can use it as a point of reference. . . but I think we also need to be open to the fact that it's a different world and, [with] the folks we are seeing. . . there are many different circumstances that redefine these stages.

Other psychologists more directly rejected the stage model framework, based on their learning from clients. For instance, Dr. Aviva described stage models as "very, very murky. I don't think there's anybody who really can defend a model of life stages." Still other participants expressed ways of conceptualizing human development that differ from the traditional models that conceptualize stages of growth as defined and sequential. For example, Dr. Odila described development as "Not so much formal stages. . . we are comprised of many different parts from every age. . . We have to integrate ourselves. . . getting older is a process of increasing complexity and integration. . ."

Some respondents shared learning from clients that development is a nonlinear process of expansion and contraction, of growth and regression. As Dr. Sunny said:

> *When you are a young child things are exciting, and the world is full of opportunity; as you get older you think you know everything, and your options begin to shrink. . . then you get to college, and you realize you don't know everything, so you have options again. . . after that, options shrink again. . . this pattern occurs approximately every 4-5 years until about age 70, when you become more aware that the everyday stressors no longer matter.*

Similarly, Dr. Julia shared the following view: "I think there is an awful lot of fluidity of the life stages that we go through and what they mean to us and how we access earlier stages of life to inform us about where to go next."

Still others noted that, through their work with clients, they had devised their own models for conceptualizing life stages. An example of this was Dr. Natasha, who described her belief that life is comprised of two stages. In the first, people operate based on received wisdom, adopting the schemas and assumptions of those around them. In the second, individuals prioritize knowledge gained through their own experience. In this connection, she described one client as:

> *. . . kind of living half his life under these assumptions and slowly questioning them. . . like "Oh, I don't have to life under these assumptions" and "be different" and "it is still okay to be different and people love me." More acceptance of themselves, and learning, understanding themselves with their own eyes and not how other people have seen them, and questioning some of the assumptions that have been placed on them. Some people never get to that stage.*

Theme 3: Clients' and therapists' life stages can influence therapeutic processes

"So, I'm trying to figure out, you know, where this developmental stage is affecting, how it's affecting my teaching, and my therapy, and my life." (Dr. Jeremey)

Psychologists who participated in our study told us that much of what they learned from clients about life stages was processed through the lens of their own development, both personally and professionally. The influence of personal development on professional development has been described by Skovholt and Starkey (2010) as one of the three legs of the epistemological stool that supports therapists' development of knowledge. Skovholt and Starkey describe empathy and effectiveness with clients as grounded in therapists' recognition and acceptance of their own humanness. Therapists use their own life experience as a way to make sense of the breadth and depth of the human condition, and they use this knowledge to better understand the world of their client. The authors explain:

> *The human story is not reserved for clients: therapists are also fully involved in the human narrative. Recognizing this not only helps the therapist live a richer and more meaningful life, but it also fosters empathy, makes it easier to relate to clients, and helps with the creation of the ultimately important therapeutic relationship.* (Skovholt & Starkey, 2010, p. 129)

An example of a response alluding to the therapist's use of their own life experience in the context of their therapeutic work was provided by Dr. Goodheart, who said:

> *A therapist can use. . . life experience to help guide younger clients. . . I find that I have noticed in my therapy [that] as I've gotten older I [have] more wisdom because I have gone through so many more of the life stages.*

In those instances where a client's and a therapist's stage of development coincided, psychologists reported using their own life experience to inform their work, while simultaneously learning from their clients about ways that they might manage their own life transitions. This is consistent with research on this topic. For example, Rosen, Miller, Nakash, Halperin, and Alegría (2012) examined whether reciprocal complementarity between therapist and client during the initial session was impacted by various dimensions of social identity, including age. They found that clients who were matched with therapists of similar age showed significantly higher levels of complementarity with those therapists than with non-age matched therapists, as assessed both by self-report and observer rating. The authors interpreted this finding as demonstrating that "shared generational reference points and the providers' experiential understating of phase of life concerns" formed a basis for an effective therapeutic alliance (Rosen, Miller, Nakash, Halperin, & Alegría, 2012, p. 193).

Examples of responses gained in the current study that were illustrative of this phenomenon include Dr. Goodheart's observation in this regard: "My practice has always been a moving bell curve where there is a larger number of clients I see who are in the same decade I am. . . Hearing about my clients' struggles normalizes my own." Or, as Dr. Arcy observed, "As I get older, it is curious, but my clients seem to get older" and Dr. Harriet M. said "I think your best clients are your own age." Dr. Jeremey shared that when clients discussed issues related to his current life stage, particularly issues related to age or health concerns, he noticed that he was more attuned to the client. Similarly, Dr. Sarah said, "I think probably because I am 60-something, I think me recognizing my life stages, that has been helpful in working with women. . . just being able to mentor them through, 'Okay, here's what you can expect to some degree'."

Conversely, some therapists discussed the difficulties in working with clients from whom they differed in life stage. As Dr. Anna said, "It can be tricky as a young therapist to deal with someone who is an older client. . . to gain their trust," and said Dr. Ellen, "I see a lot of young people and, as I get older, it can be hard to relate." Similarly, Dr. Mai reported:

> I think of that in relationship to my own stages; I was kind of intimidated in the beginning when I started doing therapy. I was this young 20-something with no kids trying to give advice to these parents who [were] much older. I [didn't] have my own kids and I didn't have the level of life experience these people did, and who am I to tell them what to do? But there are things that I learned and things that I knew that I was able to offer.

Theme 4: Current life stages may indicate what to expect from future life stages

Another theme observed in the responses of our participants was that they learned from clients who were older than they were what to expect from future life stages. Psychologists shared that working with older clients provided them with an intimate look at the challenges and opportunities that can arise as one moves through future life stages. Here therapists learned from their clients, in the professional realm, lessons that they were able to apply to their own personal development. Embodying this theme was Dr. Rick's observation that:

> . . . the personal impact might be if there are some people that I dealt with who are at life stages that I haven't faced yet, it has maybe prepared me for those life stages more than what would otherwise be the case.

Responses that illustrate this theme showed therapists wrestling with what they want for their own futures, having perhaps been influenced by what they learned from working with clients. For example, Dr. Felipe said that he learned to anticipate the future with optimism, "[It's] exciting because I have more life stages to go through yet and I have much more to learn." Similarly, Dr. Leslie noted, ". . . we see the roadmaps before we actually go into the territory. We still have to go into the territory, but we do see the maps."

Others, like Dr. Homer, reported mixed feelings about their own future based on their work with clients:

> As I approach that stage in life, I see people who have courage, and I see people [whom] I don't want to be remembered like. . . Working with older clients leads me to reflect on how I want to be remembered.

Rather poignantly, Dr. Arcy shared that working with a client with a terminal illness caused him to reflect on his own future, saying, "I was touched by a dying patient who made me think of my own end of life issues." Reporting having learned acceptance from her clients, Dr. Laura said, "I'm struggling with this in my own life right now. . . what can you change and what you need to accept as time gets shorter, as you move toward the end of life." And, in a humorous tone, Dr. Ricky observed, "I have learned to live with a certain graceful disdain for kvetching about getting older."

Dr. Kristi also shared what she had learned from clients older than herself; her comments show interplays between her own personal and professional growth and the empathy that her developmental experiences and learning have generated for her future clients:

> I think I learned the most from my older clients. I guess because I haven't gotten to where they are at yet, so at any given age that I was a therapist, if I worked with somebody older than me, I got to see. . . somebody going through [an older stage]. And certainly as I get older I can see where my own transitioning into different life stages, which I thought would be smoother in certain cases.[Some] were not and some were. I can certainly relate with clients that way.

She also noted that her professional experiences engendered some trepidation about her own future in terms of aging: "Unfortunately it makes you think of your own transition stages and where you are at, and for me that hasn't bothered me as much as when I hear the elderly people talk about where they are at."

Theme 5: Life stages both pose challenges and provide opportunities

Whether or not our participants adopted a traditional stage model for conceptualizing lifespan development, they communicated how they have learned from their clients that, throughout one's life, both internal and external events demand coping and adaptation. At various stages, and depending on our perception of our ability to negotiate change, we may perceive this demand as either a burdensome or favorable circumstance—as a challenge or an opportunity.

In terms of the challenges associated with advancing life stages, some participants said that, beyond the inherent difficulties associated with each stage, the very act of transitioning between them serves as a source of some difficulty for many clients. For example, Dr. Leslie described ". . . the challenge of giving up valued earlier stages and seeing the benefits and opportunities of the new stage. Many people have difficulty giving up a successful stage for the possible opportunity of a new stage." Along the same lines, Dr. Linda observed:

> *Most of the major life stages are not smooth transitions. . .*
> *the lesson is that each life stage has its own challenges, but*
> *that we are likely not going to transition from one to the*
> *other in a really smooth way. I think that, no matter what,*
> *it will be a shock to our system.*

Altogether our respondents spoke of the challenges that present across life stages, including Dr. McMillan's perspective on these issues as they relate to identity:

> *Struggling with your identity is a life-long process. I*
> *remember when I was a young psychologist, my colleagues*
> *talked about the identity crisis that happens. I saw it*
> *happen one time. I have learned that it is perpetual. It is*
> *constant, no matter where you are, everybody struggling*
> *with who they are.*

Related to this idea, Dr. Oliver observed: "Every stage of life has its inherent socio-cultural struggles, out of which conflicts of their character style come together."

Some therapists shared having learned from clients about the challenges inherent in specific stages of life. In this vein, Dr. Jack noted:

> *I have learned how difficult mid-life is. That's one*
> *that stands out from a lot [of others] because it is such a*
> *consistent theme. . . it has helped me learn about what that*
> *place is like and what kind of tension it presents and how*
> *difficult a transition it is to begin the process of embracing*
> *this other half of life, and how different it is when you are*
> *kind of looking down the hill as opposed to up and trying*
> *to conquer the next thing.*

Among other therapist responses was the idea that the challenges associated with a given life stage arise, in part, because clients are unprepared to transition from a previous developmental stage. An example of this can be seen in Dr. Pine's response:

> *I think being aware of the fact that a person is. . . being propelled into another life stage, that they might not be ready to embrace or to understand what the positives could be of that particular life stage. I have learned, I think, from my patients that it is important to consider that that is also an issue for them when they talk about the losses that they have experienced. . . that they are also sort of being prematurely pushed into another life stage that they may not have been able to yet prepare for.*

Again, while therapists noted the challenges associated with life stages, they also provided responses that indicated they had learned from clients about the rewards and opportunities that arise with each phase. As Dr. Doral observed, ". . . at every stage of life, there are options and opportunities for people to change." And Dr. Rick said ". . . I have become more aware of. . . how you can effectively deal with these life stages and deal with the challenges at each stage." Dr. Sunny reported having learned from clients that the challenges accompanying each of the life stages can be successfully met, saying:

> *Each life stage brings a new transition and adjustments to human beings, and every stage has ups and downs and its own difficulties to go through. But again, I think if they are resilient, they can go through the different stages.*

In connection with the responses about the opportunities presented by life stages, a number of therapists spoke of what they had learned from clients regarding the challenges associated with the final stage of life. Dr. Rachel discussed learning from a client near the end of her life that the ability to change can endure throughout one's lifespan. She said, "One thing [is] that we can grow at any stage. It's the last stage of it, but she's leaving feeling really good about the life that she has led and her contribution to the world. . ." Similarly, Dr. Cody noted, "It's never too late to make a change." Specifying the positive growth that clients have reported in relation to moving through the phases of life,

Dr. Sarah said, "As you navigate the life stages, you gain wisdom and become less judgmental."

Theme 6: Trauma can have an impact on the transition through life stages

> *"Often when people have a trauma early in life they get stuck there."* (Dr. Odila)

There is ample evidence indicating that traumatic experiences, particularly those that occur in childhood, can have a significant and enduring effect on human development (Perry & Szalavitr, 2006). Individuals who experience trauma early in life may even evidence varying degrees of disrupted neuro-development (Anda et al., 2006), and are at far greater risk for a variety of physical illnesses (Edwards, Anda, Felitti, & Dube, 2003), as well as psychological disorders (Heim & Nemeroff, 2001), occurring across the lifespan. Trauma experiences often shape how one views the world, one's interpersonal functioning, and one's self-evaluation of the capacity to manage and recover (Benight & Bandura, 2004; Foa, Keane, & Friedman, 2010; Herman, 1997).

Several of the responses we received from psychologists referred to learning from their clients about the impact of trauma on their development. As one example, Dr. Yetty shared that she had learned through her work that the traumatic effects of childhood sexual abuse are more often than not long-lasting, and can shape a person's identity:

> *When the trauma happens, at which stage of your life you are, it significantly impacts its outcome. So in my line of work it is an incredible significance when the trauma happens. You know, you find a lot of women when their trauma has happened—while they're married, for example—you find that there's oftentimes a previous long history of abuse, but it really colors who they are.*

Similarly, Dr. Odila discussed a client from whom she had learned that progression through the stages of life may be arrested due to the traumatic loss of a parent. She described the regressive behavior she observed in this client:

I once treated a young woman whose mother died when she was 11 and she presented very much as an 11-year-old girl even though she was some 10 years older than that. The goal of therapy in that case was to sufficiently work through the trauma of her mother's untimely death so as to help her get back on the developmental track.

Dr. Julia also reported having learned of the arresting impact of past trauma, even in an individual who appeared to have great resilience:

. . . there is a way in which these horrible experiences, particularly if there [are] a lot of them, really reduce [the individual's] ability to bring all of that good solid development into their adult life. It is almost like they stop.

Theme 7: Life stage impacts coping

Several of the therapists in our sample said that they had learned about how one's perception of stressful life events, and the ability to cope with these, varies with age. As discussed in Chapter 4, research indicates that the specific coping mechanisms employed by both young and older individuals, when faced with challenges, do not vary too much. Each age group typically uses problem-solving strategies, avoidance, and/or seeking of social supports as ways to cope with and endure difficult circumstances. However, the rate at which these mechanisms are applied tends to vary with age, with a trend toward the increasing use of problem-directed, rather than avoidant, strategies over the course of a lifespan (Amirkhan & Auyeung, 2007). Evidence further suggests that the ways in which individuals react to stressors tend to be consistent over the lifespan and are shaped by their perceptions of threat, along with an evaluation of their resources to cope (Jorgensen, Dusek, Richards, & McIntyre, 2009).

However, while it has been shown that older adults increasingly use problem-solving rather than avoidance methods of coping, overall rates of coping decreases with age (Brennan, Holland, Schutte, & Moos, 2012); whether reduced engagement in coping behaviors leads to greater stress for older adults is unclear. However, it has been suggested that older adults are merely more judicious in the application of coping behaviors than younger individuals, as a result of being better able to determine levels of threat and consequently their ability to cope in challenging circumstances (Aldwin, 2007).

In general, therapists reported learning about age-related variations in threat appraisal and one's ability to cope with stressors. As Dr. Iris said:

> *Clearly stages make a difference in how a person sees things or how they construe stuff. . . what they expect in life, what they anticipate, what they know. . . At 62, it's a very different world to look back on than it was at 32, or 22, or even 42, or 52, for that matter. There is something to gathering wisdom as one ages; life stages are phases rich in very grand sources of learning and development.*

Dr. Mark shared his learning that stage of life influences the ways in which individuals respond to stressful life events:

> *Someone at 20 gets breast cancer, someone at 40, someone at 60 or 70, or prostate cancer. . . as an example, you know they handle it very differently and it can be very different resources. . . coping with different ages and stages of life— different perspectives.*

Another psychologist, Dr. Peyton, discussed learning from a younger client that while the appraisal of a stressful event may be embedded within the perspective of a particular life stage, such as adolescence, life stage influences must be respected:

> *When a 15-year-old comes in and cries, let's say a young lady. . . and she's crying because her boyfriend who she felt very close to. . . had other plans and she was crying. So, my first reaction is very simple: "You're 15 years old kid, forget it. Now, this ain't a life-changing moment in your life." That's wrong! To her, at that time, in that setting, that is a life-changing event and you must deal with it in that way. . . It's so easy for us adults to say, "Oh, what the heck kid, you know, you'll be in love with somebody else in three months." And they probably will be, but that's not the point.*

Theme 8: Culture can influence life stages

A criticism of stage models of development has been that they reflect a particular path of growth, one that is rooted in a Western, 20th century reality (Sneed, Schwartz, & Cross, 2006). As such, they may not capture the rich variety of ways in which the seasons of life unfold in other parts of the world, or in individuals who do not identify with majority Western culture (Sneed, Schwartz, & Cross). Our participants shared learning from their clients that the intersection of culture and the passage through stages of life often results in deviation from traditional stages of development (see also Chapter 8).

Several of the responses conveying this theme focus on the idea that adolescence is a particularly Western culture-bound concept. For instance, Dr. Odila said, "Depending on their culture. . . some cultures don't really feature an adolescent stage of development at all, whereas in America it is a much publicized stage of life." Similarly, Dr. Clark noted:

> [A] college student from a Middle Eastern background, [was] figuring out that whole individuation [process]: "How am I going to be a functioning adult?" [It] is particularly difficult when you've got that intersection of life stage and culture. And a group of Canadian friends thinking that this is the way the transition from adolescence to adulthood works in our culture and a very different way in which life stages are conceived of or happen in another culture—that was really tough on him. Life stages are not fixed.

Dr. Ranju said he learned to question the applicability of traditional stage models altogether:

> I also have learned. . . that we tend to go through stages at our own pace and that often we revisit stages. I don't find thinking about life in stages to be very useful, especially in the U.S. when people are. . . I don't know. . . generative maybe, for so much longer. The stages are artificial or at least just not helpful once someone gets to be 25 or so.

Dr. Luke discussed learning through his work with a culturally diverse clientele that Erikson's thinking regarding the developmental tasks of the adolescent period was perhaps not so universally relevant:

> *Identity versus role diffusion, you know, a lot of kids from immigrant [cultures] have this foreclosure issue. Their parents have told them they are going to be doctors. It's a real problem in these families. I've seen it over and over again. These kids, they don't go through an identity process where they work things out and experiment and try things on . . . and find themselves.*

Dr. Luke further elaborated on learning from his culturally diverse adult clients whose progression through the stages of life was disrupted by immigration:

> *Then you have some folks from other cultures coming in as well where there were certain expectations about what was supposed to happen in their life. . . And you don't get that life stage you expected. . . It is taken away, put off by twenty years. . . So their life stages, what the expectations are about life stages. . . have shifted at least in terms of chronological age, maybe not by stage in terms of sequences—but by chronological age. . . quite a big shift.*

Theme 9: Gender can influence life stages

Traditional stage models of development often consider male identity as bound to generativity in adulthood (Erikson, as cited in Friedman, 2000), and the reduction in generativity that can accompany later stages in life has been associated with reduced self-esteem (Orth, Trzesniewski, & Robins, 2010). Traditional stage models have been criticized for failing to acknowledge women's developmental trajectories (1982). Josselson (1996), however, envisioned women's development as involving the establishment of identity during adolescence, one based on both competence and connection. She described women's progression through all life stages as characterized by an investment in developing abilities and agency as well as affiliation and interpersonal relatedness (1996).

When asked what they had learned from their clients regarding life stages, a number of therapists in our sample gave responses that referred to the struggles that both men and women experience in relation to aging. Most of these responses referred to clients in later life. One participant, Dr. Jack, discussed a male client who struggled with moving into the later stages of life:

> *I was talking about that with one my clients just today, because he is kind of approaching that stage in life and . . . I've witnessed how tragic that can be and how difficult. . . and how they tear apart relationships because they are trying to hold on to this image of youth and hold on to this path of. . . conquering one more thing and continuing to build their empire—as opposed to embracing this period of developing wisdom and more of an internal reflection; reflecting internally as opposed to conquering externally.*

Dr. Jack appears to see the development of this client through the lens of Crocker and Wolfe's (2001) argument that healthy adult development involves turning inward for sources of positive self-esteem, rather than seeking external reinforcement. Dr. Linda also discussed observing from her male clients the challenges of the decline that can happen in late life:

> *I have had a couple of men—elderly clients—who are realizing that they are losing physical and mental skills or capabilities and they are starting to deteriorate physically or mentally and they see it and they know it and how difficult that is for them.*

Dr. Steve discussed observing the differences in the developmental course of men and women:

> *Men and women age differently. Men have a much greater difficulty with aging than women do usually, which surprises me. This is reflected in the much greater suicide rate amongst older males compared to older women. I have learned that transitions are the primary cause of coping difficulties— people coping with transitions to different life stages.*

Dr. Steve also reported learning from his female clients that their struggles with aging often relate to a shift in sexual identity. He described reflecting about ". . . a woman client in her early 60's. . . having the most difficulty adjusting to the fact that she is no longer the young attractive woman that she used to be. . ."

Learning from female clients the challenges that accompany aging in a culture that values youthful appearance, Dr. Ricky noted that some "women fight aging appearance through plastic surgery. . . and worrying about wigs and make-up."

Among the participants' responses that referenced gender and midlife were some about living with the consequences of choices made earlier in life. Dr. Linda talked about a female client who was working through her choice not to have children and coming to terms with what that would mean for her:

> . . . A lady who made the decision to get married and not have children and is now struggling with "I am getting almost too old to have kids. . . I told my husband that I didn't want kids." Now she is having trouble accepting the decision that she made. I see women really struggling who are going through menopause.

And Dr. Sunny discussed learning from both male and female clients about trying to cope with relationship dissatisfaction in midlife:

> Seeing male clients in their 40s or 50s with midlife crisis issues all of sudden thinking that they haven't enjoyed life and they want to have an affair and divorce. Same with females who were involved in an arranged marriage and now they find themselves not happy in the relationship.

Concluding Thoughts

The responses to the question of what psychologists learned about life stages from their psychotherapy clients made it clear that the wisdom therapists gained through clinical work added significantly to their understanding of lifespan development. Psychotherapists shared that they learned much about the richness of human development and the multiple ways in which individuals can rise to the challenges of each stage of life. They recognized that their clients were not alone in this growth and that they, too, were growing personally and professionally. The interplay of professional and personal growth appears to mutually enrich both of these domains in their lives. Psychotherapists spoke of learning how little they knew, and how much they have come to know by observing their clients negotiate the stages of life, particularly from those clients who are more senior. Dr. Julia's statement seems to embody much of the content of therapists' response to this question, "There is a lot of flexibility in terms of how we adjust and manage with life stressors or problematic situations. This kind of fluidity is something that has consistently impressed me."

References

Aldwin, C. M. (2007). *Stress, coping, and development: An integrative perspective.* New York, NY: Guilford Press.

Amirkhana, J., & Auyeung, B. (2007). Coping with stress across the lifespan: Absolute vs. relative changes in strategy. *Journal of Applied Developmental Psychology, 28,* 298-317.

Anda, R. F., Felitti, V. J., Walker, J., Whitfield, C. L., Bremner, J. D., Perry, B. D. . . .Giles, W. H. (2006). The enduring effects of abuse and related adverse experiences in childhood: a convergence of evidence from neurobiology and epidemiology. *European Archives of Psychiatry and Clinical Neurosciences, 56,* 174-86.

Benight, C. C., & Bandura, A. (2004). Social cognitive theory of posttraumatic recovery: the role of perceived self-efficacy. *Behaviour Research and Therapy, 42,* 1129-1148.

Edwards, V. J., Anda, R. F., Felitti, V. J., & Dube, S. R. (2003). Adverse childhood experiences and health-related quality of life as an adult. In K. Kendall-Tackett [Ed.], *Health consequences of abuse in the family: a clinical guide for evidence-based practice* (pp. 81-94). Washington, DC: American Psychological Association.

Erikson, E. (1950). *Childhood and society.* New York, NY: Norton and Company.

Foa, E. B., Keane, T., M. & Friedman, M. J. (2010). *Effective treatments for PTSD: practice guidelines from the International Society for Traumatic Stress Studies* (2nd ed.). New York, NY: The Guilford Press.

Friedman, L. J. (2000). *Identity's architect: A biography of Erik H. Erikson.* Cambridge, MA: Harvard University Press.

Heim, C., & Nemeroff, C. B. (2001). The role of childhood trauma in the neurobiology of mood and anxiety disorders: preclinical and clinical studies. *Biological Psychiatry, 49*(12), 1023-1039.

Herman, J. (1997). *Trauma and recovery: the aftermath of violence—from domestic abuse to political terror.* New York, NY: Basic Books.

Jorgensen, R. S., Dusek, J. B., Richards, C. S., & McIntyre, J. G. (2009). An experimental investigation of consistency in female undergraduates' reports of coping efforts for the same versus different stressful situations. *Canadian Journal of Behavioural Science, 41,* 51-54.

Josselson, R. (1996). *Revising herself: The story of women's identity from college to midlife.* Oxford: Oxford University Press.

Orth, U., Trzesniewski, K. H., & Robins, R. W. (2010). Self-esteem development from young adulthood to old age: A cohort-sequential longitudinal study. *Journal of Personality and Social Psychology, 98,* 645-658.

Perry, B., & Szalavitr, M. (2006). *The boy who was raised as a dog and other stories from a child psychiatrist's notebook: What traumatized children can teach us about loss, love and healing.* New York, NY: Basic Books.

Piaget, J. (1959). *The language and thought of the child* (3rd ed.). Florence, KY: Routledge/Taylor & Francis Group.

Power, F. C., Higgins, A., & Kohlberg, L. (1989). *Lawrence Kohlberg's approach to moral education*. New York, NY: Columbia University Press.

Rønnestad, M. H., & Skovholt, T. M. (2003). The journey of the counselor and therapist: Research findings and perspectives on development. *Journal of Career Development, 30*, 5-44.

Rosen, D. C., Miller, A. B., Nakash, O., Halperin, L., & Alegría, M. (2012). Interpersonal complementarity in the mental health intake: a mixed-methods study. *Journal of Counseling Psychology, 59*(2), 185-196.

Skovholt, T. M., & Starkey, M. T. (2010). The three legs of the practitioner's learning stool: Practice, research/theory, and personal life. *Journal of Contemporary Psychotherapy, 40*, 125-130.

Sneed, J., Schwartz, S., & Cross, W. (2006). A multicultural critique of identity status theory and research: A call for integration. *Identity: An International Journal of Theory and Research, 6*, 61-84.

Chapter 7

THERAPISTS' FIRST-HAND LEARNING ABOUT PERSONALITY AND PSYCHOPATHOLOGY

Joanne S. West, Manuela L. Waddell, and Claudia Hinojosa

"When I look at the personality style and the psychopathology, there is a clear relationship between the two. Sometimes it doesn't look like it matches on the surface. . . but if you worked with them for any length of time you could really see it. For me the life lesson is to trust my instincts." (Dr. Kristi)

This question was designed to facilitate a better understanding of psychologists' perspectives on the relationship between the personalities of their clients and the psychological disorders with which they may have presented. We were interested in their understanding of the interplay between personality—disordered or not—and psychological dysfunction, and how it may have impacted the psychotherapy treatment. Questions regarding how personality style and psychopathology may influence each other continue to be explored in the field of psychology, and there are multiple hypotheses as to the nature of the relationship between these two constructs. Particularly the burgeoning field of "developmental psychopathology" (also sometimes referred to as "development and mental health") addresses these issues (see, for example, the work of Luthar, 2006; Sameroff, 2000; Masten, 2001;

and Rutter & Sroufe, 2000, among others). In this chapter, theories and research evidence regarding the complex interrelationship(s) between personality and forms of psychopathology will frame the narratives drawn from the clinical experience of our participating psychotherapists.

Therapist Responses to This Question

Participants' responses reflected a diversity of perspectives, including the idea that personality and psychopathology sometimes converge, or that they are related but divergent in terms of impact on the client and his or her treatment, or that the two are unrelated constructs. A number of therapists said that although the association between psychopathology and personality had face validity, they were unsure of the precise nature of that relationship. Several respondents seemed to struggle to find an answer to this question, in contrast to other questions for which their responses seemed to flow more readily. This may reflect the fact that the question asked participants to frame what they had learned from clients in terms of DSM- (or diagnosis-) related constructs, while other questions focused on more universal themes. It may also reflect a reticence on the part of many of the psychologists to label or run the risk of over-pathologizing clients. Responses of these varieties will be explored later in this chapter.

Prevalence of Mental Health Concerns

Given the high rates of mental health concerns in both the general and clinical populations, it seems likely that our sample of psychologists would have had ample opportunity to learn from clients presenting with difficulties related to personality in conjunction with a variety of psychological dysfunctions. According to the lifetime prevalence estimates from the National Comorbidity Survey replication (NCS-R), approximately 54% of Americans will meet diagnostic criteria for an anxiety, mood, impulse-control or substance disorder in their lifetime (Lenzenweger, Lane, Loranger, & Kessler, 2007). This survey indicated also that approximately 9% of American adults met DSM-IV-TR[3]

---

[3]   Note that at the time of this publication the DSM-5 is the newest iteration of the Diagnostic Manual.

criteria for a personality disorder diagnosis when asked about the previous 12 months in their lives (Lenzenweger, Lane, Loranger, & Kessler). Since personality disorders are thought to be longstanding forms of dysfunction that begin to develop prior to adulthood, the prevalence rate may actually be higher in the general population if those younger than 18 were also included in the sample (Moffitt et al., 2007).

Within clinical populations, the rates of personality disorder are significantly higher. A study of 859 users of outpatient services assessed with the Structured Interview for DSM-IV Personality (SIDP-IV) found just under half (45.5%) of these individuals met the criteria for a personality disorder diagnosis (Zimmerman, Rothschild, & Chelminski, 2005).

Comorbidity Rates

The regularity with which personality disorders and psychopathology co-occur has led some to call their dual presence "the rule rather than the exception" (Links & Eynan, 2013, p. 532,). Lenzenweger et al. (2007) found high rates of comorbidity between personality disorders and other types of psychological dysfunction, with some variations. For example, they found that comorbidity was far higher for Cluster B personality disorders than for Cluster A or Cluster C disorders. The authors attributed this finding to the possibility that the affect dysregulation associated with many Cluster B disorders may be more predictive of other forms of psychopathology (Lenzenweger et al.).

Esbec and Echeburúa (2011) note the high rates of comorbidity between certain personality disorders and specific maladaptive psychological disorders, namely schizotypal personality disorders and schizophrenia, paranoid personality disorder and delusional disorder, mood disorders and borderline personality disorder, obsessive-compulsive disorder and obsessive-compulsive personality disorder, and social phobia and anxious avoidant disorder. The significant symptom overlap among these personality and psychological disorders has formed the basis for calls to end their classification as different categories of dysfunction and to adopt dimensional classification, as has been adopted by the latest version of the Diagnostic Manual (American Psychiatric Association, 2013; Kernberg, 2012; Krueger & Markon, 2014; Shedler & Westen, 2004; Widiger & Frances, 1994).

Personality Styles on a Continuum

Everyone has a personality style, which can be both healthy and adaptive. However, a number of psychologists in our sample reported having learned from their work with clients that personality lies on a continuum, making the distinction between adaptive and non-adaptive a matter of intensity and how one's day-to-day life may be affected. For example, it can be an adaptive personality style to be quite careful and precise, which can bode well for one's work and organizational skills; however, if taken to an extreme, this same quality, increased exponentially, can manifest as an obsessive-compulsive disorder that greatly interferes with the person's quality of life.

Personality is defined as an individual's "enduring patterns of perceiving, relating to, and thinking about the environment and oneself that are exhibited in a wide range of social and personal contexts" (American Psychiatric Association, 2000, p. 686). Until recently, the field of psychology has relied on a categorical view of adaptive and non-adaptive personality, regarding the number, frequency, and duration of certain characteristics defined as maladaptive (Khoury, Langer, & Pagnini, 2014). However, this nosology has been criticized as arbitrary, because it neither reflects empirical evidence nor addresses culturally embedded variations that might be considered adaptive (Khoury, Langer, & Pagnini, 2014). For example, whereas shyness may be seen as a concern in American culture, in other cultures—such as in some Asian cultures—it may be valued as a personality asset. However, and in general, the perspective that disordered personality lies on a continuum from an adaptive personality structure to maladaptive adjustment has gained increasing support (Bernstein, Iscan, & Maser, 2007). Krueger and Markon (2014) suggest that the inclusion of a dimensional model for assessing personality can serve as the basis for continued development of an empirically supported means of understanding both adaptive and maladaptive personality functioning—even as that approach also has its critics.

In fact, there are a number of ways of thinking about the nature of the continuum from adaptive to maladaptive personality. Currently the perspective with the greatest empirical support seems to be the Five-Factor Model (FFM)(Costa & McCrae, 1985), which describes personality as a unifying structure (Krueger & Markon, 2014; Miller, 2011; Widiger, 2011). Originally designed to identify those factors that underlie general personality characteristics, the FFM has repeatedly demonstrated that it can also adequately account for those traits associated with disordered personality (Miller, 2011). Using the 30 traits identified in the FFM to assess disordered personality as maladaptive extremes of adaptive personality traits has been shown to be reliable (Few et al., 2010) and valid (Miller, Reynolds, & Pilkonis, 2004).

Within our research sample, a number of psychologists endorsed learning from clients in a way that views personality as dimensional rather than categorical. For example, Dr. Vincent said, "You get enough symptoms together and you get a disorder; so all personalities can become disorders. All personalities can become pathological with a sufficient number of symptoms." Similarly, Dr. Rose said she has learned:

> . . . that psychopathology is just a personality style that does not work as efficiently or as effectively as just the personality style. . . certainly something like a narcissistic personality disorder is just narcissistic personality style on steroids. There is no such thing as normal; it is just a matter of degree.

Dr. Sunny also noted that personality lies on a continuum, but cautioned that, while "personalities are related to disorders. . . not everybody has a disorder just because they have a particular personality." And Dr. Trayton observed ". . . there is a short path between a personality style and an Axis II disorder. So, in that sense, there's a relationship between personality style and psychopathology."

Nature of the Psychopathology/Personality Relationship

These responses from our psychologists demonstrate that many have given thought to the nature of the frequently complex relationship between personality and psychopathology. Their conclusions are reflective of the field more generally, in which multiple hypotheses regarding this relationship have been proffered. Perhaps the most comprehensive review of the ways in which personality and psychopathology are thought to interact was provided by Millon (2011), who outlined eight different hypotheses in this regard: 1) the characterological predisposition hypothesis; 2) the complication hypothesis; 3) the attenuation hypothesis; 4) the co-effect hypothesis; 5) the modification hypothesis; 6) the orthogonal hypothesis; 7) the overlapping symptomatology hypothesis; and 8) the heterogeneity hypothesis. All but the orthogonal hypothesis (which states that personality disorder and other forms of psychological dysfunction represent distinct psychological phenomena that often co-occur solely because each is common in the population), were represented in the responses from psychologists to the question we posed as to what they may have learned from clients regarding the relationship between personality and psychopathology. The other seven hypotheses are presented here along with the responses that illustrate each one.

The Characterological Predisposition Hypothesis

The characterological predisposition hypothesis asserts that maladaptive personality traits constitute the primary disorder, precipitating the secondary appearance of psychopathology, often in reaction to environmental stressors. Widiger (2011) also endorsed neuroticism as a precipitate of psychological disorder, through a pathway of reacting strongly to stress. There is empirical support for this connection. For instance, the trait of neuroticism strongly predicts psychopathology in reaction to stress (Lahey, 2009). It is believed that neuroticism may lead to negative ways of thinking about oneself and the world, and that this in turn leads to anxiety and or depression (Freeman & Garety, 2003). In a similar way, introversion and the social isolation that can accompany it have been thought to leave one vulnerable in the face of stress, perhaps resulting in psychological dysfunction (Landerman et al., 1989). For a more detailed description of the overlap between particular personality disorders and other forms of psychopathology, see Esbec and Echeburúa (2011).

Millon (2011) described the characterological predisposition hypothesis as the most commonly endorsed relationship between psychopathology and personality, and this was reflected in our study because, by far, most of the therapists characterized the relationship between personality and psychopathology in this way. An example of that type of response came from Dr. Rick, who said:

. . . certain personality styles will be more prone to psychopathology than others. And then I think that the second part of it would be that the specific personality styles would be more likely to lead to specific kinds of psychopathology. So, different personalities will tend to yield different forms of psychopathology.

The majority of psychologists reported learning from clients that the personality trait of introversion tends to predict depression and/or anxiety. As Dr. Tevin said:

. . . personality style predisposes you to pathology because certain people are born with specific traits. The one thing I have learned is that stress tends to exacerbate personality traits and that people who have certain personality traits are very predictable in stressful situations.

And Dr. Jac said: ". . . the more introverted kind of personality style. . . the more potential for depression in that personality style."

Similarly, Dr. Oliver shared learning that "Certain kinds of depressions are more likely to grow out of certain personality styles than they are others," whereas Dr. Rick noted that ". . . somebody who is shy in their personality would be more prone to problems like depression, perhaps because they are less likely to be effective socially and connecting with other people in relationships, which is a good buffer against depression." In a similar vein, Dr. Michelle noted:

. . . if you have a depressive personality structure, there is a greater probability that you will suffer major depressive episodes, which is. . . psychopathology. Highly sensitive people. . . are predisposed to psychopathology. Depressives are predisposed to it. Anxious people are predisposed to it.

Dr. Clark discussed learning about the connection between personality and disorder, stating:

Sometimes with introversion you get depression or self-medicating of negative emotions and that was a whole different presentation. You got the psychopathology being

depression and addiction with the introverts. With the
extraverts it was more antisocial and addictions that could
happen.

In contrast, and perhaps taking account of the cultural differences noted previously, Dr. Luke indicated that clinical experience had not taught him that personality influenced the development of depression or anxiety:

Will shy people tend to manifest more pathology in the
area of social anxiety and depression than other kinds of
people? I don't know if that's the case. I've never really seen
obvious connections between people who have a certain set
of personality characteristics and specific pathologies.

Some psychologists referred to learning that the manifestation of psychological disorders, other than anxiety and depression, is determined by personality. As Dr. Rachel told us: "There's a certain personality type that is more likely perfectionistic, more likely to become anorexic than they are to become alcoholic. So it's more that [personality] might inform the pathology of choice, not that we consciously choose our pathologies." Dr. Natasha spoke of learning from clients that personality disorders predict maladaptive psychological functioning: "I found that if someone is more independent or more avoidant, they end up having a different psychopathology than somebody who is more narcissistic."

The Complication Hypothesis

The second type of relationship between psychopathology and personality noted by Millon (2011) is the complication hypothesis. This theory states that it is psychopathology that influences personality and its expression, rather than that personality predicts psychological dysfunction. Just one response in our sample, from Dr. Mai, was consistent with this hypothesis:

We have personality disorders, but there are Axis I issues
like anxiety disorders and depression and those are more
ingrained in the persons' personalities—much more than

> *DSM defines. People think of the Axis I stuff as state kind of disorders but. . . Your psychopathology becomes your personality and who you are in some way. These things define who you are in some way and are thus part of your personality.*

The Attenuation Hypothesis

The third hypothesis outlined by Millon (2011) is the attenuation hypothesis, which is predicated on the idea that personality disorders constitute alternative expressions of psychopathology. The idea is that a single genetic or biological dysfunction underlies both and shapes their expression (Van Velzen & Emmelkamp, 1999). Cloninger, Svrakic, and Przybeck (1993) argue that this underlying entity is an individual's genetically determined temperament. This perspective was reflected in several psychologists' reports of what they had learned from clients. For example, Dr. Ricky said he had learned that:

> *. . . there is a blur, that there is not a clear line there, you don't go from personality style to psychopathology overnight, and I'm not sure that there is a difference. . . at what point psychopathology starts and personality style ends, I don't know.*

And Dr. Julia said:

> *I think people are born with certain temperaments, and if they are born into the wrong kind of family, if they are born into a really dramatic or anxious family, they are going to be even more highly anxious. I definitely think there is a relationship.*

Related to that idea, Dr. Aviva noted, "To me, personally, style and psychopathology are just saying the same thing."

The Co-effect Hypothesis

Next, Millon (2011) described the co-effect hypothesis, that psychopathology and personality are distinct entities often present in the same individual because of a third environmental variable. This hypothesis does not assert a common psychobiological vulnerability, but rather that personality and psychopathology may occur together as an outcome of a significant life event— for example, childhood trauma (Millon). Similarly, Widiger (2011) recognized that psychopathology and personality may share a common underlying cause, but argues that this may indicate the two are not different entities, but rather that they occur on a spectrum of alternate manifestations of a common etiology.

Consistent with this hypothesis, a number of the psychologists we interviewed indicated that they consider both personality and psychological disorder as shaped by early life experiences. As Dr. Natasha said, "first thing I learned was that [a] personality problem...the earlier it starts the more. . . severe the pathology ends up to be. If the personality structure gets affected at an early stage, the more chances of a more severe psychopathology..." And, Dr. Vincent observed that attachment issues can lead to maladaptive personality and psychopathology: "You get enough symptoms together and you get a disorder. And some of the symptoms happen early in age, being shut out by your parents. . ." Offering a specific example, Dr. Julia discussed the clients she works with who are diagnosed with anorexia and attributed that disorder, at least in part, to parenting style. In summarizing this perspective, Dr. Sunny said, "Earlier relationships with significant others [and] early traumatic experiences do really shape someone's personality and hence can lead to psychopathology."

The Modification Hypothesis

The modification hypothesis (Millon, 2011) states that personality shapes, not only the presentation of psychological disorder, but also the prognosis of the disorder. This hypothesis is supported by a good deal of evidence. As one example, in a meta-analysis of studies examining the impact of disordered personality on depression, Newton-Howes, Tyrer, and Johnson (2006) found that a co-occurring personality disorder doubled the risk of a poor outcome for individuals with depression—and the effects seem to be manifested over time. For example, Crawford et al. (2008) found in a 20-year longitudinal study that the coexistence of personality dysfunction with other forms of psychopathology makes for significantly poorer outcomes as compared to those with psychopathology alone. These authors argued that given its impact on prognosis, disordered personality should be conceptualized as a risk factor for long-term psychological dysfunction.

The assertion here is that individuals with particular personality profiles will be less responsive to treatment for comorbid psychopathology. Dr. Iris' remarks reflected this hypothesis:

> *I would think then that personality style would be the way in which one's psychopathology is worked out or manifested. I guess a way of answering that would be to say that no two depressed patients are going to ever look the same actually or no two bipolar patients are going to look the same. . . the way in which one [goes] forth in the world, in a particular way, will frame whatever pathology or health one brings with one. . .*

Dr. Felipe talked about learning that disordered personality can serve as a barrier to successful treatment, saying:

> *I think that people who have the darker side of the borderline, personality disorder, the more narcissistic, the more truly anti-social personality disorder— I guess what I have learned is that their pathology is life-long and it is really hard to get any change. They are not invested in change. They are not interested in change. They are stuck in it. Whatever personality style that you see is your strength that you have always relied on [but it] often starts to give you symptoms and starts to become psychopathology at some point.*

Dr. Yetty, in reflecting on work with individuals undergoing bone marrow transplant as part of cancer treatment, indicated learning about the ways that personality can shape the treatment of physiological dysfunction, stated: "Illness is managed best if your personality is one that is open, is one that is accepting of help from other people, and if you're one that is generally, more positive. . . willing to talk things through [and] regulate your affect."

The Overlapping Symptomatology Hypothesis

With this hypothesis, it is thought that the reason that personality disorders and other forms of psychological dysfunction co-occur is because the criteria used to diagnose each of them overlap significantly (Millon, 2011). In other words, personality disorder and other psychological dysfunctions often appear simultaneously because the mental health field applies definitions to these two classes of disorders based on common characteristics. Therefore the distinction between what were known in the DSM-IV-TR as Axis I and Axis II disorders is artificial. Evidence for this hypothesis comes from research that has examined the relationship between individual personality disorders and other forms of psychopathology. Examples of this include Widiger's (1992) conclusion that avoidant personality disorder and social phobia represent, not distinct entities, but rather overlapping constructs that differ only in terms of severity. With the inclusion of schizotypal personality disorder in the schizophrenia spectrum, DSM-5 (2013) endorses the view that a significant overlap in symptoms between this personality disorder and schizophrenia is substantial enough to merit classifying the two as differing only in terms of symptom severity.

Several psychologists in our study talked about learning from their clients that the distinction between personality and other forms of psychological dysfunction seems artificial, and that, in their experience, there is often considerable overlap between these two categories of disorder. Dr. Michelle reflected this by saying "I guess the reason I am having a hard time with the question is that sometimes they're sort of overlapped, right?" And Dr. Ranju said, "They are the same. Mental illness is basically how someone cope[s] in this world." Dr. Homer observed, "The two are mashed, intertwined, and play out in that personality style," and Dr. Laura said, "They are so intertwined, they are completely linked together."

The Heterogeneity Hypothesis

Finally, the heterogeneity hypothesis speculates that personality and other forms of psychopathology result from various combinations of internal factors, such as genetic predispositions or temperaments, as well as external factors that create a variety of vulnerabilities to facilitate the development of psychological dysfunction (Millon, 2011). Because these factors combine in various ways, the result is a heterogeneous grouping, with some individuals evidencing both personality disorder and psychopathology. Nigg (2006) endorses the importance of temperament in the development of psychopathology, but emphasizes that environmental factors must also be present for a disorder to develop. Some psychologists spoke of having learned from their clients that different patterns of interaction between and among environmental factors, individual temperament, and biological inheritance combine into individual psychological profiles that sometimes lead to personality and psychopathological dysfunction. This is embodied in Dr. Mark's statement about a particular client:

> *This taught me how personality styles can interact with things that the environment throws at you and leads you down the garden path. It wasn't one or the other. You know. . . had [my client] grown up in a different setting his dependent personality style wouldn't have necessarily led to that particular self-doubt/self-concept problem. But it was the interaction of the style and the environmental circumstances from which he came. That would be the lesson that I took away from that. . . to always pay attention to the style, character, personality—whatever you want to call it—on the one hand and circumstances the person is in on the other, and how these things play off one another.*

Dr. Sunny also talked about having learned about the combined unique influence of factors that she saw shape a certain client's dysfunction: "Earlier relationships with significant others, early traumatic experiences do really shape someone's personality and hence can lead to psychopathology. Environmental factors are an issue, coupled with the biological and inheritance issues." Indeed the overriding controversy as to the respective influences of nature versus nurture in relation to the myriad human talents and the human condition is ever-present in the thinking of psychologists.

Other Perspectives

It should be noted that Millon's hypotheses are not at all the only perspectives subscribed to by psychologists. In a somewhat different formulation, Widiger (2011) suggested that personality and psychopathology relate to one another in three different ways. Like Millon, Widiger recognized that psychopathology and personality may share a common underlying cause and, as a result, may not be different entities; however, he argued that the two represent different manifestations of a common etiology, and that they present on a spectrum. Cloninger, Svrakic, and Przybeck (1993) believed that this underlying entity is the result of an individual's genetically-determined temperament, whereas Nigg (2006), who endorsed the importance of temperament in the development of psychopathology, emphasized that environmental factors must also be present for mental disorders to develop.

Widiger (2011) further believed that there is evidence for a bidirectional relationship between personality and psychopathology, in which each shapes the presentation of the other; this is also the basis for the burgeoning field of developmental psychopathology. Participant Dr. Lewis reflected this perspective when discussing the interplay between personality and schizophrenia:

> I think the two interact together. You know. . . it's a chicken-and-egg situation. All of their behavior leads to their personality style, so their pathology influences their personality style. But I'm willing to bet that, as the years go by, personality style then turns around and influences the psychosis.

So some theorists like Widiger (2011) argue that personality and psychopathology can have a causal bidirectional relationship in which each may influence the development of the other. Unlike any of the hypotheses presented by Millon, by that line of reasoning, each of the two entities is equally influential on the other's developmental trajectory.

Treatment Considerations

Several psychologists shared with us what they had learned from clients about psychopathology and the treatment of personality disorders when these forms of dysfunction co-occur. In discussing how to deal clinically with the influence of personality on the treatment of psychopathology, a number of psychologists indicated that they had learned that personality must be addressed first in order for treatment to be successful. For example, Dr. Justin said:

> *I think the way you are as a person and the way you are as an individual is going to reveal itself in its psychopathology. And I think that you've got to change the personality or work on the personality of a person, how the person lives his life, how the person grows, how the person behaves, which then will lead to changes. . .*

And Dr. Eliza stated ". . . maybe the personality style can cover or disguise the psychopathology for a while. I think as therapy kind of peels away the different layers of the client, some of that starts to emerge."

In a related observation, Dr. Leslie discussed having learned to bring the influence of their personalities into clients' conscious awareness, saying, "I am struck about the enduring effects of overall personality patterns, and how much people are unaware of them. I see a lot of therapy involving helping people get more [of a] grip on these issues." And Dr. Goodheart discussed the ways in which personality can shape the choice of psychotherapeutic intervention, saying she had learned that:

> *. . . different personality styles adapt to different types of therapy and, because I am an eclectic, sometimes it's a trial-and-error with somebody to see if they can handle cognitive-behavioral therapy or they need more insight-oriented therapy or more reality therapy. I find that those who are more rigid and narcissistic don't last in therapy, that they are not as willing to make changes or to see other people's point of view. I find that personality styles can be highly impacted by depression and distorted thinking that goes along with it, and as people deal with their depression*

*they can adapt some changes in their personality style. So, I
do think personality style can impact their psychopathology
and then in turn can impact our ability to work with
them.*

She also reported that ". . . personality style is both adaptive and maladaptive, so psychotherapy involves understanding the ways in which one's personality style is both pathological and a survival skill or an adaptive thing at the same time." Similarly, Dr. Arcy said, "You respect the personality styles because they can be sources of strength as well [as] particular vulnerabilities."

Risks of Over-Pathologizing

In their responses to this question, several psychologists expressed concerns regarding the use of labels such as "personality disorder" or "psychopathology" to characterize their clients or the situational difficulties with which they presented. Instead, they emphasized the need to understand each client individually, within his or her own context. For instance, Dr. Martina said, "If there's an emphasis or a pressure to diagnosis, then I think sometimes we're very quick to say, 'That's their personality and this is what's going on,' rather than really taking the time to get to know them." And Dr. Ricky stated, "I don't believe in psychopathology and I don't believe in personality styles. I take each individual situation and do my best to understand them on their own terms." Also not wanting to label his clients in a pejorative manner, Dr. McMillon said "Well, I'm so ambivalent about the whole thing. I can say 'various levels of normal'."

From another perspective, Dr. Sunny shared what she had learned from clients regarding diagnosis and gender:

*I think that we are quick to pathologize anything that
goes against the norm. I think we over-pathologize women
especially and that sets young girls up to a disadvantage
almost from the start. I think that when we take the time
to get to know people and where they came from, where
their personality style was actually formed from, what
experiences along the way have made her more standoffish*

or him more extroverted, then we would be less likely to
pathologize, and psychotherapy and life in general would
go a little more smoothly.

In addition, several psychologists responded to our question by saying they rejected the very notion of personality. As Dr. Peyton said, "Well I'm kind of stumped; I don't know what personality types are." And Dr. Beach noted, "I don't even deal with personality styles." Such responses seem to suggest that part of what these psychologists learned from their clients is the negative consequences that can sometimes accompany psychiatric diagnosis. Clients and practitioners alike are acquainted with the stigma that labels can carry, and in particular the diagnosis of personality disorder, which has been perceived—even by mental health professionals—as indicating significant impairment of interpersonal functioning, often with little hope for improvement.

Cultural Considerations

Perhaps surprisingly, among the responses to the question of what they had learned from clients regarding personality and psychopathology, only two psychologists referred to cultural considerations. Dr. Doral discussed learning about the ways in which culture influences the content of delusions, saying ". . . the manifestation of delusions oftentimes is influenced sort of by the cultural and social background of the person. I am not quite sure how to answer the rest of that about personality and psychopathology." Dr. Anil said she had learned from clients to ". . . recognize the importance of culture; I think pathology is created more socially rather than personally. What we call pathology in one culture may not be pathology in the other." Here she expressed having learned about the role of culture in our concept of what constitutes normal and abnormal functioning, and the importance of developing a contextual understanding of clients (Ben-Zeev, Young, & Corrigan, 2010).

No Relationship Between Personality and Psychopathology

Although the majority of the psychologists responded to the question about what they had learned from clients about personality and psychopathology with narratives describing their understanding of the connection between these two constructs, there were clearly dissenting opinions. Some respondents indicated that they believe no relationship exists between personality and other forms of psychological dysfunction. Exemplifying responses of this type, Dr. Pines said, "I guess I don't really have an idea that there is this sort of relationship between personality styles and psychopathology," and Dr. Odila said, "I don't find an answer to that. Somehow I don't understand that connection." Dr. Luke elaborated this point:

> *Will shy people tend to manifest more pathology in the area of social anxiety and depression than other kinds of people? I don't know if that's the case. I've never really seen obvious connections between people who have a certain set of personality characteristics and specific pathologies.*

Personality and the DSM-5

The nature of a reciprocal interaction between personality and psychopathology is an open question, and one that continues to attract considerable attention within the mental health practice community. The elimination of the multi-axial system from earlier iterations of the DSM in the recently published DSM-5 seems to represent the American Psychiatric Association's current position that personality disorder is not essentially different from other forms of disorder (APA, 2013). The inclusion of both categorical and dimensional means of identifying personality characteristics perhaps best embodies the way in which we can best conceptualize what constitutes adaptive or maladaptive personality functioning. Whether or not maladaptive personality is somehow categorically different from other psychological dysfunction remains unresolved. The responses that the psychologists in our study provided to this question clearly reflect this ongoing debate.

References

AmericanPsychiatric Association. (2000). *Diagnostic and statistical manual of mental disorders* (4th ed., text rev.). Washington, DC: Author.

American Psychiatric Association. (2013). *Diagnostic and statistical manual of mental disorders* (5th ed.). Arlington, VA: American Psychiatric Publishing.

American Psychiatric Association. (2013). *Personality Disorders Fact Sheet.* Washington, DC: Author.

Ben-Zeev, D., Young, M. A., & Corrigan, P. W. (2010). DSM-V and the stigma of mental illness. *Journal of Mental Health 19,* 318-327.

Bernstein, D. P., Iscan, C., & Maser, J. (2007). Opinions of personality disorder experts regarding the DSM-IV personality disorders classification system. *Journal of Personality Disorder, 21,* 536-551.

Cloninger, C. R., Svrakic, D. M., & Przybeck, T. R. (1993). A psychobiological model of temperament and character. *Archives of General Psychiatry, 50,* 975-990.

Costa, P. T., Jr., & McCrae, R. R. (1985). *The NEO personality inventory manual.* Odessa, FL: Psychological Assessment Resources.

Crawford, T. N., Cohen, P., First, M. B., Skodol, A. E., Johnson, J. G., & Kasen, S. (2008). Comorbid Axis I and Axis II disorders in early adolescence: outcomes 20 years later. *Archives of General Psychiatry, 65,* 641-648.

Esbec, E., & Echeburúa, E. (2011). New criteria for personality disorders in DSM-V. *Actas españolas de psiquiatría, 39,* 1-11.

Few, L. R., Miller, J. D., Morse, J. Q., Yaggi, K. E., Reynolds, S. K., & Pilkonis, P. A. (2010). Examining the reliability and validity of clinician ratings on the Five-Factor Model score sheet. *Assessment, 17,* 440-453.

Freeman, D., & Garety, P.A. (2003). Connecting neurosis and psychosis: The direct influence of emotion on delusions and hallucinations. *Behaviour Research and Therapy, 41*, 923-947.

Heimsch, K. A., & Polychronopoulos, G. B. (2014). Diagnosis in the assessment process updated and revised. In E. Neukrug & C. Fawcett (Eds.), *Essentials of testing and assessment: A practical guide for counselors, social workers, and psychologists.* Pacific Grove, CA: Brooks Cole.

Kernberg, O. (2012). Overview and critique of the classification of personality disorders proposed for DSM-V. *Swiss Archives of Neurology and Psychiatry, 163*(7), 234-238.

Khoury, B., Langer, E. J., & Pagnini, F. (2014). The DSM: Mindful science or mindless power? A critical review. *Frontiers in Psychology, 5*(602), 1-8.

Lahey, B. B. (2009). Public health significance of neuroticism. *American Psychologist, 64*, 241-256.

Landerman, R., George, L. K., Campbell, R. T., & Blazer, D. G. (1989). Alternative models of the stress buffering hypothesis. *American Journal of Community Psychology, 17*, 625-642.

Lenzenweger, M. F., Lane, M., Loranger, A. W., & Kessler, R. C. (2007). DSM-IV personality disorders in the national comorbidity survey replication (NCSR). *Biological Psychiatry, 62*, 553-564.

Links P. S., & Eynan, R. (2013). The relationship between personality disorders and Axis I psychopathology: deconstructing comorbidity. *Annual Review of Clinical Psychology, 9*, 529-554.

Luthar, S. S. (2006). Resilience in development: A synthesis of research across five decades. In D. Cicchetti, D. J. Cohen (Eds.), *Risk, disorder, and adaptation.* New York, NY: John Wiley and Sons.

Krueger, R. F., & Markon, K. E. (2014). The role of the DSM-5 personality trait model in moving toward a quantitative and empirically based approach to classifying personality and psychopathology. *Annual Review of Clinical Psychology, 10*, 477-501.

Masten, A. S. (2001), Ordinary magic: Resilience processes in development. *American Psychologist, 56,* 227-238.

Miller, J. D. (2011). Exploring personality: Personality disorder relations and their implications for DSM-5. *World Psychiatry, 10*(2), 110-111.

Miller, J. D., Reynolds, S. K., & Pilkonis, P. A. (2004). The validity of the five-factor model prototypes for personality disorders in two clinical samples. *Psychological Assessment, 16,* 310-322.

Millon, T. (2011). Further thoughts on the relation of personality and psychopathology COMMENTARIE, *World Psychiatry 10,* 107-108.

Moffitt, T. E., Caspi, A., Taylor, A., Kokaua, J., Milne, B. J., Polanczyk, G., & Poulton, R. (2010). How common are common mental disorders? Evidence that lifetime prevalence rates are doubled by prospective versus retrospective ascertainment. *Psychological Medicine, 40*(6), 899-909.

Newton-Howes, G., Tyrer, P., & Johnson, T. (2006). Personality disorder and the outcome of depression: meta-analysis of published studies. *British Journal of Psychiatry, 188,* 13-20.

Nigg, J. T. (2006). Temperament and developmental psychopathology. *Journal of Child Psychology and Psychiatry, 47,* 395-422.

Røysamb, E., Tambs, K., Ørstavik, R. E., Torgersen, S., Kendler, K. S., Neale, M. C. . . Reichborn-Kjennerud, T. (2011). The joint structure of DSM-IV Axis I and Axis II disorders, *Journal of Abnormal Psychology, 120,* 198-209.

Rutter, M., & Sroufe, L. A. (2000). Developmental psychopathology: concepts and challenges. *Development and Psychopathology, 12,* 265-296.

Sameroff, A. J. (2000). Developmental systems and psychopathology. *Development and Psychopathology, 3,* 297-312.

Shedler, J., & Westen, D. (2004). Dimensions of personality pathology: an alternative to the Five-Factor model. *The American Journal of Psychiatry, 161*, 1743-1754.

Van Velzen, C.J.M., & Emmelkamp, P.M.G. (1999). The relationship between anxiety disorders and personality disorders: prevalence rates and comorbidity models. In J. Derksen, H. Groen, & C. Maffei (Eds.), *Treatment of Personality Disorders* (pp. 129-153). New York: Plenum Press.

Widiger, T. A. (1992). Generalized social phobia versus avoidant personality disorder: a commentary on three studies. *Journal of Abnormal Psychology, 101*, 340-343.

Widiger, T. A. (2011). Personality and psychopathology. *World Psychiatry, 10*, 103-106.

Widiger, T. A., & Frances, A. (1994). Towards a dimensional model for the personality disorders. In P. Costa & T. Widiger (Eds.), *Personality and the Five Factor model of personality* (pp. 19-39). Washington, DC: American Psychological Association.

Zimmerman, M., Rothschild, L., & Chelminski, I. (2005). The prevalence of DSM-IV personality disorders in psychiatric outpatients. *American Journal of Psychiatry, 162*, 1911-1918.

Chapter 8

VENTURING OUTSIDE THE BOX: WHAT THERAPISTS LEARN ABOUT CULTURE

Katherine Tighe, Joan M. Frye, and Sherry L. Hatcher

Culture is "the whole way of life of a people, from birth to the grave, from morning to night and even in sleep," wrote the English poet T.S. Eliot in 1948 (Eliot, 1948, p. 31). As has been noted across these chapters, psychologists learn much from our clients in this regard. One of the most important lessons psychologists learn regards cultural differences, cultural change, and the dimensions of culture in people's lives. To prepare this study, the authors asked 61 psychologists the following question: "What have you learned from your psychotherapy clients about culture?"

We were fortunate to pull together a rich cross-section of practicing psychologists who agreed to participate in our study. These psychotherapists come from different ethnic, religious, and socio-cultural backgrounds; their training on cross-cultural issues is varied and they practice in all types of settings, ranging from private practice in the suburbs to community clinics specializing in work with immigrants and refugees. The psychologists who participated in our research were at different points in their careers, ranging from relatively recently licensed to pre-retirement.

It should be noted that qualitative research of the variety conducted here is particularly useful as a means of looking at therapeutic process, particularly in an area such as cross-cultural psychotherapy (Hill et al., 2005; Ponterotto, 2005). Qualitative methodology can take into consideration nuanced aspects of individuals' lives and experiences in a particularly meaningful way (Hoshmand, 2005). Such rich and nuanced responses characterize the responses we gained in our research. In response to the question on multicultural learning, multiple themes of interest emerged.

Multiculturalism has arguably been one of the most powerful emphases in psychology over the last 20 years. Because of this, it is possible that therapists who have most recently graduated would have experienced the most formal education in cross-cultural issues, even while some of those longer in practice may have had more experience across a variety of clients' cultural presentations. In either case, the responses from our interviewees are thoughtful, provocative and, not infrequently, surprising.

Multicultural Awareness: Utility of the Concept

Perhaps reflecting a marked change in thinking on cultural issues over the last few decades in North America, almost all of the psychologists we interviewed reported that they had experience working cross culturally and that they believe that successful psychotherapy includes an understanding of the culture of the individual client as well as sensitivity to cultural issues more generally. Their responses suggest that most therapists in our sample gave careful consideration to cultural issues, mirroring the ethics of the profession (Sue & Sue, 2007, p. 15).

Our interviewees largely agreed with the Eliot quote that begins this chapter, often speaking of cultural influences that have shaped their own characteristic ways of perceiving and living in the world, as well as their understanding of particular psychotherapy clients. Most of our respondents conceptualized cultural forces as manifesting in multiple ways, such that the therapist would have to understand a range of cultural aspects for each client in order to successfully treat her or him.

This majority view of our participants was tempered by a few who stated they did not believe it was particularly important to examine cultural issues in the context of conducting psychotherapy. According to that school of thought, an overemphasis on culture can lead the therapist to make potentially misleading assumptions. For example, two respondents expressed the view that any trained therapist should be able to treat anyone because the universal language of emotions is a sufficient basis for therapeutic communication. One of these therapists described how cultural differences pale in comparison to the human relationship beneath apparent differences. Therapists with this perspective often advocate for learning about a client's culture simply by asking him or her about it.

What the Psychologists Say

Most respondents first spoke of their experience and learning in treating racial and ethnic minorities, and then reflected on the broader influences of culture, including within the contexts of gender, economic status, family experiences, sexual orientation, geographic location, and religious affiliation. These topics correspond to the group levels of identity as detailed by Derald Sue (Sue, 2001), as well as the dimensions of the Personal Dimensions of Identity Model, as proposed by Arredondo et al. (1996). The basic attitude of most therapists in our sample on this point can be summed up in the words of one respondent, "You can't look at culture without looking at race, ethnicity, gender, class, social environment, and myriad other things."

A number of respondent remarks expressed similar ideas. According to Dr. Trayton:

> It doesn't have to be [someone] from a racial culture. It could be from a religious culture, it could be a geographic culture. . . it could be the culture of that particular family. . . Ethnicity is just part of what is within a larger construct of differentness. I just think there are many ways of slicing the pie. Socio-economics is every bit as important as race and we could go on and on from there.

Others conceptualized culture still more broadly, such as Dr. Aviva who said:

> I don't think of culture just as ethnic, or racial, or national terms, but culture in terms of ways of responding in a

family culture, couple culture. I think that everybody brings their own culture, as it were, to the therapeutic enterprise, because part of what of they are examining is what of those people and those groups or larger groups that had an impact on them has shaped who they have become and how they have become. So I am always attempting to try to understand something about the particular kind of milieu that people grew up in and people now live in and what those—what their assumptive world is around that.

Some respondents applied a cultural perspective to a broad range of issues. Said one interviewee: "[Even] working with schizophrenics is akin to working with another culture." Another spoke about the culture of "kids who cut," and another about the specific culture of inner city life. Still another viewed the stages of the lifecycle as involving culture differences, explaining that therapists must keep in mind such differences when working with young parents, older parents, or families with grown children.

When asked what they had learned about culture from their clients, several respondents at first stated that they had either minimal cross-cultural experience or none at all, explaining or implying that they lacked racial or ethnic minority clients in their practice. One psychologist's response, typical of several others, follows:

I guess what I probably need to say is that I have not learned enough about cultural diversity. And part of that is due to the fact that my clientele tends to be like me, tends to be educated, middle class and, above all, Caucasian, suburbs—and that over the years I've not had a lot of diversity in my client loads.

Upon consideration, most interviewees who first offered a statement such as this went on to describe significant experiences with a range of cultural issues, although not necessarily with regard to racially or ethnically diverse clients. Such reports were in keeping with the majority of responses that conceptualized culture broadly. Dr. Goodheart, for example, despite initially having said she had little cross-cultural experience, went on to give examples of how culturally significant it has been for her to work with clients from a religious background different from her own. She also reported how her affluent clients bring a particular cultural issue, such as guilt over their good fortune, into the psychotherapy room.

One respondent said that he had little cross-cultural experience and suggested that this may be because he has been in private practice all his life. He expressed a fascination with ethnic and racial differences, however, saying:

> *And just the sense that there is that difference and I haven't the vaguest notion how to [work with these clients] leaves me with [a lack of knowledge in] the whole area. It's kind of daunting when you think about it.*

Uniqueness Versus Stereotyping

Nearly 30% of interviewees emphasized that belonging to specific cultural groups does not trump client individuality. An overriding theme of the responses was that there are many characteristics—global and local, universal and individual —that must be taken into consideration with all clients. The therapists we interviewed strongly expressed the belief that for a mental health professional to adopt generalizations based on stereotyped ideas of culture is deeply inadequate conceptually, and even unethical. As one psychologist, Dr. Lewis, stated, "I think cultural differences have to be respected, but it is more important to address each individual as a specific individual." This is consistent with the view of a number of experts in the field, including Nichols and Schwartz (2007). who suggest that an overemphasis on ethnicity can cause a therapist to assume great differences between therapist and client that may, in fact, not exist and which could be harmful to the therapeutic alliance and to outcome. As Dr. Odila commented about the complexity of culture manifested in an individual client:

> *It is clear to me that each member of a couple [for example] does literally come from a different cultural background. . . and that every family system is its own culture and every extended family is its own culture. I think I work to help people recognize those inherent differences as a given, as*

something that has to be understood and factored in to working out their ability to live together.

And Dr. Luke said:

Sometimes you just have a sort of difficult, obnoxious person and it has nothing to do with culture. A lot of people who do not deal with cultural issues make a lot of assumptions about something that is cultural which is really personality. . . So, separating out what's culturally the norm or typical or what is unique to that individual personality-wise is a big [issue].

For some respondents, the understanding of how to sort out cultural and personality issues emerged through thoughtful reflections on their own personal history. For example, one psychologist described learning a valuable lesson while working with a client of the same gender, age, economic background, and small town upbringing as herself. However, despite her initial assumption that they would have much in common, she found that she and her client were actually very different culturally. Dr. Sunny, an immigrant from a North African country, explained that her own unique experience of family, schooling, friends, opportunities, and other factors made her quite culturally different from someone who may have come from the same geography, spoken the same language, and shared the same religion.

Sue, Arredono, and McDavis (1992) consider insight into one's own background to be a skill required for multicultural competency. In fact, they view self-understanding in relation to one's own worldview and cultural conditioning as a core competency (Sue, Arredondo, & McDavis, 1992). This is a nuanced and psychologically sophisticated way of looking at culture and fit between psychologist and client and was reflected in comments made by several of our respondents. For example, Dr. Antonia disclosed that she is very much aware of her abilities and limitations and that she asks herself with each client, "Do I really understand this person, am I the best fit for this person?" She adds that she will refer a client to a more appropriate therapist if she believes the person will be better off working with another professional.

Cross-Cultural Training Versus Experience

Close to 50% of the psychologists we interviewed emphasized the importance of learning about specific differences across racial and ethnic cultures, whether through formal training or in collaboration with client feedback. Some stated that such learning made the therapeutic alliance more likely to prosper, while others noted it was important for diagnostic purposes, and still others explained that it simply gave them a head start in understanding their client's perspective. As Dr. Yetty remarked, "It's important to kind of have some idea about different cultures because it can then show [clients] that you have some knowledge about different ways of thinking." Or, as Dr. Michelle said:

> *I had a patient a long time ago from a South American country and he would have to educate me a lot on [his] culture, and that worked very well for us. I would say, "Well, I don't understand this," and he would say, "Oh yeah, you probably don't understand that because in my country this is important". . . or "this is the way we do things". . . or "we place value on this." He taught me to appreciate more of how his culture shaped his expectations on himself, on other people, his priorities in life.*

Several respondents mentioned how general knowledge about culture could give them an advantage in understanding their clients. As Dr. Trayton noted:

> *I've seen a fair number of Hispanic families, enough to get a sense of some of the prevailing cultural issues, [and] I have developed a certain set of expectations that I carry with me to the next Hispanic family. It doesn't mean I don't appreciate uniqueness, but it helps me with my hunches and makes me more efficient. Without this experience, some of the cultural dynamics might not have occurred to me.*

While most interviewees discussed cultural knowledge related to ethnic and racial minorities, Dr. Goodheart reported that the experience of living abroad offered an alternative perspective from which to contrast the dominant United States culture, especially as a culture of affluence:

I think having lived other places that the culture here is a little more pathological, more narcissistically fragile and driven among a certain part of our affluent community. The culture suffers in kind of a bizarre way. They can sometimes be really, really devoted to avoiding life's difficulties. And they fail. Nobody can do that. Then when they feel unhappy, they feel terribly ashamed and guilty about it because they have so much. So it's more difficult for them to talk about their unhappiness.

A vocal minority of our participants expressed the belief that the kind of training and the practical application of training commonly associated with understanding racial and ethnic differences is, in itself, a form of stereotyping. Dr. Ranju made this point as follows: "I have learned that what is taught today is mostly silly. I went to a cultural sensitivity training. . . and thought it was really not. . . useful. Africans do this, Hispanics do this. . . .all stereotypes." (It should of course be noted that a brief "cultural sensitivity training" may have included quite different content and expertise from in-depth, doctoral-level training in cultural competence.)

Two additional respondents felt that culture-specific training has gone too far. As Dr. Justin said:

If I'm working with an Asian client, or an African American client, I'm not going to automatically remember page 23 of my multicultural textbook, and say, Well, with an Asian client I'm not supposed to be sitting within five inches of them. I mean, really, I think you really have got to read the individual and not the cultural.

Dr. Aviva commented that some aspects of multicultural training have led to stilted communication between client and therapist, at times almost absurd levels:

I teach multiculturalism, I'm doing a lot of multi-culture stuff in group relations, but the way that it's getting translated in psychology is really a kind of stereotyping of, "Okay, in order to be sensitive to your culture, what I'm going to do is stereotype you by saying, 'Well, I know about

your culture and I'm going to ask you about your culture.'"
And I've even seen students, or in groups, sit down with
patients and say, "Well, tell me about your culture. What
is this? Tell me about your culture." People don't walk
around with a culture. "Tell me about your culture.". . .
You can't say to them, "Tell me about your culture" without
recognizing the absolute insanity of such a question.

However, the vast majority of our respondents who spoke of the usefulness of cultural sensitivity training also expressed the need to strike a balance between formal training in culture and an appreciation of the uniqueness of each individual. For example, as Dr. Justin explained:

I took a multicultural counseling [course]. I thought it
was very valuable, but I still take my stance. Yes, you have
to learn about Asian cultures like being too close, spatial
distance; Hispanic cultures kind of having a different way;
how some cultures don't believe in the therapeutic process. I
think that that's important and [you've] got to learn about
that, but I think that also leads to stereotypes. And that
also leads to kind of being culturally insensitive, too. You
have to be culturally sensitive to the people you work with,
but I think that you also have to take each individual
from where they're coming from and have to really try to
understand the client from where they are.

Dr. Yetty pointed out that theory knowledge, while important, has to be balanced by the personal experiences of the individual, emphasizing the need to "keep the door open for the person to tell you what their culture is, so that the relationship is authentic, not based on assumptions, or my assumptions about who people are."

Several of our interviewees also mentioned how specific training helped them to be careful to evaluate apparent psychiatric symptoms through a cultural lens before jumping to conclusions about diagnoses, thus avoiding the possibility of over-pathologizing. As Dr. Tevin said, "In some cultures, hearing voices might make you somewhat special; in our culture, hearing voices makes you labeled 'schizophrenic.'" Dr. Justin talked about having learned the importance of fully exploring and understanding a psychotherapy client's full cultural history, including lifestyle, family background, and details of upbringing before considering symptoms, in order to formulate an accurate diagnosis. This psychologist used the example of a man who had witnessed the type of violence that would typically have produced symptoms of post-traumatic stress syndrome (PTSD), but that did not in his particular case:

> *The culture with which he grew up. . . was this very violent part of one of the cities close by and growing up in a gang, so for him, that was part of the culture. It was not out of the norm on a daily/weekly basis to see an act of violence, and he was able to make sense of it within his culture, whereas another person who was never exposed to that and witnessed that might develop PTSD. You know, he really did not have any signs and I did not get the sense he was denying it. So, knowing about his culture, and not his racial culture but just his lifestyle and [the] background from which he grew up was very important in terms of diagnosis and really understanding that patient's symptoms.*

Others mentioned some important issues that their cultural training did not address, such as acculturation issues, which quite frequently arise for some minority clients. For example, several psychologists who had extensive experience working with immigrants and refugees mentioned the need to "get out of the office" and to act as a "connector" with their cultural and language minority clients. They either directly stated or implied that standard therapy may not be enough in such situations, and that a more social work-oriented approach was at least adjunctively helpful to psychotherapy for clients attempting to acculturate in North America. Others mentioned the need to further develop, within themselves, personality characteristics such as humility, flexibility, and curiosity that would make them maximally successful as therapists in working with cross-cultural issues.

A few psychologists in our sample felt that some of the ethnocultural training they had received was not particularly useful in a practical sense, because of resource constraints in the workplace. Two in particular mentioned specifically that they had been trained to refer out language minority clients or clients who were a poor fit for the therapist. Frequently they were not able to comport themselves with these guidelines because there was simply nowhere else to refer these clients. Clearly this created for them both an ethical and practical dilemma, because the American Psychological Association calls for services to be performed in the language preferred by the client (American Psychological Association, 2003). At times this requirement may, however, prove more aspirational than feasible.

Two other interviewees commented that, although multicultural training is important, it is years of experience that truly enable therapists to improve their rapport with culturally diverse clients. Both mentioned that they had been inflexible in their methods until, through failure experiences, they learned to try different and more productive approaches. While only two therapists specifically expressed the view that experience can trump cultural knowledge, the comments and stories across our interviews suggest that accruing experience and empathy has made therapists increasingly skilled and effective at working with culturally different clients (see also Hatcher, et al., 2005).

There were a few specific and additional comments about working with language-minority clients. In one, a psychologist recalled an experience where he had hired a Hindu interpreter for a Hindu-speaking client. However, this therapist had little background in languages and hired someone who spoke a Hindu dialect different from that of the client and therefore could barely speak with the client. Another said he had learned through experience and through watching native speakers working with language minority clients that clients did far better speaking in their own language with someone who understood culture-specific language and even non-verbal communication. Overall, however, there were surprisingly few comments about language issue from the therapists in our sample.

In that language has been identified as a critical issue in therapy (American Psychological Association, 2003; Biever et al., 2002), it is a curious omission. Alternatively, it is possible that the majority of the therapists we interviewed simply had not been faced with providing therapeutic services to clients who do not speak English. Or perhaps they assumed that interpreters could be called in, as necessary, though that belief would obviate an understanding of the very complex nature of both the therapeutic alliance and a need for the translator's concomitant expertise in psychological interpretation.

Cross-Cultural Therapy: Learning How to Do That

About 40% of the psychologists we interviewed described quite specifically how they conduct therapy with an appreciation for cross-cultural issues. However, while the majority of psychologists described culture as a broad concept, when discussing specific instances of their experience in working cross-culturally with clients, they reverted almost exclusively to discussing ethnicity and race.

Other Ideas for Working With Clients Whose Lives Are Different From the Therapist's

A common theme from interviewees was the need to go slowly with clients who were culturally different from the therapist in order to develop rapport and a reliable working alliance. Some therapists said it is advisable in such situations to provide solid psychoeducation regarding what therapy is and what it is not. Many therapists in our sample spoke of the need to be quite flexible and creative, in a variety of ways. Some talked about integrating Western and Eastern therapy practices that take into consideration the client's beliefs (and therefore do not explicitly or implicitly aim to convince clients of any superiority in a Western approach to psychotherapy). Several therapists said that, at the client's request, they combined therapy with more culturally traditional methods, such as working with a shaman, with a client's meditation practice, or even with the clients' culturally specific musical interests. However, there may be ethics boundaries to consider in adopting some of these practices.

The therapists we interviewed volunteered specific stories about tailoring their therapy approaches by combining contemporary and traditional cultural practices. One such story came from Dr. Mark, who at one time worked as a therapist with several large groups of refugees who had resettled in his community. He and his staff decided it would be best to work together with those community religious leaders who were respected and trusted by the therapy clients. This psychologist believed that by reaching out in this way—that is, working in the community as well as the therapy room—the therapy outcomes were far more positive than they would have been otherwise. He specifically recounted an episode in which mental health professionals were having trouble convincing Ethiopian Orthodox Christians who had been prescribed psychotropic medications to take their pills. The psychologists asked community religious leaders for help, and a priest came to the center and distributed water that he had blessed. He explained to the clients that God works in many ways, including through Western medications, and also through the holy water with which they should take their medications. Importantly, that solved the problem of compliance in this case, though the psychologists involved had to venture out of their offices reach out, and become actively involved in a relevant cultural community.

More than a few psychologists mentioned that, in order to be effective in a multicultural environment, they had to work at reaching out to connect clients to multiple resources, such as places of worship, job opportunities, and various key individuals in their communities. The idea of being "a connector" for clients to friends who speak the same language—and to the larger immigrant community more generally— appeared thematically several times in the narratives, especially among those therapists who reported having considerable experience in working with immigrant clients. Those therapists with the most experience of this nature, or who were foreign-born themselves, seemed most likely to discuss the importance of language issues in therapy, and also the potential uses of psychotherapy as an aid in the acculturation process.

For some, tailoring therapy for clients of diverse cultures meant changing or adapting their models of practice. The most frequent observation made by therapists on this point was that they had changed their style to be more directive than they might have been otherwise. Dr. Julia recalled a client who:

> . . . came with the expectations that doctors are here to tell you what to do. She expected a more directive style, and needed that in some ways, so I had to alter how I work because I don't tend to be very directive.

Dr. Lucas, recalling an episode of providing therapy to a Chinese mother, offered the following background:

> She wanted me to "tell her what to do". . . and I was most reluctant because I like to collaborate with my clients, and finally I thought to myself, Give the client[s] what

they are asking for. So I said, "When you start telling your teenage son these things, how helpful do you think it is for him to know all about your husband and your sexual relationship?" She said, "Well, I have to share with somebody." And I said, "We don't do that." And she said, "No?" And I said, "No." And I went through the reasons why [not] and she said, Okay." And she stopped doing it.

Another change to typical practice techniques that interviewees mentioned as important in working with those culturally different was the loosening of traditional therapy boundaries in order to build a working therapeutic alliance. Therapists reported that this kind of adjustment in technique avoided intimidating clients unused to Western psychological practice, and allowed them to be more successful with those for whom interpersonal trust is built on a somewhat closer relationship. Some respondents mentioned accepting small gifts from clients, attending events important to a client, and going out with them into the community to help them with acculturation issues. For example, Dr. Linda spoke of how client boundaries may be different across cultures, perhaps as a result of an expectation that the therapist is or will be a friend:

What shocks me still to this day is how you can sit with people from different cultures and how quickly they invite you into their lives. I had one woman that I saw for a while and she invited me over to different religious celebrations that they were having. Her husband had died about nine years before and they still had a yearly custom on what to do around that and she had asked me one day—having to end her session early because she was going to one of these events marking her husband's passing—and asked me if I wanted to go. It is amazing that people invite you into that part of their lives.

Providing Therapy When Third Culture Issues Dominate

Third culture issues featured prominently in the content of the sessions reported by some respondents. For our purposes here, being of a "third culture" refers to the push-pull position of a child with foreign-born parents, raised in North America, who has integrated elements from both the mainstream culture in which they live and the more traditional culture from which they have originated. About 20% of the psychologists in our sample mentioned working with clients who were brought up at least partly in the United States or Canada but who have immigrant parents at home with very different ideas about dating relationships, family roles, and quite a few other matters. Several comments captured the pain of those clients who felt pushed into traditional, cultural roles through family pressure, yet felt pulled by the larger society into making independent, Western-style decisions. Several of the psychologists spoke of their own struggle in working with client values quite different from their own. Said Dr. Julia:

> [I worked with] an Asian client. Listening to her parents' guidance was very important, despite the way that I saw it. [I wanted to tell her] "You need to get away from your home; it's dysfunctional. You need to individuate and develop a pure sense of self, separate from your family." In her culture, that's not how things work, and I really had to think about helping her within that [framework].

Most interviewees were cautious, searching for balance, trying to distinguish between cultural characteristics that yield adaptive or maladaptive value for the client in complex life situations, rather than judging any situation in absolute terms. Therapists also reported needing to manage their own feelings and values and not challenge the client's cultural perspective unless there was a therapeutic value in doing so. As Dr. Luke said:

> If somebody needs to be more assertive to survive in the American workplace, even if they come from a culture where, for example, as a woman you are not supposed to be assertive, you are going to have to work on that because that has practical survival value. So, it's not trying to have

them give up anything that they value but to add on a skill that could be situational or specific that allows them to compete and be viable.

Dr. Leslie spoke of learning to assess how closely clients identify with their cultures of origin, versus what they are "struggling to be free of." Making such a distinction can pose a difficult challenge for both client and therapist. This therapist recalled working hard at resisting the temptation to push a client to individuate from her parents when the client's choice was to follow their advice instead of doing what she herself wanted.

On the other hand, Dr. Ellen remembered having to struggle with a client who expressed attitudes that made felt uncomfortable: "I had this guy, and he was very arrogant, especially when he talked about his wife. I really had a hard time with that. I felt like taking up for her, even though he was my client."

Rather than embracing the task of managing a values clash, a few of the respondents said that they just refused to see certain kinds of clients because it brought up too many difficult feelings for them. One therapist reported that he would not treat clients who believe they are not free to live their lives as they choose. "I don't see fundamentalist clients," said Dr. Felipe; "I've seen a few, but it can be hard for me to get my head around their worldview." In a similar vein, Dr. Antonia said, "there are some cultures, frankly, that I have learned I will never understand."

Cross-Cultural Therapy and the Universal Language of Emotions

Approximately 15% of the respondents touched on the commonalities of human experience, such as the universality of emotions that go beyond one's particular culture. For these respondents, the basic principles of human wants, needs, and emotions are perceived as similar for all people, even if experienced through different cultural lenses. In discussing trauma recovery and the emotional similarities between those suffering war trauma and non-war trauma, Dr. Linda expressed the view that people are similar in many more ways than they are different. In this same vein, Dr. McMillan stated:

Everybody feels the same thing. We are all organized and wired in the same way; we have the same hormones. Culturally, the only thing that happens is we have expectations that create the feeling and our expectations are different because of cultures, but the feelings are wired in the same way.

Dr. Tom said:

I think I got to a place where I feel like I can appreciate [culture] a lot. . . but if I am doing what I am supposed to do in relating to the human being as a human being, those things fall apart as unimportant constructs.

When analyzing these varied responses, it appears to us as though respondents who were most likely to emphasize the universality of human emotions were also those who had a good deal of experience in working with cultural minorities, in particular immigrants and refugees.

How Cross-Cultural Work Affects the Therapist

Many of the psychologists we interviewed spoke about having grown as a person and a therapist as a result of their cross-cultural work. A sizable number of our respondents specifically mentioned having developed greater kindness, flexibility, and creativity as a result of working with clients across cultures. As Dr. Doral remarked, "I think I'm a much broader, tolerant, and flexible person who actually has come to enjoy cultural differences more than just tolerate differences." And Dr. Raju said, "I feel blessed that I have had so much interaction with different cultures and [because of this] I think I am a better thinker and a better listener."

Several psychologists mentioned experiencing an increase in curiosity as another benefit of their cross-cultural work in psychotherapy. Having become more inquisitive, Dr. Wilbur said, "[I am] somewhat more accepting of myself, kind of more curious about the world in general." And Dr. Juan said:

> *I have encountered cultural expressions and practices quite different from my own culture. . . I am more interested in studying my own culture and have examined some of my practices with clients whose culture is generally Eastern and not Western.*

Some interviewees spoke of having gained in confidence and worldliness as a result of cross-cultural experiences in their clinical practices. Dr. Trayton mentioned that early on she had had some trepidation about working with foreign-born clients and wondered if trust could develop as well in those therapy relationships as in the ones where she and the client were culturally similar. This psychologist said that, over time, her cross-cultural experience had ultimately been gratifying and it markedly expanded her worldview. Another therapist, Dr. Harriet M., reported that working cross-culturally helped her to further develop an interest in world religions, while Dr. Reuben experienced an expansion of his multicultural musical tastes.

Third culture differences with clients are, in fact, the theme of many of the examples given in the interviews we collected, and, according to most respondents, such differences ultimately serve to facilitate great learning for the therapist. Several of those in our sample spoke about how they have come to value and respect cultural differences, and that they have learned not to try to push clients too hard toward their own ideas of how a person should live. As Dr. Natasha said:

> *I have learned to be really careful in understanding a person's context and letting them come up with whatever works in their culture or their context, recovery, or working through different dilemmas, and not imposing my own [values] or something I might have learned in my training on "this is how it should be," such as "You should be independent" or "You shouldn't have to listen to your family."*

As Freeman and Hayes pointed out in their highly original (2002) work about how clients change therapists, the therapist can grow as a result of working with clients from culturally different backgrounds and from those who may challenge some of the most basic assumptions and values of the therapist. When a therapist allows him- or herself to be nonjudgmental and open to the uniqueness of each individual client, these ways of looking at the world invite opportunities for change and growth (Freeman & Hayes, 2002).

It appears that working cross-culturally has come to mean many different things to psychologists. For some, cross-cultural therapy means working with racial and ethnic minorities. For others, it is a broader concept that helps them work more effectively with immigrants, with clients of different religions, sexual orientations, or even with specific illnesses with which clients may present. Others have found that cross-cultural approaches help therapists better understand the dynamics of individual families, blended families, third-culture families, and extended families.

The value of therapist cultural competence in therapy is a message that the American Psychological Association (APA) has worked to promote for many years in relation to its training programs and ethics principles and codes. From the responses of our participants, it is apparent that psychologists have increasingly integrated this message into their hearts, minds, and practices.

References

American Psychological Association (A. P.). (2003). Guidelines on multicultural education, training, research, practice, and organizational change for psychologists. *American Psychologist, 58*, 377-402.

Arrendondo, P., & Perez, P. (2006). Historical perspectives on the multicultural guidelines and contemporary applications. *Professional Psychology: Research and Practice, 37*, 1-5.

Arredondo, P., Toporedk, R., Brown, S. P., Jones, J., Locke, D. C., & Sanchez, J. (1996). Operationalization of the multicultural counseling competencies. *Journal of Multicultural Counseling and Development, 24*, 42-78.

Biever, J. L., Castano, M. T., de las Fuentes, C.,,, Gonzalez, D., Servin-Lopez, S., & Sprowls, C. (2002). The role of language in training psychologists to work with Hispanic clients. *Professional Psychology: Research and Practice, 33*, 330-336.

Eliot, T. S. (1948). *Notes towards the definition of culture*. London: Faber and Faber.

Freeman, M. S., & Hayes, G. (2002). Clients changing counselors: an inspirational journey. *Counseling and Values, 47,* 13-21.

Hatcher, S. L., Favorite, T. K., Hardy, E. A., Goode, R. L., DeShetler, L.A., & Thomas, R. M. (2005). An analogue study of therapist empathic process: Working with difference. *Psychotherapy: Theory, Research, Practice, Training 42,* 198-210.

Hill, C. E., Knox, S., Thompson, B. J., Williams, E. N., Hess, S. A., & Ladany, N. (2005). Consensual qualitative research: an update. *Journal of Counseling Psychology, 52,* 196-205.

Hoshmand, L. T. (2005). Narratology, cultural psychology and counseling research. *Journal of Counseling Research, 152,* 178-186.

Nichols, M. P., & Schwartz, R. C. (2007). *Family therapy: concepts and methods* (8th ed.). Boston: Allyn & Bacon.

Ponterotto, J. G. (2005). Qualitative research in counseling psychology: a primer on research paradigms and philosophy of science. *Journal of Counseling Psychology, 52,* 126-136.

Sue, D. W. (2001). Multidemensional facets of cultural competence. *The Counseling Psychologist, 29,* 790-821.

Sue, D. W., Arredondo, P., & McDavis, R. J. (1992). Multicultural counseling competencies and standards: a call to the professions. *Journal of Counseling and Development, 70,* 477-486.

Sue, D. W., & Sue, D. (2007). *Foundations of counseling and psychotherapy: evidence-based practices in a diverse society*. Mississauga, Ontario: Wiley & Sons Canada.

Chapter 9

AN EXAMPLE OF LEARNING FROM CLIENTS CROSS-CULTURALLY: NORTH AMERICAN AND BRAZILIAN PSYCHOLOGISTS

Adriana Kipper-Smith[4]

This chapter encapsulates the research findings of a cross-cultural doctoral dissertation (Smith, 2012) stemming from Hatcher's (2012) important data about what therapists learn from their clients. The chapter expands the topic from an in-depth, cross-cultural perspective. Specifically, it highlights the role of culture in the shaping of lives and advances our understanding of how psychologists from different cultures listen, and learn, from their clients. In this research study, the narratives of North American psychologists were compared to those of their Brazilian counterparts.

---

[4]   I would like to express gratitude to my Fielding Graduate University dissertation committee, including Dr. Sherry Hatcher, my dissertation chair; Dr. Margaret Cramer, for her precise and thoughtful feedback; and Dr. Michele Harway, who guided me through the sinuous roads of qualitative research. Also, my gratitude goes to Dr. Sylvia D. Dantas from Universidade de Sao Paulo, Brazil, for her expertise and encouragement.

In 2002, Norcross, Hedges, and Prochaska stated that the main challenge for the field of psychotherapy is to find creative ways to integrate the values and worldviews of different cultures into the mainstream discourse in concert with the efficiency of evidence-based treatments. The present discussion aids in that spirit of bringing different values and worldviews closer to that goal.

Aligned with Hatcher et al.'s (2012) original research, this study explored what psychologists from the United States, Canada, and Brazil learn from their clients across the following domains: general wisdom, relationships, resolving moral and/or ethical dilemmas, coping mechanisms, courage, the relationship between personality and psychopathology, cultural differences, and developmental life stages. Of note, the two North American countries are typically described as quintessentially individualistic; Brazil, on the other hand, is a conspicuous example of a South American collectivist nation.

Why Focus on Culture?

Focusing on culture allows us to better appreciate its enormous influence on our cognitive, physical, social, and emotional development (Gardiner & Kosmitzki, 2005). Cross-cultural studies offer the opportunity for psychology to develop into a more mature science through global understanding of human behaviors and thoughts. When "folding back" the findings from other societies into the mainstream, psychologists help to enrich their discipline by studying "all that is human" (Friedlmeier, Chakkarath, & Schwarz, 2005, p. 17). Quite importantly, the exploration of cross-cultural realities bespeaks a valuable effort in addressing an increasingly globalized world. Growing diversity, particularly seen in the United States (e.g., ever-increasing numbers of Latinos, including Brazilians) demands that therapists face clinical issues and cultural backgrounds that may be different from their mainstream cultures (Leong & Lee, 2006).

Increasing psychotherapy expertise undoubtedly includes greater multicultural competency (Jennings, D'Rozario, Goh, Sovereign, Brogger, & Skovholt, 2008), and cross-cultural research between Latin American countries and non-Latin North America is especially needed. As a Latin American nation, Brazil holds an increasing status as a global force, representing a strong point of departure for the evaluation of many variables that are also pertinent to the rest of the world (Pearson & Stephan, 1998; Vistesen, 2008), particularly to other collectivist cultures. Additionally, psychology in Brazil has more than one century of history. Unlike the United States and Europe, psychology in Brazil did not start as an experimental discipline; it has gained the status of a science only very recently. Hence, the discipline has enjoyed the prestige of being much more of an art than a science. The rejection of quantification and the subsequent avoidance of science prompted Brazilian psychology to advance in qualitative, phenomenological, and psychoanalytic orientations (Hutz & Adair, 1996). Interestingly, psychotherapy in several other collectivist nations shares similarities with Brazil, especially with regard to the approach to psychology and with regard to prevalent theoretical orientations. However, it is important to keep in mind that not all collectivistic nations share with Brazil the same theoretical approach to psychotherapy.

The fields of psychology in Brazil, the U.S., and Canada do share some similarities. Each of these countries is among the nations with the highest number of psychologists per population in the world, and Brazil, the U.S., and Canada also appear to have a similar proportion of psychologists per capita (World Health Organization, 2005). When a culture has a considerable ratio of psychologists per inhabitants, it can be generally assumed that the profession of psychology is considerably valued and has an important role in the making of the collective subjectivity. This seems to be the case in these three countries.

Culture, Psychology, and Cross-Cultural Dimensions

Culture is a concept that belongs to the social world and determines how people structure and live their lives (Hofstede, Pedersen, & Hofstede, 2002). Matsumoto et al. (2008) defined culture as an informational and meaning system that is passed across generations. The creation of norms of behavior serves to prevent social chaos and provide social order, and social environments foster meaning-making structures (Matsumoto et al., 2008; Oyserman & Lee, 2008).

Contemporary views show an awareness that culture influences psychological processes, as well as the converse of this, that psychological processes also influence culture (Lehman, Chiu, & Schaller, 2004). Culture can also be aligned with the concept of worldview. According to Ibrahim, Roysircar-Dosowski, and Ohnishi (2001), worldview corresponds to the lens through which we see the world. For example, when comparing Brazilian and American worldviews, these authors maintained that Brazilians tend to be more traditional than Americans, prefer linear-hierarchical social relationships, and focus on the past and future rather than the present. In their analysis, Americans appeared to be more spontaneous and modern in their worldview. In other words, worldview defines how a person sees his or her relationship with the world, and this is inextricably related to that person's upbringing and life experiences (Sue & Sue, 2003).

Language acts as another important lens through which we see the world. It is generally accepted that language differences between countries correspond to differences in culture as well. Language, beyond the knowledge of vocabulary, includes the knowledge of what to say, when to say it, and why (Hofstede, Pedersen, & Hofstede, 2002). Based on the fact that culture influences communication, it comes as no surprise that Brazilians and North Americans greatly differ with regard to communication styles (Singelis & Brown, 1995). Independent and individualistic self-constructs generally have a low-context communication style, whereas interdependent and collectivist self-constructs tend to have a high-context communication style (Gudykunst, Matsumoto, Ting-Toomey, & Nishida, 1996; Leong & Lee, 2006).

The definitions by which individuals describe themselves and their relationships with others, especially with the groups or collectives to which they belong, corresponds to one of the most widely used concepts for understanding cultures and the cultural differences between individualism and collectivism. Oyserman and Lee's (2008) research findings confirm that the concepts of individualism and collectivism (I-C) can be understood through the extent to which either individuals or groups are seen as the basic unit of analysis. Within an individual-focus scenario, societies exist to establish individual well-being. Within a group-focus setting, individuals are seen as essentially connected to their societies and belonging to their groups. More importantly, they must fit into these units. Naturally, different cognitive processes are believed to be predominant in different cultural setups, and culture is charged with defining not only cognitive content, but also cognitive process—for example, self-concept, focus of perception, nature of relationship with others (Oyserman & Lee, 2008).

Most studies on cross-cultural differences are based on the assumption that differences in judgment and behavior are due to either individualism or collectivism (Takemura & Yuki, 2007; Triandis, 1995, 2001). From this perspective, social contexts provide a powerful and meaning-making influence. According to Oyserman and Lee (2008), these assumptions depend on which countries are being asked to define individualism and collectivism, as many nations are steadily underrepresented within this research (e.g., Latin American countries).

Individualism and Collectivism

It comes as no surprise that individualism was born from the pursuit of democracy and has largely been understood as an expression of freedom in Western culture (Zha, Walczyk, Griffith-Ross, Tobacyk, & Walczyk, 2010). As it arose from the struggle between monarchical and aristocratic society, individualism has been viewed as a product of modernity, because political and economic thought in free-market economies is focused on rewarding the individual. Though individualism promotes freedom, self-expression, wealth, and creativity, it has also been associated with loneliness, isolation, and selfishness (Chaibong, 2000).

Arendt (1998) offered a compelling viewpoint on the emergence of individualism. According to her, the concept and understanding of man after the 18th century's Industrial Revolution began to include a considerable strain of alienation with the world, as individuals became more self-centered and eager for gratification. Later on, the post-World War II period was marked by a weakening of communal values and an orientation toward consumerism. Along with consumerism, a blind acceptance of the ideas of inner truth and the true self came to be prominent in American society (Cushman, 1995).

For instance, in individualistic cultures, people buy services from others and they do not mind if the providers of these services have different views and values from theirs, something rarely seen in more collectivistic cultures. This relationship of mutual benefit tends to be superficial. However, it allows individuals and groups to do their own thing and it also fosters some degree of tolerance (Safdar, Friedlmeier, Matsumoto, Yoo, Kwantes, & Kakai, 2009; Triandis, 1993).

Since Hofstede proposed this definition about 30 years ago, individualism-collectivism (I-C) has received the most attention in cross-cultural research among all dimensions of cultural differences; it is the most widely studied dimension used to explain and predict cultural differences (Hofstede, 1980, 2002; Triandis, 1995; Oyserman, Coon, & Kemmelmeier, 2002; Fischer et al., 2009). From his survey of over 40 cultures, Hofstede (1980) proposed that the constructs of I-C are opposite poles of one dimension. It is worth noting that these constructs can only be opposites when analyzed at the cultural level and across cultures. When they are analyzed within cultures and across individuals, they tend not to be opposites but rather multidimensional gradations that change across individuals in each particular context (Triandis, 2001).

It is important to keep in mind that these constructs need to be considered carefully as well, since individuals change depending on the situation to which they are exposed (e.g., when the in-group is being threatened, most idiocentrics become more allocentric). Additionally, depending on the situation, I-C can coexist because we all carry both tendencies: "One can be individualist in relation to one person and collectivist in relation to another" (Triandis, 1993, p. 162). To further illustrate how some individualistic cultures may, depending on situational determinants, become more collectivistic, the aftermath of the 9/11 attacks in 2001 prompted individuals in the U.S. toward more collectivistic practices. Though temporary, the crisis placed group membership (i.e., American, New Yorker) in the foreground.

Members of individualistic societies tend to have goals that are often distinct from the goals of their in-group, as they are more likely to determine their social action based on personal needs and perceived personal rights. Members of collectivistic cultures tend to have goals that are compatible with the goals of their in-group, as they are more intensively guided by group norms and obligations to the in-group (Fischer et al., 2009).

Individualism has also been associated with direct and goal-oriented communication, while collectivism is associated with indirect communication, mostly grounded on partners' feelings and self-expression (Brewer & Chen, 2007). Not surprisingly, individualism has been correlated with higher expressivity and extraversion (Hofstede & McCrae, 2004). Additionally, happiness (Matsumoto et al., 2008) and creativity (Zha et al., 2010) have also been associated with this construct.

Brewer and Chen (2007) maintained that cultural differences are based on how social identification processes are represented and organized in order to regulate the balance between individual expression and social conformity. The bottom line seems to be that every society values its in-groups in a similar manner. However, the nature of the psychological attachment to the in-group is often what defines each culture (Brewer & Chen, 2007). In sum, individualistic cultures promote an independent construal of self, support the achievement of personal goals rather than in-group goals, and feature rationality and interpersonal exchange. Collectivistic cultures promote interdependent selves and favor in-group goals, stimulate relatedness, and place more emphasis on norms of behavior. Additionally, individuals from collectivistic cultures tend to endorse less emotional expression (Matsumoto et al., 2008).

In expanding on the fine differences in gradation between individualism and collectivism, research has shown that collectivists tend to be as self-reliant as individualists. However, whereas individualists praise the freedom to do what they please by themselves, collectivists think of self-reliance more in terms of not being a burden to the group (Triandis, 2001). Additionally, collectivists generally make a more distinct differentiation between in-group and out-group. By this token, personalism, a system in which a person is defined by his or her hierarchical position in the family or in the social group, is still a common trait of Brazilian culture (Garibaldi de Hilal, 2006), and may likely be a good example of the exercise of the discrepancy between in- and out-group treatment.

As mentioned earlier, the centrality of collectivism lies in the group, whether family, tribe, work organization, ethnic group, or religious organization. For instance, southern Italy, rural Greece, most parts of Africa, Asia, and Latin America are considered to be more collectivistic (Hofstede, 1980, 2009; Triandis, 1993). It is also important to note that collectivistic cultures tend to have more tolerance for cognitive inconsistency—for example, being a vegetarian but eating meat when others eat meat (Safdar et al., 2009; Triandis, 2001; Zha et al., 2010). In this manner, a good amount of tolerance for cognitive inconsistency can easily be found in Brazilian culture as well, since some forms of religious syncretism tend to be very common (e.g., being Catholic and practicing Buddhism, or being Catholic and attending Candomblé temples/*casas*, etc.).

Instead of acting as categorical truths about how cultures function, "cultural syndromes" (i.e., individualism, collectivism) should rather be seen as bridges to a more comprehensive and multilayered understanding between cultures from all parts of the world (Ponterotto, Casas, Suzuki, & Alexander, 2001; Sue, 2001; Triandis, 2001). In other words, both cultures and individuals are better understood if analyzed through bio/social/ecological lenses (Leung, 1989). In sum, categories are constructs and, as Hofstede (2002) proposed, not realities.

The United States[5]

Equality and diversity are fundamental elements in American society, and have attracted immigrants from all parts of the world for more than 200 years. Even though these values are not always equivalents of cultural reality, they are important cultural markers that foment the making of reality (Tamis-Lemonda & McFadden, 2010). The value of independence in the cultural make-up of America is tightly enmeshed with the frontier spirit, the so-called American dream, and the Protestant work ethic (Uchida & Kitayama, 2009). As a prominently modern and individualistic culture, marked by self-referentiality (Baudrillard, 1989) and masterful, "economically entrepreneurial" selves (Cushman, 1995), American society and its individuals tend to resist any identification with scenarios of powerlessness and vulnerability (Harris, 2009). The correspondent loss of relatedness likely prompts individuals to value power over connection.

As the cradle of individualistic democracy and the West's most powerful nation, the U.S. also has one of the world's largest populations of psychologists. For these reasons, this country potentially represents an optimal source of cross-cultural comparison, which may ultimately impact the debate on cultural trends. Becoming a psychologist in the U.S. requires a doctorate. After the attainment of a doctoral degree,

---

[5]   When speaking of culture, the United States is more thoroughly discussed in this section because the vast majority of the North American participants came from the United States; only two participants in this sub-sample of the original study were from Canada.

license to practice is granted for those who pass standardized state licensing examinations and other state by state requirements. Americans' individualism, consumerism, and technocratic tendencies inevitably influence the practice of psychotherapy (McWilliams, 2005a). In the U.S., the majority (70-90%) of counselors and psychologists report using cognitive-behavioral therapy (CBT; Hays, 2009; Sato, 1998). CBT seems to incorporate many of the values present in American culture, including assertiveness, personal independence, rationality, verbal ability, behavioral change, and the primacy of goal-directed tasks (Frank & Frank, 1993; Hays, 2009).

Of note, psychology practice in different countries remains an important area for further research and exploration. For a discussion of how psychotherapy is regulated and practiced in other individualistic and collectivistic countries, please refer to Smith (2012). It appears that research on psychotherapy is especially sparse in the case of collectivist cultures, where few or no studies published in English can be found. Even though some researchers have proposed the internationalization of psychology and psychotherapy, international research on therapy factors is still lacking.

Brazil and the Field of Psychology

Brazil is a country with a history of mixing the traditional and the modern; it is also much more about mixture than diversity: of races, of religions (syncretism), and of cultures (Garibaldi de Hilal, 2006). The coexistence of poverty and technological sophistication results in a cultural make-up marked by incongruities (Mendes, 2002; Pellegrini, 2000). Brazil has the largest economy in Latin America; however, approximately one-third of households are considered poor when compared to rich countries in the indexes of urban population, adult literacy rate, and gross domestic product per capita (Bornstein, 2010).

Although the country's levels of poverty have substantially changed over the past two decades, the incidence of poverty acts as a primary deterrent to achieving a healthy individual development and/or pursuing one's dream. An example of this can be found in the great number of street children in Brazil; poverty profoundly impacts the way these children see and plan for their future (Raffaelli & Koller, 2005). The country's vast wealth coexists with its unrestrained poverty, and access to social opportunities is greatly modulated by class and racial hierarchies. Moreover, Brazilian culture seems to be predisposed to cultural integration and biculturalism, given that race relations tend to be more subtle, and consequently more complex, than in the U.S. (McGoldrick, Giordano, & Garcia-Preto, 2005).

Unlike the U.S. slogan "separate but equal," Brazilians usually say "different but united," which reflects the way the country's hierarchical and relational system is organized (DaMatta, 1991). The importance of family constitutes a central cultural value, and includes non-blood kinships. Brazilians are also known for their extreme gregariousness and positive outlook on life. This latter aspect seemingly contributes to the culture's tendency toward conflict avoidance (Hofstede, 2009). While notions of privacy and having one's own space are prominent aspects of American culture, Brazilians generally do not entertain such concerns. What seems to be emphasized in this culture is the need to be considerate and to acknowledge others' needs, moods, and problems. Even though relationships are emphasized, the importance of accomplishments has recently taken on greater significance in Brazilian culture (McGoldrick, Giordano, & Garcia-Preto, 2005).

For the most part, Brazil can be considered an interdependent and collectivist culture (Gouveia, Albuquerque, Clemente, & Espinosa, 2002; Gouveia, Vasconcelos, Queiroga, Franca, & Oliveira, 2003; Omar et al., 2007; Spencer-Rodgers, Peng, Wang, & Hou, 2004; Vikan, Camino, & Biaggio, 2005). Despite this, signs of biculturality may be seen in characterizations of the country as egalitarian and individualist (DaMatta, 1991). Indeed, Brazil has some characteristics of individualistic cultures, such as being highly industrialized and "Westernized," especially Southern Brazil (Van Horn & Marques, 2000). As members of a more collectivistic culture, Brazilians are prone to focus on relatedness, harmony, and the improvement of larger group (Ribas, Jr., 2010).

Though research has suggested that collectivist nations tend to be less concerned with self-disclosure and have fewer affectionate relationships than individualistic cultures (Cheng & Kwan, 2008), Brazil seems to have a unique collectivist make-up whereby relationships tend to be highly affectionate. Unlike Asian collectivist cultures, Brazilians tend to be very affective and emotional (Pearson & Stephan, 1998). Additionally, as in individualistic cultures, Brazilian culture also seems to emphasize intimacy. For this reason, comparing North American and Brazilian cultures requires taking into account their multiple divergent and convergent aspects.

In 2005, the World Health Organization (WHO) published statistics for the number of psychologists per 100,000 inhabitants in several countries. A few of these numbers include Argentina (121.2), Denmark (85), Finland (79), Switzerland (76), Norway (68), Germany (51.5), Canada (35), Brazil (31.8), the U.S. (31.1), and Ecuador (29.1). Canada, Brazil, and the U.S. are among the nations with the most psychologists in the world (seventh, eighth, and ninth respectively). Additionally, these countries have a similar proportion of psychologists per capita. The combination of these factors has particular importance to this study, as it likely allows a more equitable cross-cultural analysis.

A five-year undergraduate program in Brazil includes a two-year internship (including a minimum of 500 direct contact hours), which qualifies the candidate for licensure as a psychologist. In 2004, Hutz, McCarthy, and Gomes stated that there were 140,000 licensed psychologists in Brazil. In that same period of time, less than 1% of these psychologists held doctoral degrees (Neto & Arruda, 2006).

Psychology is a respected profession in Brazil. Three types of professional organizations support and regulate the profession (regional councils, the National Association for Graduate Study and Research in Psychology/ANPEPP, and regional syndicates). However, none of these is equivalent to the American Psychological Association (Hutz, McCarthy, & Gomes, 2004). A blend of European and North American traditions has created a unique type of psychology employed in Brazil, where phenomenological, experimental, and psychoanalytic orientations coexist. Although cognitive-behavioral, humanistic, and biological perspectives have gained considerable ground in Brazilian psychological territory, psychoanalytic orientations to clinical practice remain the most frequently used (Hutz, McCarthy, & Gomes, 2004). Perhaps because it can be creatively applied to the understanding of social realities, psychoanalysis in Brazil is more alive than ever (Mendes, 2002). Moreover, "analysis" is synonymous with psychotherapy in Brazil, and it evokes a certain social status (Bastos-Turner, 2008). At the same time, though it appears to be a much-respected occupation, psychology has also been described as a predominantly feminine, young, and underpaid profession in Brazil (Pereira & Neto, 2003).

Due to its emphasis on social responsibility, Brazilian psychology seems to be more oriented toward work with disempowered groups. Psychology in Brazil, particularly psychoanalysis, serves a demand for personal expression that a dictatorial government formerly suppressed. As a movement, it boomed in the '60s and '70s and it is still a force creatively applied to social realities (Mendes, 2002). Ferreira Neto (2008) stated that the field of psychology in Brazil has gradually been reoriented from its classic configuration (i.e., individual treatment, mostly grounded on medical models) to what is called *clinica do social* ("the clinic of the social"). This pragmatic reorientation of the psychological field, influenced by Italian democratic psychiatry, aims to be accessible to the most pauperized and largest segments of the Brazilian population. In this context, therapy and politics, subjectivity and citizenship, intersect. Philosophy, sociology, and psychoanalysis represent different knowledge areas that demand articulation with the professional practice of psychologists (Ferreira Neto, 2008). Psychology has incorporated the North American tenets that regard this field as primarily a science. However, Brazilian psychology has also kept its close ties with the exercise of psychology as art (Hutz & Adair, 1996).

Learning From Clients

From a research scenario eminently focused on psychotherapy outcome and its related issues of efficacy and effectiveness (e.g., Seligman, 1995; Hunsley & Lee, 2007), the scope of psychotherapy research has gradually come to incorporate new areas of investigation. Studies concerning the effects of clients on the personal and professional lives of therapists are likely to develop even further, for example, therapists' self-awareness (Williams, 2008); what's on the therapist's mind (Robert, Elliott, Buysse, Loots, & Corte, 2008); and therapists' dreams about clients (Guy, 1987; Spangler, Hill, Mettus, Guo, & Meymsfield, 2009). Such development will probably foster new areas of investigation with the potential to enrich the conspicuously inadequate knowledge about the effects of psychotherapy upon psychotherapists. Ultimately, it may also bridge the gap between research and practice.

Several master psychologists have affirmed that the very best moments of their professional experiences are associated with being changed by their clients (Freeman & Hayes, 2002; Kottler, 1993;

Yalom, 1989, 2000): "Troubled, yet resilient, clients who work tirelessly through adversity in counseling seem to inspire counselors" (Freeman & Hayes, 2002, p. 13). According to these authors, therapists tend to welcome challenging clients because they ultimately inspire hope, challenge the therapist's basic assumptions, and potentially broaden the therapist's world.

Present Study and Its Inquiry

The aforementioned dissertation followed the same research protocol proposed by Hatcher et al. (2012). A few modifications were related to the translation and interpretation of the original protocol, which were performed by the author of this chapter. Because beliefs and realities are socially and contextually constructed, this study's approach was "discovery-oriented" to the extent to which similarities of experience were conceptualized and theorized (Jennings, D'Rozario, Goh, Sovereign, Brogger, & Skovholt, 2008; Rudestam & Newton, 2007).

Twelve licensed psychologists of various ages and levels of experience, affiliated with the psychoanalytic/psychodynamic theoretical orientation, were interviewed in Brazil. This theoretical orientation was selected because most Brazilian psychologists tend to be psychoanalytic/psychodynamic. Hence, those selected from the larger sample of North American participants in the original research by Hatcher et al. (2012) who ascribed to this theoretical orientation were chosen for this study. Narrowing the theoretical orientation facilitated the cross-cultural analysis between the U.S. and Brazil.

A purposeful sampling strategy was used to identify psychologists with doctoral-level degrees and different ranges of clinical experience in Brazil (Patton, 2002). The material from the interviews collected in Brazil was translated and subsequently coded. Additionally, this study also employed a co-rater/second coder in order to improve accuracy in the coding process. The second coder was asked to read all of the interview transcripts and compare them with the code book. Qualitative methods are designed to study the multilayered, complex, and ongoing subject of human lived experience (Polkinghorne, 2005). The evidence from these experiences, provided through different accounts, was analyzed in order to produce a core description.

The research was anchored in a qualitative methodology. It took an interpretivist perspective on the responses that psychologists from two different cultures gave to the proposed questions (Schwandt, 2000). The starting point of this research was the observation and analysis of data gleaned from interviews, rather than hypotheses (Babbie, 2005). Much more than being simply "collected," the data were integrated in a way that gave them substance and meaning (Kazdin, 2003).

The primary concepts were organized into main themes and categories. The method was largely based on the qualitative analytic method detailed by Miles and Huberman (1994), which uses sequential steps to identify and confirm thematic categories. The categories that emerged from the interviews were established through a manual coding process that emphasized repetitions, similarities, and differences, also noting patterns and clustering (Bernard & Ryan, 2010; Miles & Huberman, 1994).

Participants

The sample participants in Brazil consisted of 12 psychodynamically oriented, doctoral-level licensed psychologists. The majority of respondents had more than 20 years of experience, a sizable minority had 6-10 years of experience, and a few participants had 11-20 years of experience. In terms of age, respondents were evenly divided between two age groups, age 31 to 40 and age 41 to 50. No participant was younger than 30. Somewhat more than half were female.

The sub-sample derived from the original U.S. and Canada was also comprised of 12 psychodynamically-oriented, licensed psychologists. Half of the respondents had 11-20 years of experience, a considerable minority had more than 20 years, and a few participants had 6-10 years. In terms of age, the majority of participants were between 41 and 50, a sizable minority were older than 60, and a few participants were evenly divided between ages 31 to 40 and 51 to 60. More than half of the participants in this sub-sample were female.

Because some differences were found in the participants' narratives, it is possible that they represent the cultural make-up from which they emerged. In regard to gender and its influence on the quality of the narratives, no significant differences were found. As in the original study, both female and male psychologists were candid about their clinical experiences, offered ample case examples, and seemed to be remarkably aware and appreciative of the impact that their clients had in their lives. Hence, gender has not been used as a comparison variable. As mentioned above, the cultural constructs of individualism and collectivism (I-C) are used to establish connections, interpret potential differences, and promote a better understanding of the categories.

The North American and Brazilian participants herein mentioned are each identified by pseudonyms derived from common names in their respective cultures. The use of first name only, instead of "Dr. X," was chosen for two main reasons. First, Brazil has a more informal culture in which it is more natural and expected to call someone by their first name, and the use of "Dr." before the first or last name is more unusual than in North American settings. Second, utilizing first names only may potentially represent an exercise in cultural relativism, as opposed to ethnocentrism.

North American and Brazilian Narratives

The process of establishing differences in the participants' narratives must of necessity remain somewhat tentative, for there is a constant risk of perceiving different narratives through different lenses. The nuances encountered in the North American and Brazilian psychologists' discourses warrant attention, for they are likely enunciating different standpoints from which these two groups process and understand their learning from clients. Of note, both groups of participants had several years of experience in private practice, which is a finding in its own right. Unlike novice and training therapists, they have considerable experience from which to draw when they focus on their learning. Not surprisingly, both Brazilian and North American psychologists noted that they believe they have learned more from their clients than from books.

General Learning

The first question (see also Chapter 1) focused attention on the general learning that psychologists accumulated through their experiences with clients. Participants from the U.S. and Canada stated that their learning inspired changes in their original perspectives. They also focused on resilience, gratitude for previous life experiences that prompted them to become psychologists, the courage involved in coming to therapy, and on overall realizations that a few therapists experienced regarding insight, the process of change, and the origins of self-esteem.

Dr. Michelle, an American psychologist in her 40s with more than 10 years of clinical experience, offered a strong example of the relationship she had with a client and how it helped her to gain insight into her own struggles. She noted having a client whose three children had ADHD. Before Dr. Michelle had her own children, she shared that at first she felt rather judgmental of one client's feelings toward her sons, thinking, "How can you say that about your children?. . This is pathological. . . She doesn't have empathy for her own children. . . She is being too harsh and punitive. . . blah, blah." Although acknowledging this client's "hard edge," when Dr. Michelle later had a son with ADHD, she reported reflecting on this client's comments, and noted that they helped her to gain perspective on her own experience. Dr. Aviva, another American psychologist with over 20 years of clinical experience, shared her view of therapists as "fellow travelers" who unavoidably change as the therapeutic process evolves.

From Dr. Michelle's learning experience with a client whose son had ADHD, and later having the experience of her own son having ADHD, to Dr. Aviva's view of therapists as "fellow travelers," North American psychologists shared their shortcomings, their therapeutic errors, and how their practices helped them to improve their views on technique and on their own roles in the therapeutic process. These psychologists also referred to insight, self-esteem, and change processes.

Many of the participants from the U.S. and Canada courageously shared their experiences of learning from clients by noting that they feel changed by them. These changes reportedly occurred in the ways they incorporated new perspectives into their personal and professional lives (e.g., by becoming more compassionate with themselves or by realizing that both therapists and clients are changed in the therapeutic process). Interestingly, the tone and nuances of their narratives seemed chiefly to reflect technical elements of the therapeutic process (e.g., therapeutic errors) and a more structural realm of psychotherapy concerning individual strengths (e.g., resilience, self-esteem, courage) and weaknesses (lack of insight, etc.). Obviously they addressed process-oriented instances (e.g., changes in the therapist, the process of career choice, etc.); however, the North American psychologists' main thematic categories tended to be focused on *figure* (i.e., the therapeutic process and individual potential) rather than on *ground* (i.e., the context of psychotherapy and its role).

The nature of the categories gleaned from the narratives of Brazilian psychologists is thought provoking. Although most of them also focused on being changed by their clients and inevitably altering their perspectives, there appeared to be a more visceral and boundless component to their stories, as they referred to the expansion of their own lives through the lives of clients. Additionally, several of them focused on the role of psychotherapy and psychoanalysis, and on the limits of being a therapist. In comparison to their North American counterparts, Brazilian psychologists focused more on ground than on figure. Moreover, such a ground seems to more boundlessly connect the person of the therapist with the person of the client. Of course, not all Brazilian participants would perfectly fit this description. However, those are the group trends and voices that stood out to this researcher that were confirmed by the second coder.

As noted earlier, the Brazilian psychologists seem to have had a more unified pattern of response to this first question, with fewer emerging categories. This finding would be more striking if it had continued throughout the transcripts; however, that was not the case, as both groups eventually found a balance in terms of the number of categories. Because this first question was open-ended and more general, it is important to note that Brazilian psychologists seemed to share more similarities than divergences in regard to their first impressions on what they learn from clients. Because more categories and outliers were found in the North American sample, it could be implied that a more fluid expression of heterogenic standpoints may well be the result of a more individualistic cultural fabric.

Furthermore, only psychoanalysts were interviewed in Brazil, whereas the interviewees from the U.S. and Canada were psychologists who were affiliated with both psychoanalytic/psychodynamic theoretical orientations and other theory orientations, such as CBT. This may bring up several important issues. Firstly, being a psychoanalyst may prompt psychologists to be more philosophic, visceral and, perhaps, more boundless. To this end, it remains unclear whether their connection with clients and the perception of their learning with them is determined by their degree of individualism/collectivism or by the culture of their professional disciplines. The response patterns to the following questions are expected to shed light on this issue.

Secondly, because psychoanalysis is not as much in the mainstream in American psychology as it was several decades ago, more dissonant views of its foundational tenets are to be expected. Additionally, there is possibly less cohesion among U.S. psychoanalysts as a group than among the Brazilian participants. However, it is important to note that Brazilian psychoanalytic territory is not a unified and theoretically linear block of knowledge, either. Not unlike American psychoanalysis (Greenberg & Mitchell, 1983), different theoretical approaches, with their own perspectives, languages, and formulations, are characteristic of Brazilian psychoanalysis as well.

Relationships

In the question about relationships (see also Chapter 2), North American psychologists focused on the complexity of human relationships and on the struggle to find balance in these relationships. They talked about the processes of approximation and withdrawal, noted that these processes are present in every relationship, and reported learning that perfect relationships do not exist. The narratives of North American participants emphasized instrumental factors such as the importance of having good communication between partners, and the primacy of love in order to hold things together. Participants from this group shared a sense of surprise at what they discover in their work with clients, especially that being close to another human being can often be terrifying. They also noted that accepting reality involves letting go of idealized and romanticized images. Finally, they conveyed that their clients have prompted them to improve their own relationships.

Not as restricted to the territory of love and romantic relationships, Brazilian participants focused their narratives on more general relationship configurations. Only a few of these participants focused on couples. This finding may be explained by both language differences and by cultural context. Brazilian participants expressed a rather fluid concept of relationships, and this fact probably has several cultural explanations. As a collectivistic culture, Brazilians are in relationships with one another all the time. They are also less strict in regard to the hierarchical lines that define the status of different relationships. Although the idea of family and its structure remains an important Brazilian institution (DaMatta, 1991), other relationships (friends, neighbors, co-workers) are often perceived to be within the family group (DaMatta, 1991; Van Horn & Marques, 2000).

Because of the possible influence of language differences in the word *relationship*, Brazilian participants were prompted to focus on romantic and close relationships. In spite of this, these participants still tended to approach this issue more generally than did North American participants. Several participants understood this question as a supplement to the first question, and their themes emphasized the close and powerful relationships they had developed with their clients. They also more readily referred to their personal lives as being much changed by their clinical experience. "This is all very beautiful," as Alfredo, a Brazilian psychologist, noted, adding that "there is no way" for therapists not to question their own lives when they are dealing with the lives (and relational matrices) of others.

Although these differences seem substantial, there were a few points of convergence in the narratives of Brazilian and North American participants. Both groups seemed to agree that romantic relationships are extremely complex, paradoxical, unconscious, and formed either by connection and disconnection, or by pursuit and withdrawal. However, the Brazilian participants once again emphasized the multiple characters of love relationships and their inherent transmutability. Several participants also noted that therapeutic work promotes a certain "lightness" in relationships. It is important to note that the majority of Brazilian participants used the word "lightness" in their discourses which, in the context of their interviews, generally meant freedom and/or absence of rigidity.

Overall, it appears that participants from the U.S., Canada, and Brazil emphasized different aspects of relationships. Whereas North American psychologists focused on the pragmatic and behavioral components of relationships, Brazilian psychologists focused on the therapist-client relationship, and on the role of psychotherapy in changing people's relationships and lives in general. The responses to this question suggest another thought-provoking marker, as the idea of relationships in the discourses of Brazilian psychologists seems to be less defined and bounded than in the discourses of North American psychologists. Although an immediate correlation with collectivism cannot be assured, this finding suggests that a more collectivistic culture may also be understood through the ways in which individuals feel connected with and related to one another. This confirms previous studies which proposed that collectivistic cultures stimulate a great deal of relatedness (Markus & Kitayama, 1991; Matsumoto et al., 2008; Fischer et al., 2009). In this manner, the culture of the professional discipline of psychoanalysis (i.e., North Americans being psychodynamic and Brazilians being analytical) does not seem to play a distinguishing role.

Moral and Ethical Dilemmas

The third question (see also Chapter 3) introduced the much more specific issue of moral and ethical dilemmas. North American participants focused on the importance of an awareness of gray areas because everything is contextual. They pondered the concepts of right and wrong, and expressed complex and mature views of what constitute moral or ethical violations. Additionally, they talked about the roles of guilt and shame, and of integrity and courage. Overall, they emphasized the intricacies of ethical behavior, an ability to understand their clients' context while suspending their own personal judgment, and an awareness of how human suffering can prompt therapists to step outside of their professional boundaries.

Interestingly, the narratives of Brazilian participants could be condensed into one category, which highlighted the theme of the inherent struggle involved in being a therapist and having to deal with ethical and moral issues which, at times, collide with the therapist's views. These participants seemed to be more explicit about the ways in which they explained the interplay of therapists' and clients' ethical boundaries, and about how their relationships with clients have changed them. Not unlike the North American participants, they also referred to the knowledge that experience has afforded them in regard to gray, less black-and-white areas, and they noted that therapists cannot act as a moral tribune.

Brazilian participants also shared the difficulties involved with listening to clients who cross moral and ethical boundaries. It is possible that these participants were referring to the ethical relativism present in Brazilian and other collectivistic cultures, in which loyalty to one's group tends to override social rules (Scheper-Hughes, 1992; Hofstede, 2009). Whether or not ethical relativism permeated and potentially explained their comments, Brazilian participants seemed to have tackled a very important issue when, surprisingly, they raised more clear boundaries between their ethics and that of their clients. Carmen and Joana, Brazilian psychologists, even reported questioning whether they could go on listening to certain clients. In a more subtle way, the common factor throughout their narratives seemed to be a reflection on the role of psychotherapy and analysis for both clients and therapists. Of note, the ethics code for Brazilian psychologists was reformulated and a new version, the third in the history of psychology in Brazil, was implemented in 2005, which is shorter, less descriptive, but relatively similar to the APA and CPA ethics codes.

Coping Mechanisms

The fourth question (see also Chapter 4) was also content-specific, and focused on coping mechanisms. North American participants noted that psychotherapy fosters the development of coping skills in both clients and therapists, highlighting the fact that therapists can learn new coping mechanisms from their clients. They shared about learning from their clients how to improve their tool boxes of coping mechanisms. They also reported being inspired by their clients' coping strategies. At the same time, they noted that certain coping mechanisms can turn into psychopathology. North American participants discussed the importance of being open, mindful, and even humorous in relationships with others, noting that these are important coping mechanisms. Overall, North American participants talked more directly about different coping mechanisms. Additionally, they highlighted the role of psychotherapy in the teaching of those coping mechanisms.

Brazilian participants similarly emphasized the role of the therapeutic process in the teaching of coping mechanisms, stressing the fact that their experiences with clients fostered their own emotional development. They noted that their clinical practices have prompted them to develop an emotional reserve that helps them to deal both with their own lives and with their interventions with clients. Participants from this group also emphasized the role of psychotherapy in bringing to consciousness what is still unconscious, and in fostering hope. Not surprisingly, some participants highlighted the context of private practice and an overall contemporary subjectivity. Only one participant more directly emphasized coping mechanisms, highlighting the role of infancy in their development (i.e., the extent to which childhood experiences shape personality and correspondent coping styles).

In analyzing this response pattern, it can be noted that Brazilian participants did not focus on coping mechanisms per se, but rather on the overall learning of coping strategies that they accumulated through their work with clients. Although there seems to be a certain resemblance between this concept and what North American participants reported (i.e., that therapeutic work fosters the development of coping mechanisms for both clients and therapists), Brazilian participants more peripherally touched on specific coping mechanisms. However, language differences may have played a role in their responses. The word *coping* is often accepted without translation in Brazilian psychological academic settings; though several participants required that this expression be elucidated. Hence, it was rephrased as "mechanisms to deal with problems and adversities." Despite this rephrasing, many participants referred to defense mechanisms, a term most likely learned during their psychoanalytic training. Interestingly, a few North American participants also referred to defense mechanisms as well.

Overall, within a rather tangential style of response in regard to coping mechanisms, Brazilian participants once again focused on collective subjectivity and the role of psychotherapy. Additionally, they more readily addressed their learning as a byproduct of psychotherapy, noting that the therapeutic relationship fosters the development of an emotional reserve. Conversely, North American psychologists placed more emphasis on the curative sphere of psychotherapy, especially in the role of therapists as providers of coping strategies. It remains unclear whether this finding refers to different cultural fabrics or to the different levels of cohesiveness, power, and influence of their respective professional disciplines (e.g., psychodynamic psychotherapy as compared to psychoanalysis).

Courage

The fifth question (see also Chapter 5) focused on courage. Several North American participants asserted that coming to therapy is an exercise in courage because it requires one to confront and lay bare the difficult and shameful parts of oneself. They explained that their clients' courage to keep coming to therapy inspires therapists to face anything, and gives them hope in helping other clients. One North American participant noted that courage might actually entail not confronting things, but "sucking it up and taking time."

Brazilian participants also reported learning that coming to therapy is an expression of courage; the courage to dissolve bad situations, to leave one's comfort zone and "plunge into the sea." However, one main difference seems to have emerged: Brazilian participants referred to the therapist's daily courage to listen to disturbing life stories and still be able to offer support. They noted that the privilege of being a therapist required courage. The responses to this fifth question resulted in rather similar and consistent narratives, and the subject of courage seems to have been distributed, in both groups, across several questions, especially the first one. However, the participants' responses suggest that Brazilian psychologists tend to feel slightly more comfortable with their own personal limits, as they referred to the courage needed in order to keep listening to their clients. Again, there appears to be no clear causality to explain this discrepancy in content. Nonetheless, we may hypothesize that the concepts of relationality and intersubjectivity, along with the shift to affectivity (Mitchell, 2003), may be further developed in the context of North American psychoanalysis.

Additionally, the findings for this question may be aligned with the cultural contexts from which they derived. For instance, whereas North American participants referred to courage as necessary to confront shameful parts of oneself, Brazilian participants more often alluded to a perspective of rupturing comfort zones and "breaking up situations." While subtle, this may reference the social and "radical" role of psychoanalysis in Brazil.

Personality Style and Psychopathology

The sixth question (see also Chapter 7) focused on personality style and psychopathology. North American participants emphasized the connection between personality style and psychopathology, stating that psychopathology is merely a personality style that doesn't work. Several participants also noted that some personality styles—sensitive, temperamental, depressive, introverted, and poor affect regulation skills—seem to be more prone to develop psychopathology. "They are predictable conflicts that can be expected within a character style," American participant Dr. Oliver noted. Some participants also shared that their clients gave them a certain level of validation for their own perceived differences as therapists. A few participants referred to the struggles that women and men face in contemporary society, as they discussed the fact that anything against the norm tends to be pathologized. One North American participant reported being struck by the endurance of personality patterns, and at how difficult it is for people to be aware of their own personality style.

Brazilian participants vehemently emphasized their hesitancy to adhere to psychodiagnostic labels, explaining that these labels can hinder the way therapists listen to their clients. They argued that diagnostic labels prompt therapists to overlook unique ways of experiencing suffering. They defended the idea that the process-oriented understanding of each individual, where they were raised and lived, along with the amazing changes people are capable of, justifies their disinterest in categorical structures and stereotypes. One Brazilian participant more directly but still allusively noted that personality differences can be clearly perceived in the transference relationship, and the impact of such transference reverberates in the person of the therapist. Of note, some participants focused on the role of individualism in contemporary society, how it places individual pleasures above any collective good and, consequently, enables psychopathology to develop everywhere.

An analysis of the narratives of these two groups suggests that they seem to agree about the interconnection between personality styles and psychopathology; however, while North American participants touched on the risk of pathologizing anything that goes against the norm, Brazilian participants seemed more cognizant of their hesitance to adhere to psychodiagnostic manuals. Furthermore, Brazilian participants focused on the process of psychotherapy and its role in challenging the limits imposed by different psychopathologies and taking structural organizations to the limit. Additionally, some participants highlighted the fact that contemporary society and contemporary subjectivity are likely to promote certain pathologies. As expected, North American participants chiefly focused on the structural instances of personality and psychopathology, especially when they approached the likelihood of certain personality styles to develop psychopathology.

In the narratives of North American participants, there was little reference to the social context in the development of psychopathology, whereas in the narratives of the Brazilian psychologists in the sample presented an emphasis on the social context. Additionally, although North American participants were alert to the risk of over-pathologizing differences and traits that are against the norm, they seem on the whole to more fully comply with the status quo of psychodiagnostic categories. After all, they have all been trained in the *Diagnostic and Statistical Manual of Mental Disorders* (DSM). Ethnocentrisms apart, the fact is that psychodiagnosis is considered the prime work of the majority of competent and respectable North American psychologists, and it is important to be mindful of the cultural context from which these narratives emerged. Therefore, Brazilian participants may have more freedom to differ and work apart from diagnostic labels. However, it is important to note that Brazilian psychologists also utilize the DSM, which constitutes the main source of diagnostic classification in that country.

Additionally, and as previously noted, the fact that the North American group of participants is likely not as homogenous as its Brazilian counterpart may also have implications for the content of their narratives. It is important to keep in mind that culture-specific or emic values and beliefs about mental health cannot be readily applied in the diagnosis of culturally different individuals, and overcoming ethnocentrism in psychological research remains a challenge (Gardiner & Kosmitzki, 2005; Hanks, 2008; Vicary & Bishop, 2005). Finally, the fact that Brazilian participants once again referred to the social context as a vital enabler of psychopathology highlights the importance of cultural background in the understanding of subjectivities.

Cultural Differences

The seventh question (see also Chapter 7) focused on cultural differences. North American participants reported learning with clients from a different culture than theirs, i.e., clients from either a foreign country or different ethnicity. These participants noted that they learned how to better understand differences in regard to the concepts of self, family, child-rearing, marriage, and even how one perceives psychotherapy. They shared that these experiences prompted them to develop a greater respect for cultural differences. One of the participants talked about affluent clients and defined them as a different culture than his. Moreover, in sharing their thoughts about cultural differences, North American participants contended that it is important to pay attention to differences by valuing one's culture of origin because it has a pervasive impact on one's life. Despite these differences, they also reported learning that human beings share several similarities. Finally, one participant succinctly indicated the fine and often difficult balance between therapists' and clients' belief systems (e.g., when the therapist is a liberal and the client is a conservative Christian).

Brazilian psychologists also reported learning from clients who were different from themselves in terms of race, ethnicity, language, sexual orientation, and gender. They noted that this learning helped them to better understand their own place in the world. Some participants highlighted learning experiences in working with clients with different sexual orientations and different genders, and one of these participants noted that people, in the end, tend to be very similar. Several Brazilian participants focused on the importance of an awareness of how cultural differences are perceived by both clients and therapists, noting that the individual's emotional experience of cultural differences is more important than the differences themselves. One participant stated that if one tries to get rid of the past, this past invariably ends up "coming out through [one's] sweat." Finally, several participants described the cultural context of private practice as an environment generally populated by the wealthy. Due to this, they shared learning that the context of private practice has its limitations, which can be better dealt with when psychologists also work in different settings, such as community mental health centers or non-profit organizations. One of these participants reported learning that, in the context of private practice, symbolic misery is more pervasive than economic misery.

In analyzing this question's response pattern, it appears that both groups focused on their learning from clients who are diverse in culture, be it a diversity of geography, race, ethnicity, or sexuality. Additionally, both North American and Brazilian participants seemed to agree that people ultimately have more in common than appearances alone may suggest. Brazilian participants talked about a greater array of cultural differences, which included sexual orientation, language, and gender. This may not suggest that Brazilian participants are more attuned to cultural differences, but it does suggest that these participants appear to feel more comfortable discussing more diverse aspects of culture. Additionally, they may be exposed to diverse elements of culture more often than the North American participants. In the narratives of North American participants there was mention of the potential struggle when therapists and clients have radically different belief systems; however, this issue was very briefly touched upon. Brazilian participants tended to emphasize the importance of self-awareness of one's culture, and they also talked about the context of private practice as a niche for the affluent.

Both groups appeared to be deeply affected by their learning from clients who were culturally different. The fact that a greater array of cultural differences seemed to have been evident in the narratives of Brazilian participants presents only a tentative understanding of this difference. As explained above, both groups of psychologists may be equally attuned to cultural differences; however, it is possible that, in comparison with Brazilian participants, North American participants lack exposure to cultural differences. It is also possible that cultural differences are more easily and smoothly incorporated into Brazilian culture. After all, it is well-known that Brazilian cultural make-up is marked by incongruities, and that such a culture is predisposed to cultural integration and biculturality (McGoldrick, Giordano, & Garcia-Preto, 2005; Mendes, 2002; Pellegrini, 2000). Furthermore, contextual factors involved in private practice, i.e., the culture of private practice, constitute another important element of comparison. Although one North American participant described his affluent clients as a different culture, there was no clear mention of the context of private practice in the narratives of North American participants.

Life Stages

The eighth question focused on life stages (see also Chapter 6). North American participants differed as to whether their clinical experience ratifies the existence of stages or rather questions that existence by pointing out its arbitrariness. Some participants focused on midlife clients who taught them the importance of "[gazing] inward" as opposed to "conquering externally." Other participants reported learning from older clients about their own plans (and fears) regarding getting old and/or dying. In highlighting the importance of identity development, independent of chronological age, participants went from conceptualizing this within Erikson's framework ("Erikson had a lot right") to questioning the very existence of stages ("Do they exist?. . . I don't think they are right or accurate"). Nonetheless, North American participants seemed to agree that different phases of life are more complex and multilayered than any categorical stage can anticipate. Additionally, participants shared that their experience in clinical practice prompted them to value what their clients can teach them rather than any theoretical knowledge.

Several of the Brazilian participants expressed different opinions about which life stage, from adolescence to older adulthood, they considered to present more challenges. More importantly, several participants reported learning that, regardless of the client's age or stage, they deeply affect the therapist's life, from the "lovely life force" present in a 20-year-old to older clients who function as a footnote for their therapists. Similar to the North American participants, several Brazilian psychologists also noted that they had learned that spirals and circles, rather than stages, may represent a better conceptualization of life's growth. Additionally, on a more pragmatic note, one participant reported learning that he changes his techniques as he works with clients at different life stages. Finally, and not surprisingly, a few participants expressed their concerns regarding what they called an extension of adolescence in both directions: "The acceleration of what once was called childhood. . . and the monumental delay of what would be getting old." They contended that, in contemporary society, children want to become adolescents prematurely (e.g., in terms of dress code, expressions, etc.), while midlife individuals engage in desperate attempts to look and feel younger, like adolescents.

Both North American and Brazilian participants seem to agree that therapists learn from clients who are in different life stages (or spirals), because in cases where they are older than their clients they can relive an earlier stage, or in cases where they are younger than their clients they can anticipate aging scenarios. Additionally, the two groups also appeared to hold similar viewpoints in regard to life stages, and they emphasized the primacy of life's processes. This question seemed to have generated a vigorous discussion for both North American and Brazilian psychologists. Brazilian participants, in particular, seemingly aligned the concepts of categorical life stages with the notion of diagnostic categories. North American participants instead focused on different ages, questioned the existence of stages, and proposed the existence of changes in relational configurations. Thus, both groups emphasized processes rather than stages. Some of them also shared that their experience has taught them more than their books. Brazilian participants focused on crucial and problematic life stages, proposed the existence of spirals instead, and raised cultural and contextual notes about the extension of adolescence in contemporary society.

Although in response to this question Brazilian and North American participants presented several intersecting lines of thought, differences of opinion could also once again be found in contextual notes about society in general. In this instance, Brazilian participants seemed to be more comfortable trying to make sense of the world outside the walls of their private practice. This may have to do with the history of psychology in that country. First, it is important to keep in mind that notions of privacy, and what one's private space means, greatly differ between Brazilian and North American culture, whereby Brazilians seem to be less concerned with privacy boundaries. Brazilian culture emphasizes how considerate one can be, and acknowledging others' needs, moods, and problems is a key criterion of good behavior (McGoldrick, Giordano, & Garcia-Preto, 2005).

Furthermore, because Brazilian culture is, after all, predominately interdependent and collectivistic, it can be expected that the psychologists interviewed there would portray a more prominent focus on relatedness, harmony, and the improvement of the larger group (Ribas, Jr., 2010). More specifically, within the context of that country's concept of psychoanalysis, psychoanalytic thought has been applied to the understanding of social realities, given that psychoanalysis served as a space for the expression of realities and potentialities that the dictatorial government had suppressed from the 1960s to the 1980s (Mendes, 2002).

Additional Learning

Similarly to the first question, the ninth and last question was open-ended (see also Chapter 10), North American psychologists emphasized the fact that they have acquired a wealth of knowledge from their clients, including a better understanding of gender differences, human suffering, and the parallel ways in which clients and therapists grow and mature together. Noting their assumptions that their clients are unaware of their effect on them, North American participants also reported learning that "you just never know what people are capable of and you have to let them surprise you." Notably, a few participants focused on the role of psychotherapy in prompting clients to see outside the box and beyond black-and-white thinking. Additionally, they noted the importance of being careful, respectful, and ethical in their work with clients. A few other participants talked about emotional and biological instances that can represent obstacles to growth, and one participant reported learning that "every person is capable of being liked."

Brazilian participants chiefly focused on describing psychotherapy as an art of reciprocal influence, sharing that their clients have helped them to learn and grow as therapists. Joana, a Brazilian psychologist, described the therapeutic encounter as a "bioactivity" which "is as important to them [clients] as it is to me." Along with their North American counterparts, Brazilian participants also expressed the idea that their clients know very little about the extent to which they influence therapists' lives. Additionally, some participants focused on the ethical role of the therapist in caring for and respecting clients' lives. Finally, Brazilian participants focused on psychotherapy as a way of helping clients to face the worst within themselves so that they can begin the process of healing. The role of psychotherapy in contemporary society was also highlighted, because it opens space for the exercise of calm, reflection, and reconstruction.

An analysis of the narratives of North American and Brazilian participants reveals meaningful similarities. Both groups candidly shared how profoundly affected they have been by their psychotherapy clients, and that their experiences with clients have promoted considerable growth, both personal and professional. Both groups also emphasized the importance of being careful and extremely ethical in the therapeutic setting, because clients' lives are exposed, and significant damage can take place. Remarkably, both North American and Brazilian psychologists talked about the role of psychotherapy in stimulating clients to think outside the box by challenging dualistic ways of perceiving life experiences, and in promoting reflection and calm while clients delve into their "box[es]" and "dream." Brazilian participants specifically noted that psychotherapy represents a movement that goes against the tide.

It is noteworthy that so many narratives were strikingly consonant in this last question. Differences, of course, also appeared; however, they came from single voices/outliers that referred to more structural and pragmatic domains of psychotherapy (i.e., biological and emotional obstacles to growth). The main themes were closely aligned and complemented each other as part of a cultural quilt-making that ultimately seemed to reveal a cohesive and lively culture of psychology or psychoanalysis in both countries. This finding potentially represents the bridge between worlds referred to in the introduction of this chapter.

Weaving Cultures: Individualism, Collectivism, Psychotherapy, and Learning

Several research studies maintain that psychotherapy in countries with an individualistic cultural make-up is generally geared toward the development of a sense of agency, along with the development of clients' control over their thought processes, emotions, and behaviors. In the U.S., "entrepreneurial selves" (Cushman, 1995) are promoted and primed to resist any scenario associated with powerlessness and vulnerability (Harris, 2009). Hence, concepts of communality and relatedness can be easily linked to vulnerability, because they contradict the paradigm of self-sufficiency. The cultural construct of powerful selves seems to better fit the quest for self-sufficiency, while relatedness and connection with others may often be deemphasized.

In analyzing research findings, it may be hypothesized that the underdeveloped research on what therapists learn from their clients has something to do with these ideas of vulnerability and powerlessness. As

Orlinsky et al. (2005) noted, the trademarks of contemporary scientific culture are objectivity, impersonality, and efficacy. The processes of allowing oneself to learn and subsequently acknowledging such learning are more closely related to concepts such as subjectivity, absence of neutrality, and being a person in the therapeutic setting. The cultural make-up in vogue in both the scientific community and in North American society as a whole may help to explain why psychotherapy research has been biased toward therapies rather than therapists.

In collectivist cultures, the emphasis is generally placed on strengthening of the client's self while at the same time emphasizing communality. Additionally, psychotherapy tends to be geared toward the development of agency and becoming a constructive member of society (Sato, 1998). As is well known, Brazilian culture tends to value a sense of belonging, and social values are the main guiding principles. Additionally, a larger number of collectivistic practices are considered primary, the in-group is stressed as a survival unit, and the welfare of the collective is the supreme value. Moreover, psychology in Brazil has also been characterized as pluralistic and critical of rigid theoretical frontiers (de Sa, 2007).

The analysis of participants' narratives indicated that nearly all of the categories that emerged from Brazilian participants contained references either to the social role of psychotherapy or psychoanalysis or to the context of private practice and contemporary subjectivity. In contrast, very few categories of this nature emerged from the narratives of American participants. The findings of this research have confirmed the importance of highlighting Brazilian and North American cultural contexts in psychology as media for a better comprehension of the immense complexity present in the territory of cross-cultural psychology.

As noted earlier, one of the ramifications and meanings of being a psychologist in Brazil involves being a socially and politically charged professional, as there seem to be opportunities that highlight and prime a contextually focused approach to psychology (Gouveia, Albuquerque, Clemente, & Espinosa, 2002; Gouveia, Vasconcelos, Queiroga, Franca, & Oliveira, 2003; Stevens & Wedding, 2004; Vikan, Camino, & Biaggio, 2005). Thus, Brazilian psychology tends to be closely aligned with social justice (de Sa, 2007) and the attempt to utilize psychology, psychotherapy, and analysis as instruments of social change (Mezan, 1998).

Brazilian psychology and especially psychoanalysis serve a demand for personal expression, which was suppressed by the decades of dictatorial government. It comes as no surprise that therapy, politics, philosophy, sociology, psychoanalysis, subjectivity, and citizenship intersect in the context of Brazilian psychology (Ferreira Neto, 2008). Even though the territory of psychology in Brazil has incorporated North American tenets that more closely align this field with science, Brazilian psychology seems to have kept its identity closer to the exercise of art (Hutz & Adair, 1996). The lyricism seen in the interviews of Brazilians participants constitute a good example of this.

The current study has confirmed previous research regarding the fact that psychotherapists learn from their clients, and the idea that therapists rely extensively on practical experience with clients when trying to address difficult therapeutic situations (Morrow-Bradley & Elliott, 1986; Skovholt & McCarthy, 1988). It has also provided corroboration for the fact that psychologists change—"undergo transformations"—as they conduct clinical work (Guy, 1987).

Several participants in this research shared the impression that their clients are unaware of their influence on them. Here lies perhaps one of the most powerful areas for future exploration. As Casement (1991) noted, positive therapeutic gain is associated with clients' becoming aware that therapists can learn from them. Such learning can only take place through the exercise of empathy which, not surprisingly, corresponds to the main mechanism that promotes change for both clients and therapists (Kahn & Fromm, 2001). Perhaps, at some level, clients who greatly benefit from the therapeutic process have learned about their influence on their therapists; in other words, perhaps these clients have learned that the expansion of their own personalities also facilitated the broadening of the personalities and lives of their therapists.

Several participants in this research stated passionately that they have learned and changed because of their work with clients. North American and Brazilian psychologists both provided numerous examples of situations in which they found themselves changed. Of course, the process of change through learning is not readily evident; instead, changes are potentially perceived through the presence of new thoughts, feelings, and attitudes (Wick, 2001). As Victoria, an American psychologist, stated:

I think my clients always make me stop, not to minimize my issues or problems, but to know that it's possible to get through things and get a different perspective—to grieve something and feel better. Just that it is possible. I don't think I knew that going in to this profession.

Paul, another American psychologist, contended:

I am not sure if I've learned this from one client but more from seeing many clients in psychotherapy for so many years. . . it's just a continual process throughout life of always looking at yourself and always trying to understand yourself and deepen that understanding, and then along that way things begin to shift. And life is slowly transformed, our problems are slowly transformed, and conflicts are slowly resolved.

Finally, as Poeta, a Brazilian psychologist, stated: "I find myself wondering about my life when I listen to the suffering of others; it adds new elements into my own life."

In the current research, experienced therapists tended to offer a great array of thematic connections, and they tended to conceptualize their clients, their experiences, and their learning in very complex ways. This makes sense in light of Rønnestad and Skovholt's (2003) research. These authors proposed eight developmentally oriented phases of therapist development, from the "conventional helper," which encompasses different levels of training, to the more advanced levels of post-graduate phases, which are defined by exploration, integration, individuation, and integrity. Moreover, although the participants in the current research often expressed a hesitancy to comply with categories and developmental stages, it seems relevant to note that several narratives from both North American and Brazilian psychologists appeared to fit into more advanced stages, spirals, or circles of professional development. Rønnestad and Skovholt (2003) maintained that professional development and growth take place when openness to new experiences and learning is demonstrated. That corresponds to one of the categories that emerged in this study (i.e., "Clients give therapists the chance to expand their own lives, as long they are open to the unexpected"). Regardless of how they decide to approach psychotherapy, therapists do take risks and, in doing so, they step into a different realm of engagement that begets multifold learning opportunities.

Throughout the interviews that North American and Brazilian participants offered, there appeared to be another recurring theme. Many therapists talked about the role of psychotherapy and psychoanalysis in changing people's lives, in offering different perspectives to overcome dualistic thinking, and in fostering a space of reflection that potentially creates singularity and difference (i.e., by going against the tide). Additionally, in helping people to connect with themselves, psychotherapy potentially helps them to be more connected with others. This seems to represent a different take on the role of psychotherapy from its beginning at the end of the 19th century. Then, the emergence of individualities, overshadowing of communal goals, and alienation from the world as individuals became more self-centered and avid for gratification, aligned psychotherapy with individualistic goals (Arendt, 1998). Now it appears that psychotherapy potentially represents a force that promotes not only connection but generosity, and ultimately mental health.

Of note, both North American and Brazilian participants seemed to be equally disclosing and courageous in their answers. It appeared obvious that they have learned from their clients. There are, of course, different varieties of wisdom that preceded the therapists' experience with their clients. However, the analysis of their narratives suggests that it was only through their relationships with their clients that they found validation and actual connection with those theories. As Sigmund Freud maintained in *Studies on Hysteria* (1895/2000), his clients were his "instructors," teaching him about the meaning of symptoms and about therapeutic techniques: "Listening became, for Freud, more than an art, it became a method, a privileged road that his patients mapped out for him" (Gay, 2006, p. 70). Listening to clients and to the differences each one of them provides seems to be a privileged road, indeed. The maturation of psychoanalytic thought over a hundred years has indicated that such a road needs to be continually built by both therapists and clients. Their interaction, connection, alliance, "the analytic third" or, simply, relationship, engenders a type of learning that is capable of changing the lives of those involved in this process.

There seems to be an emergent need for psychologists to become more aware of different cultural contexts as they also become aware that not all psychological phenomena can be explained by only one paradigm (McGruder, 2004; Stevens & Wedding, 2004; Watters, 2010a, 2010b). Exploring other realities—the focus of this research—allows for the development of other forms of intervention that may better meet, for instance, the needs of immigrants or other minorities. Additionally, it offers a new understanding of how the profession of psychology can be based on remarkable points of agreement between two very different nations, and yet display significant differences in regard to the understanding of psychologists', psychotherapists', or analysts' roles in society.

This cross-cultural study gives voice to different sociocultural identities that contribute to the development of therapists and, accordingly, their clients. It potentially offers new ways to understand the role of therapy for psychotherapists, as it provides new insight and likely more clarity on the effects therapy has on therapists' lives and professions. Moreover, the efforts involved in the investigation of a culture that is characterized as less individualistic than that of North America (the U.S. and Canada) may imply applicability to other cultures that are more community-oriented.

This study has attempted the construction of a cultural quilt that enlightens not only how therapists in various stages of professional development experience their learning with clients, but also how they perceive such an influence across two different cultures, those of Brazil and North America. It has helped in the development of a sensibility that is apparently rare in the field of psychotherapy, namely the humanization of the healing connection between two persons (McWilliams, 2005a). The statements of both Brazilian and North American participants seem to be powerful evidence of the role psychotherapy has in therapists' lives.

The territory of qualitative research is inherently a fertile ground for critical conversations about democracy, ethnicity, globalization, community, and freedom. It is through this lens that researchers observe the world, make it more visible and, potentially, transform it. In interpreting and making meaning of the world, qualitative research can also be a force to confront the evidence-based movement (Denzin & Lincoln, 2005).

References

Ali, A. (2001). Medical psychology in Canada. *Journal of Clinical Psychology in Medical Settings, 8,* 15-20.

Arendt, H. (1998). *The human condition* (2nd ed.). Chicago, IL: The University of Chicago.

Babbie, E. (2005). *The basics of social research* (3rd ed.). Belmont, CA: Thomson Wadsworth.

Bastos-Turner, G. (2008). *Cross-cultural comparison of stigma towards mental illness and help-seeking between Americans and Brazilians.* Doctoral dissertation, University of the Rockies. Proquest 3308538.

Baudrillard, J. (1989). *America.* New York, NY: Verso.

Bernard, H. R., & Ryan, G. W. (2010). *Analyzing qualitative data: Systematic approaches.* Thousand Oaks, CA: Sage.

Bornstein, M. H. (2010). *Handbook of cultural developmental science.* New York, NY: Taylor & Francis Group.

Brewer, M. B., & Chen, Y-R. (2007). Where (who) are collectives in collectivism? Toward conceptual clarification of individualism and collectivism. *Psychological Review, 114,* 133–151.

Casement, P. J. (1991). *Learning from the patient.* New York, NY: Guilford Press.

Cheng, S-T., & Kwan, K.W.K. (2008). Attachment dimensions and contingencies of self- worth: The moderating role of culture. *Personality and Individual Differences, 45,* 509-514.

Cushman, P. (1995). *Constructing the self, constructing America: A cultural history of psychotherapy.* Reading, MA: Addison-Wesley.

DaMatta, R. (1991). *Carnivals, rogues, and heroes: An interpretation of the Brazilian dilemma.* Notre Dame, IN: University of Notre Dame Press.

DaMatta, R. (1997). *A Casa e a rua: Espaco, cidadania, mulher e morte no Brasil* [*The house and the street: Space, citizenship, women, and death in Brazil*]. Rio de

Janeiro: Editora Guanabara. Denzin, N. K., & Lincoln, Y. S. (Eds.). (2005). *The Sage handbook of qualitative research* (3rd ed.). Thousand Oaks, CA: Sage Publications. de Sa, C. P. (2007). Sobre a psicologia no Brasil: Entre memorias historicas e pessoais [On social psychology in Brazil: Among historic and personal memories]. *Psicologia e Sociedade, 19,* 7-13.

Ferreira Neto, J. L. (2008). Praticas transversalizadas da clinica de saude mental [Transverse practices in the mental health clinic]. *Psicologia: Reflexao e Critica, 2,* 110-118.

Fischer, R. et al. (2009). Individualism-collectivism as descriptive norms: Development of a subjective norm approach to culture measurement. *Journal of Cross-Cultural Psychology, 40,* 187-213.

Frank, J. D., & Frank, J. B. (1993). *Persuasion & healing: A comparative study of psychotherapy.* Baltimore, MD: Johns Hopkins University Press.

Freeman, M. S., & Hayes, B. G. (2002). Clients changing counselors: An inspirational journey. *Counseling and Values, 47,* 13-21.

Freud, S. (1895/2000). *Studies on hysteria.* New York, NY: Basic Books.

Friedlmeier, W., Chakkarath, P., & Schwarz, B. (2005). *Culture and human development: The importance of cross-cultural research to the social sciences.* New York, NY: Taylor & Francis Group.

Gardiner, H. W., & Kosmitzki, C. (2005). *Lives across cultures: Cross-cultural human development* (3rd ed.). Boston, MA: Pearson Education.

Garibaldi de Hilal, A. V. (2006). Brazilian national culture, organizational culture and cultural agreement: Findings from a multinational company. *International Journal of Cross-Cultural Management, 6,* 139-166.

Gay, P. (2006). *Freud: A life for our time.* New York, NY: W.W. Norton & Company.

Gouveia, V. V., Albuquerque, J. B., Clemente, M., & Espinosa, P. (2002). Human values and social identities: A study in two collectivistic cultures. *International Journal of Psychology, 37,* 333-342.

Gouveia, V. V., Vasconcelos, T. C., Queiroga, F., Franca, M.L.P., & Oliveira, S. F. (2003). A dimensao social da responsabilidade pessoal [The social dimension of the personal responsibility]. *Psicologia em Estudo, 8,* 123-131. Retrieved from http://www.scielo.br/scielo.php?script=sci_arttext&pid=S1413-73722003000200013&lng=en&nrm=iso

Greenberg, J. R., & Mitchell, S. A. (1983). *Object relations in psychoanalytic theory.* Cambridge, MA: Harvard University Press.

Gudykunst, W. B., Matsumoto, Y., Ting-Toomey, S., & Nishida, T. (1996). The influence of cultural individualism-collectivism, self-construals, and individual values on communication styles across cultures. *Human Communication Research, 22,* 510-543.

Guy, J. D. (1987). *The personal life of the psychotherapist: The impact of clinical practice on the therapist's intimate relationships and emotional well-being.* New York, NY: Wiley.

Hanks, T. L. (2008). The Ubuntu paradigm: Psychology's next force? *Journal of Humanistic Psychology, 48,* 116-135.

Harris, A. E. (2009). The socio-political recruitment of identities. *Psychoanalytic Dialogues, 19,* 138-147.

Hatcher, S. L., Kipper-Smith, A., Waddell, M., Uhe, M., West, J. S., Boothe, J. H.. .& Gingras, P. (2012). What therapists learn from psychotherapy clients: Effects on personal and professional lives. *The Qualitative Report, 17,* 1-21.

Hays, P. (2009). Integrating evidence-based practice, cognitive-behavior therapy, and multicultural therapy: Ten steps for culturally competent practice. *Professional Psychology: Research and Practice, 40,* 354-360.

Hochschild, J. (1995). *Facing up to the American dream: Race, class, and the soul of the nation.* Princeton, NJ: Princeton University Press.

Hofstede, G. (1984). *Culture's consequences: International differences and work-related values.* Beverly Hills, CA: Sage.

Hofstede, G. (2002). Dimensions do not exist: A reply to Brendan McSweeney. *Human Relations, 55,* 1-8.

Hofstede, G. (2009). Hofstede's cultural dimensions: Brazil. Retrieved February 16, 2010 from http://www.geerthofstede.com/hofstede_dimensions.php?culture1=11&culture2=95#compare

Hofstede, G., & McCrae, R. R. (2004). Personality and culture revisited: Linking traits and dimensions of culture. *Cross-Cultural Research, 38,* 52-88.

Hofstede, G. J., Pedersen, P. B., & Hofstede, G. (2002). *Exploring culture: Exercises, stories, and synthetic cultures.* Boston, MA: Intercultural Press.

Hunsley, J., & Lee, C. M. (2007). Research-informed benchmarks for psychological treatment: Efficacy studies, effectiveness studies, and beyond. *Professional Psychology: Research and Practice, 38,* 21-33.

Hutz, C. S., & Adair, J. G. (1996). The use of references in Brazilian psychology journals reveals trends in thought and research. *International Journal of Psychology, 31,* 145- 149.

Hutz, C. S., McCarthy, S., & Gomes, W. (2004). Psychology in Brazil: The road behind and the road ahead. In M. J. Stevens & D. Wedding (Eds.), *Handbook of international psychology* (pp. 151-168). New York, NY: Brunner-Routledge.

Ibrahim, F., Roysircar-Dosowski, G., & Ohnishi, H. (2001). Worldview: Recent developments and needed directions. In J. G. Ponterotto, J. M. Casas, L. A. Suzuki, & C. M. Alexander (Eds.), *Handbook of multicultural counseling* (pp. 425-456). Thousand Oaks, CA: Sage Publications.

Interest section on culture and psychotherapy (n.d., para. 2). In Society for Psychotherapy Research. Retrieved from http://www.psychotherapyresearch.org/displaycommon. cfm?an=1&subarticlenbr=89

Jennings, L., D'Rozario, V., Goh, M., Sovereign, A., Brogger, M., & Skovholt, T. (2008). Psychotherapy expertise in Singapore: A qualitative investigation. *Psychotherapy Research, 18*, 508-522.

Jennings, L., & Skovholt, T. S. (1999). The cognitive, emotional, and relational characteristics of master therapists. *Journal of Counseling Psychology, 46*, 3-11.

Kahn, S., & Fromm, E. (2001). *Changes in the therapist.* Mahwah, NJ: Lawrence Erlbaum Associates.

Kanazawa, Y. (2007). Psychotherapy in Japan: The case of Mrs. A. *Journal of Clinical Psychology, 63*, 755-763.

Kazdin, A. E. (2003). *Research design in clinical psychology.* Boston, MA: Allyn & Bacon.

Kottler, J. A. (1993). *On being a therapist.* San Francisco, CA: Jossey Bass.

Lehman, D. R., Chiu, C-Y., & Schaller, M. (2004). Psychology and culture. *Annual Review of Psychology, 55*, 689-714.

Leong, F.T.L., & Lee, S-H. (2006). A cultural accommodation model for cross-cultural psychotherapy: Illustrated with the case of Asian Americans. *Psychotherapy: Theory, Research, Practice, Training, 43*, 410-423.

Leung, K. (1989). Cross-cultural differences: Individual-level vs. culture-level analysis. *International Journal of Psychology, 24*, 703-719.

Markus, H. R. (2008). Pride, prejudice, and ambivalence: Toward a unified theory of race and ethnicity. *American Psychologist, 63*, 651-670.

Markus, H. R., & Kitayama, S. (1991). Cultures and the self: Implications for cognition, emotion, and motivation. *Psychological Review, 98,* 224-253.

Matsumoto, D. (2001). *The handbook of culture and psychology.* New York, NY: Oxford University Press.

Matsumoto, D., et al. (2008). Mapping expressive differences around the world: The relationship between emotional display rules and individualism versus collectivism. *Journal of Cross-Cultural Psychology, 39,* 55-74.

Matsumoto, D., Takeuchi, S., Andayani, S., Kouznetsova, N., & Krupp, D. (1998). The contribution of individualism vs. collectivism to cross-national differences in display rules. *Asian Journal of Social Psychology, 1,* 147–165. doi: 10.1111/1467- 839X.00010

Matsumoto, D., Weissman, M., Preston, K., Brown, B., & Kupperbusch, C. (1997). Context- specific measurement of individualism-collectivism on the individual level. *Journal of Cross-Cultural Psychology, 28,* 743-767.

McGoldrick, M., Giordano, J., & Garcia-Preto, N. (2005). *Ethnicity and family therapy* (3rd ed.). New York, NY: The Guilford Press.

McGruder, J. (2004). Disease model of mental illness and aftercare patient education: Critical observations from meta-analysis, cross-cultural practice and anthropological study. *British Journal of Occupational Therapy, 67,* 310-318.

McWilliams, N. (2005a). Preserving our humanities as therapists. *Psychotherapy: Theory, Research, Practice, Training, 42,* 139-151.

McWilliams, N. (2005b). Response to Norcross. *Psychotherapy: Theory, Research, Practice, Training, 42,* 156-159.

Mendes, E.R.P. (2002). Social realities and psychoanalysis. *International Forum of Psychoanalysis, 11,* 81-82. Retrieved from http://www.pep-web.org/document.php?id=ifp.011.0081a

Mezan, R. (1998). Figura e fundo: Notas sobre o campo psicanalitico no Brasil [Figure and ground: Notes on the psychoanalytic field in Brazil]. *Percurso, 10*(20), 7-18.

Miles, M. B., & Huberman, M. A. (1994). *Qualitative data analysis.* Thousand Oaks, CA: Sage.

Mitchell, S. A. (2003). *Relationality: From attachment to intersubjectivity.* Hillsdale, NJ: Analytic Press.

Morrow-Bradley, C., & Elliott, R. (1986). Utilization of psychotherapy research by practicing psychotherapists. *American Psychologist, 41,* 188-197.

Neto, S. P., & Arruda, J. R. (2006). Aonde vai a psicologia? Reflexoes sobre o presente, o passado e o futuro da psicologia como ciencia, profissao e ensino [What is the future of psychology? Some considerations about the past, present, and future of psychology as a science, profession, and study]. *Boletim da Academia Paulista de Psicologia, 26,* 45-52.

Omar, A., Delgado, H. U., Ferreira, M. C., Assmar, E. M. L., Souto, S. O., Gonzales, A. T., & Galaz, M. F. (2007). Colectivismo, justicia y ciudadania organizacional en empresas Argentinas, Mexicanas y Brasileiras [Collectivism, justice, and organizational citizenship in Argentinean, Mexican, and Brazilian organizations]. *Revista Mexicana de Psicologia, 24,* 101-116.

Orlinsky, D. E., Rønnestad, M. H., Gerin, P., Davis, J. D., Ambühl, H., Davis, M. L. . .& Schröder, T. A. (2005). The development of psychotherapists. In D. E. Orlinsky & M. H. Rønnestad, *How therapists develop: A study of therapeutic work and professional growth* (pp. 3-13).Washington, DC: American Psychological Association.

Oyserman, D., Coon, H. M., & Kemmelmeier, M. (2002). Rethinking individualism and collectivism: Evaluation of theoretical assumptions and meta-analysis. *Psychological Bulletin, 128,* 3-72.

Oyserman, D., & Lee, S.W.S. (2008). Does culture influence what and how we think? Effects of priming individualism and collectivism. *Psychological Bulletin, 134*, 311- 342.

Patton, M. Q. (2002). *Qualitative research & evaluation methods* (3rd ed.). Thousand Oaks, CA: Sage Publications.

Pearson, V.M.S., & Stephan, W. G. (1998). Preferences for styles of negotiation: A comparison of Brazil and the U.S. *International Journal of Intercultural Relations, 22*, 67-83.

Pellegrini, T. (2000). Aspects of the contemporary production of Brazilian culture. *Latin American Perspectives, 27*, 122-143.

Pereira, F. M., & Neto, A. P. (2003). O psicologo no Brasil: Notas sobre seu processo de profissionalizacao [Psychologists in Brazil: Notes about their professionalization process]. *Psicologia em Estudo, 8*, 19-27.

Polkinghorne, D. E. (2005). Language and meaning: Data collection in qualitative research. *Journal of Counseling Psychology, 52*, 137-145.

Ponterotto, J., Casas, J. M., Suzuki, L. A., & Alexander, C. M. (Eds.). (2001). *Handbook of multicultural counseling* (2nd ed.). Thousand Oaks, CA: Sage Publications.

Poortinga, Y. H. (2005). The globalization of indigenous psychologies. *Asian Journal of Social Psychology, 8*, 65-74. doi: 10.1111/j.1467-839X.2005.00157.x

Prieto, J. M., & Garcia-Rodriguez, Y. (2004). Strengthening psychology in Spain. In M. J. Stevens & D. Wedding (Eds.), *Handbook of international psychology* (pp. 351-369). New York, NY: Brunner-Routledge.

Raffaelli, M., & Koller, S. H. (2005). Future expectation of Brazilian street youth. *Journal of Adolescence, 28*, 249-262.

Ribas, R. C., Jr. (2010). Central and South America. In M. H. Bornstein, *Handbook of Cultural developmental science* (pp. 232-339). New York, NY: Taylor & Francis Group.

Ritchie, P. L-J., & Sabourin, M. E. (2004). Psychology in Canada. In M. J. Stevens & D. Wedding (Eds.), *Handbook of international psychology* (pp. 75-91). New York, NY: Brunner-Routledge.

Robert, C., Lee, W. C., & Chan, K-Y. (2006). An empirical analysis of measurement equivalence with the INDCOL measure. *Personnel Psychology, 59*, 65-99.

Robert, P., Elliott, R., Buysse, A., Loots, G., & Corte, K. (2008). What's on the therapist's mind? A grounded theory analysis of family therapists reflections during individual therapy sessions. *Psychotherapy Research, 18*, 48-57.

Rønnestad, M. H., & Skovholt, T. M. (2001). Learning arenas for professional development: Retrospective accounts of senior psychotherapists. *Professional Psychology: Research and Practice, 32*, 181-187.

Rønnestad, M. H., & Skovholt, T. M. (2003). The journey of the counselor and therapist: Research findings and perspective on professional development. *Journal of Career Development, 30,* 5-44.

Rudestam, K. E., & Newton, R. R. (2007). *Surviving your dissertation: A comprehensive guide to content and process* (3rd ed.). Los Angeles, CA: Sage Publications.

Safdar, S., Friedlmeier, W., Matsumoto, D., Yoo, S. H., Kwantes, C., & Kakai, H. (2009). Variations of emotional display rules within and across cultures: A comparison between Canada, USA, and Japan. *Canadian Journal of Behavioral Sciences, 41*, 1- 10.

Sanchez-Burks, J. (2002). Protestant relational ideology and (in) attention to relational cues in work settings. *Personality Processes and Individual Differences, 83*, 919-929.

Sanchez-Sosa, J. J. (2007). Psychotherapy in Mexico: Practice, training, and regulation. *Journal of Clinical Psychology, 63*, 765-771.

Sato, T. (1998). Agency and communion: The relationship between therapy and culture. *Cultural Diversity and Mental Health, 4*, 278-290.

Scheper-Hughes, N. (1992). *Death without weeping: The violence of everyday life in Brazil.* Berkeley: University of California Press.

Schwandt, T. A. (2000). Three epistemological stances for qualitative inquiry. In N. K. Denzin, & Y. S. Lincoln (Eds.), *Handbook of qualitative research* (2nd ed., pp. 189-213). Thousand Oaks, CA: Sage.

Seligman, M. (1995). The effectiveness of psychotherapy: The Consumer Reports study. *American Psychologist, 50*, 965-974.

Singelis, T. M., & Brown, W. J. (1995). Culture, self, and collectivist communication: Linking culture to individual behavior. *Human Communication Research, 21*, 354- 389.

Singelis, T. M., Triandis, H. C., Bhawuk, D.P.S., & Gelfand, M. J. (1995). Horizontal and vertical aspects of individualism and collectivism: A theoretical and measurement refinement. *Cross-Cultural Research, 29*, 240-275.

Skovholt, T. M., & McCarthy, P. R. (1988). Critical incidents: Catalysts for counselor development. *Journal of Counseling and Development, 67*, 69-72.

Skovholt, T. M., & Rønnestad, M. H. (1992). Themes in therapist and counselor development. *Journal of Counseling & Development, 70*, 505-515.

Smith, A. K. (2012). What psychologists report learning from their clients: Cross-cultural comparison of North American and Brazilian psychologists (Doctoral dissertation). Available at ProQuest Dissertations and Theses database. (UMI No. 3493717)

Spangler, P., Hill, C. E., Mettus, C., Guo, A. H., & Heymsfield, L. (2009). Therapist perspectives on their dreams about clients: A qualitative investigation. *Psychotherapy Research, 19*, 81-95.

Spencer-Rodgers, J., Peng, K., Wang, L., & Hou, Y. (2004). Dialectical self-esteem and East-West differences in psychological well-being. *Personality and Social Psychology Bulletin, 30*, 1416-1432.

Stahl, J. V., Hill, C. E., Jacobs, T., Kleinman, S., Isenberg, D., & Stern, A. (2009). When the shoe is on the other foot: A qualitative study of intern-level trainees' perceived learning from clients. *Psychotherapy, Therapy, Research, Practice, Training, 46*, 376- 389.

Stevens, M. J., & Wedding, D. (2004). International psychology: An overview. In M. J.

Stevens & D. Wedding (Eds.), *Handbook of international psychology* (pp. 1-21). New York, NY: Brunner-Routledge.

Stewart, M. W. (2001). Medical psychology in New Zealand. *Journal of Clinical Psychology in Medical Settings, 8*, 51-58.

Sue, D. W. (2001). Surviving monoculturalism and racism: A personal and professional journey. In J. Ponterotto, J. M. Casas, L. A. Suzuki, & C. M. Alexander (Eds.), *Handbook of multicultural counseling* (2nd ed.). Thousand Oaks, CA: Sage Publications.

Sue, D. W., & Sue, D. (2003). *Counseling the culturally diverse: Theory and practice* (4th ed.). New York, NY: John Wiley & Sons.

Takemura, K., & Yuki, M. (2007). Are Japanese groups more competitive than Japanese individuals? A cross-cultural validation of the interindividual-intergroup discontinuity effect. *International Journal of Psychology, 42*, 27-35

Tamis-Lemonda, C. S., & McFadden, K. E. (2010). The United States of America. In M. H. Bornstein, *Handbook of cultural developmental science* (pp. 299-322). New York, NY: Taylor & Francis Group.

Triandis, H. C. (1993). Collectivism and individualism as cultural syndromes. *Cross-Cultural Research, 27*, 155-180.

Triandis, H.C. (1995). *Individualism and collectivism.* Boulder, CO: Westview Press.

Triandis, H. C. (2001). Individualism and collectivism: Past, present, and future. In D. Matsumoto (Ed.), *The handbook of culture and psychology.* New York, NY: Oxford University Press.

Triandis, H. C., Leung, K., Villareal, M. J., & Clack, F. (1985). Allocentric versus idiocentric tendencies: Convergent and discriminant validation. *Journal of Research in Personality, 19*, 395-415.

Uchida, Y., & Kitayama, S. (2009). Happiness and unhappiness in the East and West: Themes and variations. *Emotion, 4*, 441-456.

Van Horn, K. R., & Marques, J. C. (2000). Interpersonal relationships in Brazilian adolescents. *International Journal of Behavioral Development, 24*, 199-203.

Vicary, D. A., & Bishop, B. J. (2005). Western psychotherapeutic practice: Engaging Aboriginal people in culturally appropriate and respectful ways. *Australian Psychologist, 40*, 8-19.

Vikan, A., Camino, C., & Biaggio, A. (2005). Note on a cross-cultural test of Gilligan's ethic of care. *Journal of Moral Education, 34*, 107-111.

Vistesen, C. (2008, May 20). Brazil's economy: Not emerging anymore? [Web log message]. Retrieved from http://globaleconomydoesmatter. blogspot.com/2008/05/brazils- economy-not-emerging-anymore.html

Watters, E. (2010a). The Americanization of mental illness. *The New York Times.* Retrieved from http://www.nytimes.com/2010/01/10/ magazine/10psyche-t.html

Watters, E. (2010b). *Crazy like us: The globalization of the American psyche.* New York, NY: Free Press.

Wick, E. (2001). Hearing the unspoken: From hypnotherapist to comatherapist. In S. Kahn & E. Fromm, *Changes in the therapist.* Mahwah, NJ: Lawrence Erlbaum Associates.

Williams, E. N. (2008). A psychotherapy researcher's perspective on therapist self- awareness and self-focused attention after a decade of research. *Psychotherapy Research, 18,* 139-146.

World Health Organization (WHO). (1979). *Schizophrenia: An international follow-up study.* New York, NY: John Wiley.

World Health Organization (WHO). (2005). *Mental health atlas 2005.* Geneva, Switzerland:

World Health Organization. Retrieved from http://www.who.int/mental_health/evidence/atlas/global_results.pdf

Yalom, I. D. (1989). *Love's executioner & other tales of psychotherapy.* New York, NY: Harper Collins.

Yalom, I. D. (2000). *Momma and the meaning of life: Tales of psychotherapy.* New

York, NY: Perennial Books.

Yalom, I. D. (2002). *The gift of therapy: An open letter to a new generation of therapists and their patients.* New York, NY: Harper Collins.

Zha, P., Walczyk, J. J., Griffith-Ross, D. A., Tobacyk, J. J., & Walczyk, D. F. (2010). The impact of culture and individualism-collectivism on the creative potential and achievement of American and Chinese adults. *Creativity Research Journal, 18,* 355-366.

Chapter 10

DEEPENING WISDOM

Joanne S. West and Sherry L. Hatcher

Semi-structured interview protocols frequently end with a final, open inquiry about whether there is any further information respondents would like to add. This type of question can serve as a means for respondents to express themselves, free from any influence of the researcher-constructed questions (Foddy, 1993). It also encourages reflection and elaboration on responses to the earlier, structured questions (O'Cathain & Thomas, 2004; Singh, 2007). In addition, an unstructured closing question can facilitate participants in generating new themes perhaps not captured by earlier inquiry. All of these factors allow for exploration and ideas for further investigation and research (Spörrle, Gerber-Braun, & Fösterling, 2007).

In the present study, our therapist respondents were asked whether there *was any other variety of wisdom that they had gained from their psychotherapy clients that they would like to share* with the researchers. Fifty-eight of the 61 participant psychotherapists responded to this "anything-else" question with rich elaborations on themes that had arisen in answer to earlier questions and that contributed further to our narrative data. Respondents reinforced the overriding theme that psychotherapists gain valuable wisdom from their clients that affects their professional and personal lives. In reporting these experiences, therapists clearly convey a sense of deep-seated respect for their psychotherapy clients.

This chapter will present the major themes that arose in response to the final, open-ended question of our interview protocol, including representative quotations situated in the context of relevant psychological research and theory.

Importance of the Therapeutic Alliance

"In psychotherapy the relationship is very important. The patient needs to know that you really care about them and you really care about their success. And they begin to work as a team. They do their assignments. They come in for sessions on a regular basis. . . Patients who feel invested seem to work harder, and seem to feel something they never got as a child, which is that connection with somebody who cares." (Dr. Tevin)

Research has demonstrated that the therapeutic alliance is a significant predictor of successful psychotherapy outcome across therapeutic approaches (Krupnick, et al., 1996; Horvath & Bedi, 2002; Orlinsky, Rønnestad, & Willutzki, 2004) and that the psychotherapist's ability to establish and maintain a therapeutic alliance with warmth and empathy is a "common factor" central to treatment outcome (Hatcher, 1999; Lambert, 1992; Mallinckrodt & Nelson, 1991; Norcross & Goldfried, 2005).

Therapist participants in our study also reported learning from their clients that the working alliance is a critical factor for successful therapy. As Dr. Trayton observed, "I think I am more than ever appreciative less of technique than of the therapeutic context and relationship itself." And Dr. Sarah offered the following: "The key to success and working with clients in psychotherapy is whether you have a good rapport with that person," adding:

It is not just the knowledge and the education that we have to become psychotherapists but I think you have to have the skills to relate to people and I think one of the things I should emphasize is the quality of your relationships with others.

Two therapists spontaneously remarked on their views as to the greater importance of relationship than knowledge of technique. For example, Dr. Oliver said, "Out of relationships is where [the therapy] really has to grow. There are a lot of knowledgeable people who don't make very effective psychotherapists," and Dr. Tevin observed, "I think the combination of good clinical skills and good 'bedside manner' makes one a much better therapist than one who is just purely scientific."

What Makes a "Good Therapist"?

> *"People benefit just by having somebody who is a good listener. . . You need a strong curiosity to be a good therapist. You have to be actually interested in other people's lives and you have to communicate that to your client. . . You also have to appear quite human. . . fallible as well, you can't work on too much and you have to make clients accountable for making the changes that they said they wanted to make. . ."* (Dr. Cody)

A theme related to that of the importance of the therapeutic alliance emerged from the responses of participants who identified the qualities and attitudes that they believed typify a "good therapist." These were similar to the qualities that Ackerman (2003) and others have identified as the collection of attributes and behaviors or "common factors" that positively impact the "working alliance" across therapeutic orientations (Frank & Frank, 1991; Norcross, Goldfried, & Marvin, 2005; Stricker, 2008). These attributes include, among others: flexibility, honesty, trustworthiness, confidence, warmth, and openness (Ackerman, 2003).

Behaviors attributed to therapists who help create collaborative therapeutic alliances and therefore are more likely to help achieve positive client outcomes include exploration, reflection, accurate interpretation, affirmation, and attending to client experience (Ackerman, 2003), along with a focus on affect and emotional expression (Blagys & Hilsenroth, 2000).

Psychologists in our study demonstrated that they overwhelmingly value this same variety of attributes and actions in fostering a positive therapeutic alliance. For example, Dr. Tevin reflected on the need for a collaborative process involving affirmation, saying that, "number one

[is] being a cheerleader for the patient and number two. . . [is] being a role model for a patient. . . We're partners in success." Dr. Steve talked about the importance of therapists' listening:

> *That is something that needs to be worked on for therapists and clients. . . being able to listen. . . and watch your fellow human beings can be one of the most rewarding, interesting activities for all human beings, especially therapists.*

With regard to the importance of attending to clients' experience, Dr. Juan noted that "clients want the therapist to take them seriously."

Dr. Anil asserted the need to acquaint clients with their own inherent resilience in saying:

> *I am amazed by the resources that people have. . . Some of these people are afraid to use their resources and solve their problems; therapy is first and foremost that place where you try to find out ways [for clients] to use their own resources.*

A similar perspective on successful therapeutic work was shared by Dr. Eliza, who said:

> *One thing I have learned from the therapy is the importance . . . to focus on what are the client's strengths. . . what have they accomplished and build on those. I have one particular client with schizophrenia and. . . if I don't do it. . . he will. . . review his accomplishments in the session. . . such as "I have gone so many days without drinking; I haven't been gambling.". . . And I think that's a good thing to do with clients, is. . . focus on what have been the positives and what they accomplished.*

Psychologists also reflected on the need for successful therapists to be aware of their personal issues in order to successfully manage countertransference.[6] As Dr. Viola observed: "Each time. . . I sit with a person. . . and put aside my own experiences and my own wishes and let their story unfold and. . . that's worked well for me."

Dr. Iris said: "...if I can recognize my own issues. . . I have a better chance of working effectively with [clients]—not just recognize, but also be able to sequester and deal with. . . my own issues."

Similarly, Dr. Justin shared the following viewpoint:

> *I think you have to acknowledge countertransference; you have to acknowledge things are going on and then you've got to then work with it yourself. If you're not able to do that then you're not doing any benefit to anybody.*

Psychotherapy Clients Shape the Therapy

> *"It's not about me and what direction I want to go in."*
> (Dr. Viola)

Psychotherapists in our study were clear that they had learned that the client is an active participant in therapy, and that it is the clients themselves who help determine the pace, direction, and success of the working relationship. This reflects a humanistic perspective that the client is an active participant, and able to generate viable solutions to his or her own problems if offered a facilitative environment, regardless of the technical intervention provided by the therapist (Bohart & Tallman, 1999). This finding also reinforces research demonstrating that it is the client who helps determines whether or not the relationship will be therapeutic (Bachelor, 1995). All of this is consistent with more recent therapeutic modalities, across theory orientations, that stress co-construction and relational philosophies of psychotherapy (Greenberg & Mitchell, 1983; Neimeyer & Mahoney, 1995; Mitchell, 2000)

---

[6]   Countertransference here refers to a therapist's feelings, cognitions, and behaviors that occur in response to the dynamics occurring in the therapeutic relationship, either originating from the therapist's unresolved issues or from the maladaptive behaviors elicited by the client (Gelso & Hayes, 2007).

Narrative responses that described the active influence of clients in a collaborative alliance with the therapist included that of Dr. Penelope, who said:

> *I like to think theoretically, I like to work from a theoretical place, but it's very clear to me that the way in which you work is in terms of what theoretical frame you work from in very large part shaped by your client.*

Dr. Peyton observed that it is the client who will determine whether the relationship is viable: "The rocket science is: how do you know when you have a relationship and when you don't? The answer is, the client will tell you. That's the beautiful part."

Or, as Dr. Iris told us:

> *Every client has their own timing and I have to respect it. I can't make them get better, it's their choice what they want to do and they will set the end point of a therapy or a change process. I can't do that for them... so I have to trust that the client is going to have their own process and I need not insist on its being my process or my perception of their process.*

Dr. Iris further expanded on her response, illustrating comfort with the idea of the client's active shaping of the therapeutic process, and the fact that this attitude has developed and solidified for her over the course of her career:

> *When I was very much younger, a very green therapist, I would struggle [if they] didn't get where they could get to. . . Was that my fault? Or I'd blame them. You know, here I had all this wonderful stuff that I could offer and often they just weren't taking it. So, over time, what I've learned is to let that go. . . and if the person has gotten as much as they can get from me, even if it is a little bit in my perception, then it's all that they needed at that point or wanted at that point, and they have that choice.*

Working With Trauma and Vicarious Trauma

"There are things that scar us and things that scar our patients. . . part of our job is to help them [clients learn] that you can turn suffering into something useful." (Dr. Cash)

Some of the therapists in our sample talked about their work with clients who had experienced trauma. Evidence for the potential negative effects on therapists working with traumatized clients has been clearly documented (McCann & Pearlman, 1990). It can manifest in disruption of the therapist's view of self, others, and the world as a result of empathic engagement with the client and exposure to the traumatic imagery presented by clients in therapy sessions (Ortlepp & Friedman, 2002). As Dr. Peyton observed, "I know more about psychological trauma than the average person knows on the street because I have been through it vicariously [with clients] a number of times."

However, not all research has found that the outcome of trauma is necessarily entirely negative (Linley & Joseph, 2004). Some research has found positive outcomes of trauma, in the form of people marshalling resiliency in addition to any untoward effects (Linley & Joseph, 2004). Similarly, those who experience vicarious trauma exposure can develop compassion, satisfaction, and even personal growth in working effectively with clients who have experienced trauma or loss (Stamm, 2005 as cited in Craig & Sprang, 2010). For example, Dr. Wilbur's response suggests that his work has taught him that trauma can lead to personal growth:

I guess what I learned ... is that things can get really, really, really bad and there's always somebody that's got it worse. . . I hate this expression, but I'm going to say it anyway: no pain no gain. . . . It's true . . . we always learn the most from difficult situations. I mean nobody learned a life lesson from winning a beauty pageant. . . Losing the love of your life is a life lesson.

The Therapeutic Change Process

"Change is hard." (Dr. Leslie)
"It's never too late to change." (Dr. Clark)

Psychologists in our group discussed the change process in therapy. Therapeutic change is generally conceived as the outcome of a strong supportive therapeutic alliance (Wolfe, 2005) that manifests over time, and progresses stage-wise (Prochaska, 2000). Therapists reflected on the challenges that change poses for their clients, and observed that those in psychotherapy often determine whether or not change will take place, especially because motivation for change is one of the few things therapists typically cannot directly impart to their clients. For instance, Dr. Sarah noted:

> *...the major thing that I have learned is that as much as you try to push someone to see what path is right for them, or what they should do, or how they should solve their problems, or show them guidance to help them change their way of thinking, unless they are ready, it may not be helpful; it may not work. People need time to perhaps change, or sometimes they will never change.*

And, as Dr. Mark observed, "It's, on the one hand, wanting to be helpful. . . because this is a helping profession. . . doing the best you can in [utilizing] all your skill, wisdom, and theories. . . but also understanding it isn't always going to work."

The above narratives seem to indicate that therapists have employed motivational techniques to encourage clients toward positive change, while recognizing that it is the client who will ultimately determine whether or not change takes place. Reinforcing this is Dr. Antonia's observation:

> *What I have learned is that people are sometimes stuck in their situation, and no matter how much you help them to realize it, they may never realize it. . . People need time to change, or perhaps sometimes they will never change.*

Despite the challenges involved, therapists maintain their hope in the possibility of change. As Dr. Steve put it: "I have learned from my clients in general is that it is never too late to change."

Client Resilience

"My patients teach me, on a daily basis, that the human mind is incredibly durable. . . not only from the standpoint of what we can sustain. . . or the types of horrific experiences we can absorb and still function, but also the ability to venture into new ways of thinking. . . and trying things even in spite of hopelessness and a sense of powerlessness. This kind of resiliency that people have, you can tap and get them hoping again. . . It is incredible how strong and resilient human beings are." (Dr. Tom)

Our group of psychotherapists reflected on client resilience in response to our final interview question, perhaps building on their responses to Questions 4 and 5.[7] Uniformly, respondents conveyed their admiration for their clients' capacity to endure and rebound from adversity, often with valiant displays of resilience. They increasingly cited the construct of resilience, commonly defined as a dynamic set of processes by which individuals use their inner strengths in order to adapt to challenges (see, for example, Luthar, Cicchetti, & Becker, 2000).

Positive change in psychotherapy, in part as a byproduct of client resiliency, is reflected in the responses of many of the therapists in our sample. As Dr. Mike said, "I think that the clients I work with truly appreciate patience and listening and trust and allowing them to use whatever style or methods or strategies they have to figure things out for themselves." Or, as Dr. Mai noted, "Therapy is first and foremost that place where you try to find. . . ways. . . to use their own resources."

Bonanno (2008) has observed that some mental health practitioners working with survivors of trauma or loss have underestimated the

---

[7]   Question four: What have you learned from your psychotherapy clients about coping mechanisms? Question five: What have you learned from your psychotherapy clients about courage?

capacity for resilience in particular clients, perhaps as a result of working with populations that have had considerable difficulty in "bouncing back" from trauma. Similarly, there were some respondents in our study who reflected on having been surprised by their clients' resilience. For instance, Dr. Cash remarked, "People's ability to adapt and recover is much greater than we ever expected." And Dr. Maya observed:

> *People really are surprising, are capable of things that you would not expect them to be capable of, amazing strength. . . I am learning that people can be pretty powerful within their own lives. . . powerful, capable of change, strong.*

Although resilience has sometimes been thought of as an elusive trait that one either does or does not possess, it is now widely believed to be a commonly occurring human quality, even if present in more or less abundance across individuals (Masten, 2001). Other researchers have noted that resiliency involves employing adaptive strategies in challenging situations (Lyubomirsky, Sheldon, & Schkade, 2005). Therapists in our study seemed to share this perspective on resiliency: "It is the courage [clients] show and the fact that the human spirit is so strong that you see some people who are really down and out who bounce back. That's always amazing to me," said Dr. Linda. As Dr. Sarah remarked, "The thing that I value the most . . . is the indomitable will of the human spirit." And Dr. Laura observed, "what kinds of things humans can stand. . . just horrible decisions that people are faced with, that they manage, and going on with a productive life afterwards."

Reflections on Theory Orientation

> *"I think the whole holistic movement in psychology is going to be more and more important as we try to put people back together again rather than separate them into all these different specialties."* (Dr. Mike)

At the foundation of each psychologist's understanding of therapy clients and their problems lies the therapist's theoretical orientation. While some therapists adhere to the case conceptualization, therapeutic goals, and techniques prescribed by one of the major schools of psychotherapeutic thought, others identify an integrated approach, combining conceptualization and/or intervention and "common factors" from across theories and practices, in order to optimally respond to the needs of individual clients (Norcross & Goldfried, 2005).

At times the therapists in our study spontaneously discussed their theoretical orientations in response to our final research question, and the majority of those responses seemed to reflect the application of an integrated approach. This may be because, in some sense, many therapists use integrative approaches, whether or not they are so-named. For example, a psychodynamic therapist may naturally work with a client to correct cognitive distortions and a cognitive behavioral therapist may even work with transference phenomena.[8] In this context, Dr. Rose discussed the shift in her orientation across her career, stating:

> *I started psychodynamic. I went to CBT and practiced that for a while and I eventually returned to psychodynamic. . . .human beings are capable of doing very animalistic, primitive things. . . but if you are talking about developmental stages, even though we stem from animal origins, there is still hope that we can behave better.*

Similarly, Dr. Doral reflected on the fact that she uses both Adlerian and psychodynamic thinking in conducting psychotherapy:

> *I . . . believe...there are many events that are tied into why somebody might be struggling, some Adlerian stuff comes back, that it's like a string with a series of knots on the string and. . . there typically are one or two key things. . . the old psychodynamic stuff talked about pathogenic secrets. . . and that if you untangle one of those more critical ones, a lot of the others just melt away. . .*

And Dr. Penelope spoke of selecting among theoretically grounded interventions in response to client characteristics as follows:

---

[8]   Transference refers to the usually unconscious displacement of feelings and thoughts associated with a figure in the client's past onto the therapist (Gabbard, 2008).

> *I like to think theoretically. . . it's very clear to me that the way in which you work. . . is in very large part shaped by your client. There are some people who are just psychodynamic clients and there are some people who are just Carl Rogers clients.*

Regardless of whether a therapist chooses a single theoretical or integrated approach to psychotherapy, participants in this study acknowledged the importance of developing a sound theoretical basis for one's psychotherapeutic work. In referring to the observations of therapists practicing according to different theory orientations and working with the same clients in a training format, Dr. Muhomba noted:

> *[I was] watching a pure narrative therapist, a pure solution-focused therapist, and an Eriksonian kind of therapist. . . interviewing the same client. And it is just interesting to see how we do what we do and how much our model informs what we do. . . it creates a different interaction. . . with that client. . . You need a good method, and then on top of that you can develop personal style.*

However, not all respondents embraced an integrative approach, and some reflected the "camps" that sometimes exist between the theoretical approaches of different schools of psychotherapy. An example of this was reflected in Dr. Peyton's response:

> *The analytical types go to great lengths to find out the relationship between the parents and the child. Carl Rogers. . . said something like. . . why don't you ask them "What was the relationship between you and your parents?" Why go through all that crap of association and lying on the couch turning the lights low?*

Psychotherapy: Art and/or Science?

"I think the problem is in training we were taught the scientific aspect of psychotherapy but were never taught the art of psychotherapy. . . I think the art of therapy is number one. . ." (Dr. Trayton)

Another theme that arose in the responses of participants to our open-ended question was a consideration as to whether psychotherapy is an art, a science, or some combination thereof, thus reflecting a ubiquitous debate within the field. Responses from our participants indicated that most of us view therapy as an art that is grounded in science.

In some writings, psychotherapy has been described as either the art of applying technique in the moment-to-moment interaction with clients (Friedlander, Escudero, & Heatherington, 2006), or as a combination of empirically supported interventions and the art of applying these with flexibility and creativity (Hofmann & Weinberger, 2006). Some participants reflected this perspective. For example, Dr. Antonia said, "I think psychotherapy is an art itself. It is not just the knowledge and the education," and Dr. Muhomba noted:

> *I use my left brain to determine where the posts are. . . and I use my right brain to go as far as I can. . . .with a hunch. . . as long as it doesn't go outside the boundaries of propriety and what is cogent or helpful for the client.*

Beutler (2009) has argued that it is not possible, or even desirable, to remove those human factors influencing therapeutic outcome in favor of adopting a rigidly scientific medical model. Dr. Reuben seemed to share this perspective:

> *It's an irrational wish. . . on the part of psychology to emulate natural sciences. . . We don't explain like the chemist does. We aim to understand. . . We have tried it now since Wilhelm Wundt had his laboratory and Weber and Fechner had their brass instruments—and where are we? We still don't understand each other. The only avenue available to us at this time and maybe others in*

the future is to return to philosophy as the basic grounding for psychological understanding.

Spiritual/Religious Beliefs of Therapists and Their Clients

"The other change is to bring the spiritual and religious into my practice. If you do it in a judicious way—with the client taking the lead and my just asking questions about worldview—if the client likes to go there, we go there." (Dr. Arcy)

The theme of acknowledging and even incorporating clients' spirituality and/or religious beliefs into the therapeutic process appeared in the responses of some of the psychologists in our study. Developing competence in working with a range of religious/spiritual beliefs and practices is thought to represent part of developing necessary multicultural competence (APA, 1992). As Dr. Arcy observed:

In my early days as a psychotherapist, I was agnostic/ atheist. . . And I tried to be respectful of people's religious and moral backgrounds. . . But the more I grew and the more I came to work with people, [the more I] bring spiritual and religious [beliefs] into my practice.

Opening the door to clients' expressing their spiritual or religious beliefs in psychotherapy can aid them in benefitting from such coping mechanisms as self-regulation, self-soothing, and meaning-making (Crawford, Wright, & Masten, 2006). This idea was reflected in a response from Dr. Lucas:

Spirituality is an important component, and the way I think of spirituality is meaning. . . to have meaning in life. Some clients think of it as religion but meaning is important, and making meaning. . . I find there is more time spent on that [component of my practice] in the last five years than before.

Therapists expressed awareness of the challenges that spiritual or religious beliefs can pose for clients in terms of developing their own ways of making meaning, as, for instance, in Dr. Juan's response:

> *I remember a particular client who said her parents had raised her with specific [religious] traditions. . . but her grandma has taught her [otherwise] and she had spent more time with her grandma. . . and now as an adult she had to deal with that [conflict].*

The work of psychotherapy can further allow therapists an understanding of the structure and comfort that clients' beliefs can provide them; for instance, as Dr. Harriet M. reported:

> *I have wise clients like a Muslim woman whose husband had a massive stroke, and she takes care of him. . . She has a lot on her plate. I think I learned from her. She really uses her Muslim faith. . . She talks about how grateful she is. . . I just stand back and I am a little bit in awe of the greatness of her. . . spirit.*

Lessons Learned from Psychotherapy Clients

> *"You learn from your patients. YOU LEARN FROM THEM."* (Dr. Peyton)

The psychotherapists in our study reported learning important lessons from their clients, often expanding on their earlier responses to the first question presented in our interview protocol.[9] That this learning took place and was recognized by these therapists across a wide range of lessons learned indicates an open attitude toward learning, an openness often nurtured over many years of practice. "You have to be allowing the person to teach you," said Dr. Oliver.

Some psychotherapists spoke of the wisdom they had gained in broad terms, such as Dr. Homer, who said: "I gained wisdom from every client. There is another aspect of the universe that I learn from

---

[9]   Question 1: Please give an example of some important life lesson you learned from one or more of your psychotherapy clients.

every client—how they look at life, how they look at relationships, their health issues." And Dr. Wilbur asserted, "I feel like I learn something from every single patient I see. I mean I really LOVE them—well, not every single one of them, but most of them."

Other therapists spoke of their psychotherapeutic work as enhancing their own interpersonal functioning. As Dr. Rose reported, "I think [this work] helps me with compassion." Or as Dr. Ellen said, "I've learned to like people more. . . I've gotten more comfortable with silences." And Dr. Linda offered the following observation, "When I sit there and listen to what [clients] have learned from their struggle. . . they are imparting wisdom to me. They don't even know it." Similarly, Dr. Antonia reported:

> *When we are challenging others in therapy to communicate effectively or teaching them how to. . . work at relationships, it is practice for us, too. I don't think a lot of people realize that. You will often hear [therapists] talk about something that happened with their client, and then a month later there was something in their own family where you could deal with it because you had just talked about it with your client. It's good clients don't know or they would be asking us* to pay *them.*

One unique response revealed the lessons that Dr. Jack had learned about the psychological experiences of the opposite sex: "I work with a lot of women, and my female psychotherapy patients taught me a lot about [being] a woman in the world. . . understanding the other half of humanity."

A second relatively unusual response came from Dr. Rick, who noted that working as a therapist has taught him the value of sharing one's concerns with another person:

> *The overriding thing that I get is that when . . . I am in a bad place emotionally the best thing to do most times is to talk to somebody. . . What I take from that . . . in terms of improving my life, being able to listen to others and gather lessons they can teach me. . .*

Therapists' Reactions to Their Careers

"It's a great career for learning to be compassionate and feeling connected to everybody. . . Some of my patients report having that same experience from therapy. . . They feel their hearts kind of opening up, which is such a lovely thing." (Dr. Michelle)

In response to our final interview question, psychotherapists reflected upon their careers and revealed some of their accompanying feelings about working in this field. Some spoke of a realization that there are limitations to what both they—and psychotherapy—can offer clients, and how they must work toward accepting that fact, even though they wish they could help everyone who comes to them for assistance. For instance, Dr. Goodheart shared, "I guess [there is a] sense over time of being humbled by the limitations on what psychotherapy can do, but also learning that that's okay." Dr. Trayton offered a similar response:

"I move between feeling very wise and very naïve. . . there are days I practice I feel that I'm this incredibly wise savant and other times when I feel . . . I have very little to contribute to the person I am seeing."

A number of therapists reflected on the rewarding nature of their work. For example, Dr. Jeremey said, "Being able to be privy to some else's story, to the narrative their life. . . is a blessing really, I think, for both parties." And Dr. Steve said, "Doing therapy well is really hard work and. . . exhausting. It is extremely rewarding personally." Dr. McMillan offered a further personal reaction:

I think it is such a luxury [to be a psychologist]. I love my patients, I love my work and I love the opportunity to be with people as they heal. . . that's a real privilege and I treasure it."

What Working With Psychotherapy Clients Gives to the Therapist

> *"I have a depressive constitution myself and so my liability in life is to see the glass as half empty. [This is] a great occupation for me because I see so many people surviving adversity and overcoming adversity and being courageous that it has really helped me feel like. . . if they can do that I should be able to pull myself up."* (Dr. Michelle)

Participants revealed that their work as psychotherapists had benefitted them personally in a number of ways. Many spoke of an enhanced ability to cope with adversity and overcome challenges. "I feel like I always get something from them, whether it's some insight about myself or [the] thought that I can overcome challenges" said Dr. Julia. And, in speaking about a client who had faced serious adversity, Dr. Sunny observed:

> *I am so in awe that you can get up every day after that and put your shoes on and get dressed and go on about your life. If that were me, I might just keep going through the motions. I might never actually try again.*

Along the same lines, Dr. Justin responded, "I think [being a therapist] can change you as an individual in the sense that you see that [clients] can do it."

Other respondents reflected on the sense of connectedness and openness to others that their work has given them. This is how Dr. Cody expressed the sentiment:

> *I feel like I have a richer sense of humanity by having these clients share their problems and failings with me. I often feel like I have some kinship to them after a period of time where we've experienced some things together, and then I am glad that they entrusted me with the ability to help them.*

In a similar vein, Dr. Michelle told us:

> *I think it's expanded my compassion and sense of connectedness, and that's a really neat thing. Interestingly, some of my patients report having that same experience from therapy, which I think is really cool.*

And Dr. Odila added, "I've learned that getting to connect with another human being at an honest and authentic and vulnerable level heals us both."

One unique, albeit poignant, response was from Dr. Carmen, who reported that her work has made her grateful: "When I have to witness just what people really have to go through, it make me feel very lucky. . . So it's made me appreciate and be grateful for all the things I have."

Unsolicited Reactions to the Research Task

Following their responses to our final open-ended question, many respondents provided reactions to the research study as a whole, reflecting a sense of gratitude for having had the opportunity to ponder these questions and reflect on their practice of psychotherapy. These included Dr. Oliver's feedback, "I appreciate thinking about these things. I think this is a good study. . . I think an effective psychotherapist needs to learn from his patients every day." Finally, as Dr. Anna told us:

> *I mentioned this study to a colleague of mine and he quoted some famous therapist who said, "Everything I've learned I've learned from my patients." That may be a bit extreme, but I think we shouldn't underestimate how much therapists get back in the way of knowledge, wisdom, and empathy when they do this work.*

References

Ackerman, S. J. (2003). A review of therapist characteristics and techniques positively impacting the therapeutic alliance. *Clinical Psychology Review, 23*, p.1-33.

American Psychological Association. (1992, December 1). *American Psychological Association Ethical Principles of Psychologists and Code of Conduct.* Retrieved October 30, 2001, from http://www.apa.org/ethics/code.html

Bachelor, A. (1995) Clients' perception of the therapeutic alliance: A qualitative analysis. *Journal of Counseling Psychology, 42*, 323-37.

Beutler, L. E. (2009). Making science matter in clinical practice: Redefining psychotherapy. *Clinical Psychology-Science and Practice, 16*, 301-317.

Blagys, M. D., & Hilsenroth, M. J. (2000). Distinctive activities of short-term psychodynamic interpersonal psychotherapy: A review of the comparative psychotherapy process literature. *Clinical Psychology: Science and Practice, 7*, 167-188.

Bohart, A. C., & Tallman, K. (1999). *How clients make therapy work: The process of active self-healing.* Washington, DC: American Psychological Association.

Bonanno, George A. (2008). Loss, trauma, and human resilience: Have we underestimated the human capacity to thrive after extremely aversive events? *Psychological Trauma: Theory, Research, Practice, and Policy, 5*, 101-113.

Craig, C. D., & Sprang, G. (2010). Compassion satisfaction, compassion fatigue, and burnout in a national sample of trauma treatment therapists. *Anxiety, Stress, and Coping, 23*, 319-339.

Crawford, E., Wright, M.O.D., & Masten, A. S. (2006). Resilience and spirituality in youth. In P. L. Benson, E. C. Roehlkepartain, P. E. King, & L. Wagener (Eds.), *The handbook of spiritual development in childhood and adolescence* (pp. 355-370). Newbury Park, CA: Sage.

Delaney, H. D., Miller, W. R., & Bisono, A. M. (2007). Religiosity and spirituality among psychologists: A survey of clinician members of APA. *Professional Psychology: Research and Practice, 38*, 538-546.

Foddy, W. (1993). *Constructing questions for interviews and questionnaires: Theory and practice in social research.* Cambridge, MA: Cambridge University Press.

Frank, J. D., & Frank, J. B. (1991). *Persuasion and healing: A comparative study of psychotherapy* (3rd ed.). Baltimore, MD: Johns Hopkins University Press.

Friedlander, M. L., Escudero, V., Heatherington, L. (2006). Therapeutic alliance in psychotherapy. *Therapeutic alliances in couple and family therapy: An empirically informed guide to practice.* (pp. 9-29). Washington, DC: American Psychological Association.

Gabbard, G. O. (2008). *Textbook of psychotherapeutic treatments.* Arlington, VA: American Psychiatric Publishing, Inc.

Gelso, C. J., & Hayes, J. A. (2007). *Countertransference and the therapist's inner experience: Perils and possibilities.* Mahwah, NJ: Erlbaum.

Greenberg, J. R., & Mitchell, S. A. (1983). *Object relations in psychoanalytic theory.* Cambridge, MA: Harvard University Press.

Hatcher, R. L. (1999). Therapist views of treatment alliance and collaboration in therapy. *Psychotherapy Research, 9*, 405-423.

Hofmann, S. G., & Weinberger, J. (2007). The art and science of psychotherapy: An introduction. In S. G. Hofmann & J. Weinberger (Eds.), *The art and science of psychotherapy* (xvii-2). New York, NY: Routledge.

Horvath, A. O., & Bedi, R. P. (2002). The alliance. In J. C. Norcross (Ed.), *Psychotherapy relationships that work: Therapist contributions and responsiveness to patients* (pp. 37-69). New York: Oxford University Press.

Krupnick, J. L., Sotsky, S. M., Simmens, S., Moyher, J., Elkin, I., Watkins, J., et al. (1996). The role of the therapeutic alliance in psychotherapy and pharmacotherapy outcome: Findings in the National Institute of Mental Health Treatment of Depression Collaborative Research Project. *Journal of Consulting and Clinical Psychology, 64*, 532-539.

Lambert, J. J. (1992). Psychotherapy outcome research: Implications for integrative and eclectic therapists. In J. C. Norcross and M. R. Goldfried (Eds.), *Handbook of psychotherapy integration*. New York: Basic Books.

Linley, P. A., & Joseph, S. (2004). Positive change following trauma and adversity: A review. *Journal of Trauma and Stress, 17*, 11-21.

Luthar, S. S., Cicchetti, D., & Becker, B. (2000). The construct of resilience: A critical evaluation and guidelines for future work. *Child Development, 71*, 543-562.

Lyubomirsky, S., Sheldon, K. M., & Schkade, D. (2005). Pursuing happiness: The architecture of sustainable change. *Review of General Psychology, 9*, 111-131.

Mallinckrodt, B., & Nelson, M. L. (1991). Counselor training level and the formation of the psychotherapeutic working alliance. *Journal of Counseling Psychology, 38*, 133-138.

Masten, A. S. (2001). Ordinary magic: Resilience processes in development. *American Psychologist, 56*, 227-238.

Mitchell, S. A. (2000). *Relationality: From attachment to intersubjectivity* (vol. 20). Mahwah, NJ: Analytic Press.

Neimeyer, R. A., & Mahoney, M. J. (Eds.). (1995). *Constructivism in psychotherapy*. Washington, DC: American Psychological Association.

Norcross, J. C., & Goldfried, M. R. (Eds.). (2005). *Handbook of psychotherapy integration* (2nd ed.). New York: Oxford.

O'Cathain A., & Thomas K. J. (2004). "Any other comments?" Open questions on questionnaires—a bane or a bonus to research? *BMC Medical Research Methodology, 4*(25). Retrieved from http://www.biomedcentral.com/1471-2288/4/25

Orlinsky, D. E., Rønnestad, M. H., & Willutzki, U. (2004). Fifty years of psychotherapy process-outcome research: Continuity and change. In M. J. Lambert (Ed.), Bergin and Garfield's *Handbook of Psychotherapy and Behavior Change* (5th ed., pp. 307-389). New York: Wiley.

Ortlepp, K., & Friedman, M. (2002). Prevalence and correlates of secondary traumatic stress in workplace lay trauma counselors. *Journal of Traumatic Stress, 15,* 213-222.

Prochaska, J. O. (2000). How do people change, and how can we change to help many more people? In M. A. Hubble, B. L. Duncan, & S. D. Miller (Eds.), *The heart and soul of change* (pp. 227-255). Washington, DC: American Psychological Association.

Singh, K. (2007). *Quantitative social research methods.* Los Angeles, CA: Sage Publications.

Sporrle, M., Gerber-Braun, B., & Forsterling, F. (2007). The influence of response lines on response behavior in the context of open-question formats. *Swiss Journal of Psychology, 66,* 103-107.

Stricker, G. (2008). Milestones in psychotherapy integration. *Psychotherapy Bulletin, 43,* 25-29.

Wampold, B. E. (2006). The psychotherapist. In J. C. Norcross, L. E. Beutler, & R. F. Levant (Eds.). *Evidence-based practices in mental health: Debate and dialogue on the fundamental questions* (pp. 200-208). Washington, DC: American Psychological Association.

Wolfe, B. E. (2005). Integrative psychotherapy of the anxiety disorders. In J. C. Norcross, M. R. Goldfried (Eds.), *Handbook of Psychotherapy Integration* (2nd ed., pp. 263- 280). Oxford University Press.

Postscript

WHAT WE HAVE LEARNED FROM THIS RESEARCH

Sherry L. Hatcher

In sum, the therapists we interviewed regularly expressed admiration for their patients' resiliency and their means of dealing with trauma; they emphasized the importance of the art of psychotherapy and, in addition to theory and science, the essential nature of relationship—both in their lives overall, and for success in the psychotherapy process and outcome. Psychologists who participated in our study offered abundant examples of the ways in which they have benefitted from being a psychotherapist and their sense of privilege in this work, albeit it is difficult work where success is not always guaranteed. They communicated that their clients are important people in their lives whom they cherish and respect and whose confidence and trust are a privilege and a blessing in their own lives.

A Personal Note

When I began this research project with my doctoral students almost five years ago, I had recently announced the closing of my 25+ year clinical practice in a community where I had lived and worked for 45 years, but from which I moved for family reasons.

In that difficult process, I was deeply affected and impressed by the reactions of my psychotherapy clients to the news that I would be relocating, even as I announced this almost a year in advance of my departure so as to allow time for us to work through the endings of our therapy collaborations. This event was one key inspiration for my initiating the research project upon which this book is based. I learned so much from my own psychotherapy clients over the many years I practiced, and I have the definite sense that those relationships were mutually important, educative, and impactful.

For example, I have learned from my psychotherapy clients, among the many things detailed in this volume, that important leave-takings piggyback on past ones and that not only do relational endings connect with one's personal history and personality, but they also offer the opportunity to learn about how to create better kinds of life endings.

Up to the very conclusion of my private practice work with those about whom I care so very much and was sad to leave, I continued to learn from them, much as they expressed value and learning in our work together, including about the inevitable endings that occur throughout each of our lives.

It is not surprising, though nonetheless quite fascinating and reassuring, to see that colleagues from this country—and beyond—report similar and ongoing experiences of learning from their psychotherapy clients. This is an aspect of the therapeutic relationship that bespeaks a mutual reciprocity in learning, both for improving our skills as practicing clinical psychologists and, serendipitously, for benefit in our personal lives as well. Most of our psychotherapy clients may not know that we, as psychologists, experience learning along with them—learning that we cherish—and that we use this knowledge for the benefit of our future clinical work with others, for our teaching, and indeed also for betterment of our own lives.

Appendix A: Background Questionnaire

Code Number _____Date_____ Research Interviewer_____

1) Highest educational degree. . . in (name field)_____
2) As a psychotherapist what is your primary theoretical orientation? (Please circle one):

   a) Psychodynamic/Psychoanalytic
   b) Cognitive-Behavioral
   c) Behavioral
   d) Existential
   e) Transactional Analysis
   f) Humanistic
   g) Eclectic or Integrative
   h) Other_____(list)

3) For how many years have you practiced as a psychotherapist (including your internship)?

   a) 1-5
   b) 6-10
   c) 11-20
   d) 20+

4) In what types of clinical setting(s) have you worked? (Examples: clinic, hospital, etc.)

5) List the percentage of clinical hours/per week you currently engage in:

   a) Short-term therapy_____
   b) Long-term therapy_____
   c) Both short- and long-term therapy_____
   d) Assessment_____
   e) Neuropsychology_____
   f) Other_____

6) Please list licensures and certifications you currently hold (without identifying your geographical location)._____

7) Age: (Circle one of the following)

   a) 20-30
   b) 31-40
   c) 41-50
   d) 51-60
   e) 60+

8) Gender: a) female _____ b) male_____

9) Religious preference (Circle one)

Catholic
Protestant
Jewish
Mormon
Baptist
Buddhist
None
Other (specify)_____

10) Ethnicity (Circle one)

American Indian or Alaskan Native
Asian or Pacific Islander
African American, not of Hispanic origin
Hispanic
Caucasian, not of Hispanic origin
Other (specify):_____

Appendix B: Semi-Structured Interview Questions and Prompts

1. General Question:

Please give an (anonymous/disguised) example of some important life lesson you have learned from one or more of your psychotherapy clients.

2. What have you learned from your psychotherapy clients about relationships?

3. What have you learned from your psychotherapy clients about resolving moral or ethical dilemmas?

4. What have you learned from your psychotherapy clients about coping mechanisms?

5. What have you learned from your psychotherapy clients about courage?

6. What have you learned about the relationship between personality style and psychopathology?

7. What have you learned from your psychotherapy clients about individual cultural differences?

8. What have you learned from your psychotherapy clients about life stages?

9. Is there any other variety of wisdom you have gained from your psychotherapy clients that you would like to share at this time?

PROMPTS/FOLLOW-UP questions for interviews relating to the semi-structured interview questions above:

1. Ask the participants to note at least one example for each of the above questions (while preserving client confidentiality and anonymity—disguising material as necessary).

2. What, if anything, stands out for them and how have these examples affected them: a) emotionally, b) behaviorally c) in their clinical work with other psychotherapy clients?

3. Follow up on other issues of interest.

READER NOTES: